The Other Britain

The Other Britain

A *New Society* Collection
Edited by
Paul Barker

Routledge & Kegan Paul
London, Boston, Melbourne and Henley

This edition first published in 1982
by Routledge & Kegan Paul Ltd
39 Store Street, London WC1E 7DD,
9 Park Street, Boston, Mass. 02108, USA,
296 Beaconsfield Parade, Middle Park,
Melbourne, 3206, Australia, and
Broadway House, Newtown Road,
Henley-on-Thames, Oxon RG9 1EN
Set in 10 on 12pt Palatino by
Rowland Phototypesetting Ltd, Bury St Edmunds, Suffolk
and printed in Great Britain by
Redwood Burn Ltd, Trowbridge, Wiltshire

Library of Congress Cataloging in Publication Data

The Other Britain.

Contributions originally published in New Society.
1. Great Britain—Social conditions—1945—Addresses, essays, lectures.   I.
Barker, Paul.   II. New society.
HN385.086 1982   306'.0941   82-7689

ISBN 0-7100-9308-X   AACR2
ISBN 0-7100-9340-3 (Pbk)

Contents

Introduction

Paul Barker

England is in the eye of the beholder. I have my England; you have yours. What we see of a country is partly objective reality, and partly a pot-pourri of childhood memories, prejudice and expectation.

This book is twenty writers' Englands, or more precisely (given its geographical spread) their Britains. It is what they see; not necessarily what others would see: they aren't just cameras. But a camera is *one* of the things they are.

New Society – where all these pieces first appeared – tries to combine various traditions of writing in its own weekly pot-pourri. It has remained devoted to the essay, for example; and many of these have been brought together in collections by their authors (E. P. Thompson, Angela Carter, John Berger, Jeremy Seabrook, E. J. Hobsbawm, among them). But another tradition has been that of sheer social observation – extended, detailed reporting, usually by journalists on our staff or by full-time writers, but also, sometimes, by academics.

I would distinguish such social reportage from 'essays' by the fact that a very high proportion of each piece consists of trying to be as objective as you can, despite the subjectivity of anyone's eye or ear. To see and to listen are very difficult skills.

With reporting of this order, *New Society* has tried to fill the gap left by the decline of documentary journalism everywhere outside the television screen. (John Grierson's true heirs work for *Panorama*.) Words on a page have great advantages over broadcast pictures. You can get more information in; it is easier to refer

1

back to them; and they are one person's view – not, like all mass media, a kind of joint creation.

This is not to deny that an editor has something to do with what appears in his magazine. I approve of Cyril Connolly's remark, about *Horizon*, that he regarded himself as presiding at a table to which many different kinds of guests were invited. Even so, some writers wrote for *Horizon*, and some did not. The same goes for *New Society*.

Being a weekly, *New Society* has always had some functions that relate simply to keeping track of week-by-week events and pronouncements. But I would, myself, be happy for it to be judged by the quality of the writers that, over the years, it has given a hearing to, and to whose development it has sometimes been crucial.

No writers of ours have ever, I think, been edited for their opinions. The only requirement has been the level of the argument or the reporting. There hasn't been a unity of voice (which would be very tedious), but undoubtedly there is a unity of tone. Speaking, of course, as a biassed witness, I would describe this tone as rational, humane, unsectarian, unsnobbish.

*   *   *

When I was interviewed once for a more Establishment job than *New Society*, and I was pressed to produce a political position, I said it was 'libertarian anarchism': perhaps that is why I wasn't made an offer. Certainly, *New Society* has always been a bit of an outsider magazine: not within the Magic Circle that Ian Macleod wrote so angrily about in a famous article in the *Spectator*.

Outsiderism has penalties, as well as advantages. But I think it has helped the magazine get on to new ideas, and new writers, very early. And at least, by one means or another, *New Society* has managed to be (so far) one of the few magazines of its kind that has succeeded, most years, in staying in the black, with no subsidies from rich men, quangos or dubious international agencies. This has allowed us to keep doing what we've wanted to do. A rare freedom.

*   *   *

This collection is called *The Other Britain* because it presents a world, or set of worlds, that are all too seldom written about with sympathy in much of the press. Or, if with sympathy, only in the context of a news story – something which requires an urgent, immediate point to be made. But the continuities of how we live in Britain escape that sort of scrutiny.

It is also The Other Britain in the sense that it is, largely, the Britain of the underdog. Like the whole idea of documentary reporting, this puts *New Society* in a certain 1930s tradition (Mass-Observation, George Orwell, *Picture Post*) which I am happy to be thought to belong to.

This is not, of course, the whole of Britain. Nor is it, even, the whole of the lives of the people written about here. For a start, the picture is probably a sadder one. But, against that, there is the vigour of Peter Woods's banger racers, the ingenuity of Howard Parker's joyriders, or the cheerful vulgarity of Angela Carter's Oss-watchers and Stuart Weir's women on a night out. In selecting pieces, I have tried, in fact, to make sure that the total effect is not too plangent. In my own piece on Bradford, for example, I was very much concerned to bring out how impressed I was with the Bradford Asians. This is not to ignore their problems; but it may counterbalance some of the easier sort of analysis you often read.

To chronicle social change is a tough task. Daily journalism often has to be too quick to get it quite right; academic research is often very, very slow. *New Society* has tried to nip in between the two, hoping to combine speed with the longer view.

The speed has sometimes been very fast, for pieces of this length and quality. Both Ian Walker's and Paul Harrison's articles about soccer fans were written on the Sunday after a Saturday match, delivered to me at our offices on the Monday, and printed on the Tuesday. Ian Walker's is, I think, one of the best accounts I have read of how it all seems from the supposed hooligan's side. Paul Harrison was just about the first writer to make the tribal analogy, which has since been much explored. He also showed an attractive sympathy with the ordinary working people who lived in the areas that these phenomena marred. This is a point which Radical Chic writers took a long time to grasp. When *New Society* published a special opinion poll survey in late 1979, to try to measure public opinion as we entered the 1980s, it was notable how strong a faith in our public institutions people still had, including faith in the police. But the strongest fears about increased lawlessness were expressed by the working-class respondents – those whose usual phlegmatism is shown in David Selbourne's account of a doctor's waiting room. They were at the sharp end of most of it.

Of the academic authors in this collection, I should especially mention Norman Dennis. He represents a tradition of description, and attention to observed detail, which all too many British social scientists have foregone in a failed attempt to match German cloudiness or French pyrotechnics. In the 1950s, he was one of the authors of that classic study of the Yorkshire coalfields, *Coal is Our Life*. There have been few similar attempts since to pin down what a job of work is *like*. (Huw Beynon's *Working for Ford* is an honourable exception.) Dennis later became one of the bitterest and most powerful critics of planning: which, living in the Tammany-land of the north-east, he had reason to be.

But most of the writers of these pieces are younger. Ian Walker, with his remarkable gift for getting into other people's lives (as in his account of an Ulster Protestant family), is still in his twenties. So is Helen Chappell, who, like Ian Walker, is one of the young journalists *New Society* has consistently tried to discover and give scope to. (As well as theirs, the pieces by Tom Forester, Paul Harrison, Stuart Weir, David White and Michael Williams were all written as staff articles.)

Jeremy Seabrook has written for us so regularly over the years that, like Angela Carter, he almost feels to be a member of the staff. Like her, he is a characteristic part of the magazine's tone. I do not always agree with the gentle melancholy of his view of working-class life today. But that matters less than his extraordinary ability to establish sympathy with people (as in the article on South Wales which rounds off this collection).

*   *   *

This book comes out at a time when it serves as a kind of twentieth birthday card for *New Society*. There have been *New Society* collections of other sorts: *Arts in Society* (1977) brought together pieces on the mass arts; *A Sociological Portrait* (1972) was more directly social-scientific. This is the most journalistic.

Perhaps that is an appropriate way to mark our second decade, because it is certainly one in which we have had a fair number of journalistic coups. The best-known, probably, was the article on child benefits which we printed on 17 June 1976. Originally published anonymously, it was by Frank Field and contained a detailed account of the cabinet discussions in which the Labour government tried to ditch this particular commitment.

On the following Monday I had the pleasure of going along to the House of Commons to hear *two* debates about the article – one on its significance for social security, another on its breach of the Official Secrets Act. To his credit, Callaghan, who had only just taken office as Prime Minister, didn't deny that the article was true. Nor did he have Frank Field and me prosecuted – though both of us had interesting conversations with Commander Roy Habershon of Scotland Yard about where we got our information from. ('It's a conspiracy of silence' is the main Habershon comment I remember from my own interview. On the principle that the only way to keep a secret is to keep it, I myself told no one at all the name of our informant, who was, I am glad to say, undiscovered by the usual mole-hunts in the civil service.)

That article was one of the few we in the press ever publish which changed anything. Child benefit was introduced, after all; and the present Official Secrets Act was finally discredited, as were attempts by both Labour and Tory governments to tighten it up. After the fuss over the article had died down, Frank Field and I helped set up a pressure group for an Official *Information* Act. One of these days, I hope we will get it.

I am also, during the decade, rather proud of the series of articles by E. P. Thompson on jury vetting, which we ran in 1979 under the overall title of 'The State of the Nation'. The series was awarded the George Orwell Memorial Prize (the second time *New Society* had won it). As Edward Thompson noted when he reprinted them in his *Writing by Candlelight*, these and other articles of his had been published in *New Society* in spite of legal risks, such as contempt of court. He amicably described '*New Society*'s hospitality to a dissenting view' as 'heartening evidence that the closure of our democratic institutions is not yet complete'.

It has always seemed to me important to coat-trail in one way or another. Our printers got rather worked up about a cover I designed for an academic article by Professor Randolph Quirk on taboos in language. It showed the famous Droeshout head of Shakespeare murmuring, in a comic-book bubble, 'Where the bee sucks, there suck I.' However, with a long, old-style ∫, *sucks* read very ambiguously. The printers eventually relaxed their first embargo after a late-night telephone conversation with me. But their reaction, and some of the readers' letters we got, underlined Professor Quirk's point admirably.

We have often been the first to note awkward truths. In 1977, for instance, Professor Peter Hall was remarking that in inner cities the main entrepreneurial drive now came from the much-maligned immigrants and their families. It was also in 1977 that Remi Kapo wrote a bitter little article on Brixton called, with deliberate irony, 'It couldn't happen here'. When, in the spring and summer of 1981, it did happen here, several readers pointed out the accuracy of Kapo's predictions. (Ken Pryce, whose piece is reprinted here, was another accurate Cassandra.)

Those riots prompted my one signed editorial. While I was walking through Toxteth among the smell of burning, doing some of the background research for it, I suddenly found myself face to face with Michael Williams, who was on the way back to Lime Street with the raw material for his article in this collection. We had a quiet glass of beer together before going our separate ways. At a garage in Upper Parliament Street, I saw the polite sign: 'Sorry but we cannot supply petrol in cans.'

*   *   *

In this collection there are various common threads, and some deliberate counterpointings. There are two views of soccer fans, for example (or three, if you count Lincoln Allison's jaunt into Aberdeen); two of prostitution; and two of rock culture, Ian Walker on skinheads and Peter Marsh on the early punks (both of whom deserve credit for getting out there and seeing and listening, not just opining). There are several views of ethnicity. The city of Liverpool appears more than once, and so does South Wales. We have reports from both sides of the Northern Irish divide. There is, deliberately, very little on London, that over-reported city. This is The Other Britain in that sense, also.

But my main hope is that it reads well, as a whole, and as a portrait of aspects of the country that are often ignored. Britain has more sides to it, and more strengths, than it is currently fashionable to acknowledge.

January 1982

1
Skinheads: the cult of trouble

Ian Walker

Skinheads streaming out of Camden Town underground tonight look hard and they know it. The crop is the style, but it can also be the weapon: it'll nut you if you look too long or you don't step out of the way, if you're wearing the wrong uniform or follow the wrong team. Outside the Electric Ballroom four Special Patrol Group men stand staring at the line of skinheads waiting to pay £3.00 to see UB40, staring at the anti-fashion parade.

The smart look is sta-prest trousers, Ben Sherman shirts and polished Dr Martens. The tougher look is a short-sleeved shirt displaying the tattoos, bleached Levis with the braces hanging loose round the legs. The real hard cases have tattoos on their faces. One has a small cross on each cheek. Most of the girl skins look really young, about 13, and are dressed like the boys in shirts, jeans and boots. But some wear short skirts, like one black skinhead girl who's got brown monkey boots over black fishnet tights.

The police point and giggle at all the girls in mini-skirts. Now and again they try to show who the real tough guys are by frogmarching the odd skinhead to the back of the queue.

Skins: the image is white convict, the music is black. (Remember Norman Mailer's article on the cult of hip, 'The white Negro'?) Groups like UB40 – the name comes from the DHSS code for the unemployed – are now called two-tone because they put black and white musicians together to play ska, an early form of reggae coming out of Jamaica, and popular with the first wave of British skinheads in the 1960s.

It is not just skinheads who are into two-tone. Punks, Rastas, rude boys (skins in mohair suits), and a few long-hairs, are here too. But inside the Electric Ballroom, this huge and airless hall, it's the skinheads who make the atmosphere charged. . . . There's a loud crack and heads turn. But it's just a skin who's finished his can of Coke and smashed it on the floor.

A skinhead tries to make an art form out of *machismo*. He walks, chin out military style, with a duck-splayed swagger. He sucks hard on his cigarette, chews his gum with a vengeance. He doesn't smile too much, unless he's with his mates at the bar. The only time a skin looks somehow vulnerable is when he's dancing – never with a girl, always either alone or with other skins – with his eyes half-closed, dipping his shoulders rhythmically. Skinheads are great dancers.

'It's just fashion, innit?' says a 16-year-old from south London, watching his mate zap the Space Invaders in the bar, rocking gently to the reggae of Reality, the warm-up band. Two girls – one has MINI-SKIN N4 DODGER painted on the back of her army-green jacket – run full-tilt through the bar, scant regard for drink or bodies. Skin girls aim to be as street-tough as the boys. They strut to the front of the queue at the women's toilets. No one complains.

Although skin boys don't hang out with skin girls, every now and again a boy will just waltz up to a girl, kiss her violently for a couple of minutes, before moving off wordlessly. Girls are okay for kissing and fucking, but you don't talk to them, not in public anyhow. These boys, with their POW haircuts and markings, their enamel Union Jack badges, their polished boots – these boys don't get too upset if they're taken for fascists. Fascism is a laugh.

A boy in a red Fred Perry tennis shirt greets his friend with a Nazi salute, grinning. Another skinhead wandering round the bar has WHITE POWER written in blue on his T-shirt. A black roadie for UB40 stops and scowls at him, but the white supremacist ignores the challenge, walks on by.

At 10.30, UB40 come on stage and there's a rush from the bars as the skins make for the front of the hall. Two Rastafarians and six whites in this band. 'This is one of our Rock Against Thatcher numbers,' says the frontman. A few half-hearted cheers. 'Are there only 50 people here into Rock Against Thatcher?' He gets a bigger cheer. A drunk skinhead staggers through the packed dance floor, trying to kick the guy running away from him, before giving up the chase and collapsing on the floor. Everyone ignores him. Be cool.

The final encore over, the lights come on, and the plastic pint pots are ceremoniously crunched. West Ham skins sing 'Wembley' (pronounced Wemballee) on their way out, throwing down the gauntlet to the Arsenal.

It's not picked up. It's been a quiet night, after all. Police are back on duty outside as the dancers spill out, dripping with sweat this warm night, and traipse down the street for the underground train home. Home to their parents, most of them, though there is one last pleasure to be squeezed out the night: to chant and sing and look tough on the tube. Scaring the straights is half the fun.

It always has been. Seat-slashing Teds, mass-rioting mods and rockers, football thugs, skinheads, drug-taking hippies, foul-mouthed punks. . . . Sub-editors write headlines, politicians fire moralism from the hip, youth movements come and go.

Skinhead first arrived in the late 1960s. It was a sort of male working-class backlash against mods grown too narcissistic, effeminate and arty. Football fans discovered a style. I remember 4,000 Manchester United skinheads on the terraces at Elland Road, Leeds, in 1968. They all wore bleached Levis, Dr Martens, a short scarf tied cravat-style, cropped hair. They looked like an army and, after the game, went into action like one.

Skinheads never really disappeared from the football terraces. But the clothes, like skinhead music (soul, ska, home-grown rabble-rousers like Slade), went out of fashion, until the punk movement turned style inside out, starting in late 1976. A new generation of skins started following the band called Sham '69. 'If punks are about anarchy, then skinheads are the most anarchist going,' Jimmy Pursey, the band's frontman, once told me in his Hersham flat, above a bookie's. 'They fight, run riot, don't give a fuck about anything.' Pursey withdrew from the Rock Against Racism carnival in Brixton later that year because he feared that his supporters might smash the whole thing up. Sham '69 folded the next year.

Mark Dumsday never liked Sham '69 anyway. He has been a skinhead for two years, he is 18, and moved to London a year ago after working on a fairground in Southend, his home town. He now lives in a short-life ex-council flat in King's Cross. He gets £23 a week from social security.

It's five in the afternoon. We're sitting in front of a black and white portable TV, here in the living room of this fourth-floor flat in Midhope House. Mark says he usually gets up around two, watches television, then goes out for a drink, or to a gig, or whatever. His father is a welder. His mother works for Avon cosmetics.

'When I was at home,' he says, 'I didn't get on very well with them. Now it's sweet. All right now. They don't mind me being a skin. They quite like it, like the haircut, think it's tidy.' He's looking at the TV. Shots of bikini-clad women on Caribbean beaches. The Eversun commercial.

Why did Mark first get his crop? 'I dunno. I used to hang around with bikers, the Southend Hell's Angels. In August '78, when I came off the fair, I had a crop. It was something different at the time. At Southend there was only about ten of us. Now there's loads of 'em.'

The tattoo on his right arm is a caricature of a skinhead. 'Most skins have got this one,' he says, pointing to it. 'Or a lot of the BM [British Movement] skins have got the phoenix bird.' Pictures of Debbie Harry and Olivia Newton-John on one wall, and of the West Indian reggae artist, Peter Tosh, smoking a joint on another. 'Yeah, I like a blow. I don't know any skinheads who don't.'

He left school at 16 without taking any exams. 'I was hardly ever there. Used to bunk off all the time.' He's thought about getting a job as a despatch rider, but he's happy enough on the dole. He has no girl friend. 'I don't bother going out with them,' he grins. I ask him why it is that skinheads always hang out in all-male groups. Is it that they don't know how to talk to girls? 'That's rubbish,' he says. 'Anyone can pick up a bird. Anybody.' But Mark has never picked up a skin girl. 'I think a girl with a crop looks silly.'

Skinhead isn't fashion, he says; but he's not sure what it is at all. What does he get out of it? 'Not a lot.'

Two young Glaswegian women, both with dyed blonde hair and one of them tattooed, arrive with shopping bags. 'They're just staying here,' says Mark. 'Ain't got nowhere else to go . . . No, the only thing that's kept skinheads going is it's not commercial, like punk was and mods are. I want to stay one till I'm 21.'

Why? 'Dunno. Stuck it out two years. Might as well make it five.
If I quit, I'll probably turn biker.'

A lot of the skins who used to live on this estate are now inside,
but Mark has stayed pretty clean. 'I only have one offence against
me. For possession.' Of drugs, that is – 'speed', amphetamines.
'I'll have it occasionally, not very often. A lot of skins are into
glue, but I've never done that. If you can't afford the right stuff,
don't do that.' The television picture distorts. Mark gets up,
fiddles around with the aerial, which is stuck in the grille of a gas
fire. One of the Glaswegians notices a mark on the back of his
head. She asks him what it is. 'Scar,' he says. A woman on the
box, now in focus, reckons that boa constrictors are very popular
pets now. Mark sits down again.

Life here, the way he tells it, is one long struggle against the
law. 'The Old Bill were up here the other night. Took me curtains
away to analyse them. Went right through the place. They went
downstairs and asked this geezer, "Is that bloke upstairs a
nutter?"'

A prostitute who lived on this estate was murdered. Most of
her body was found in Epping Forest; police expected to find the
rest here, in Midhope House. 'The cop was saying, "You did it,
didn't you? I think you done it." I just laughed.' Mark says he did
know the prostitute. 'Didn't like her either.' A sudden strong
smell of varnish as the two women start painting their nails.

'Yeah,' Mark continues. 'You do get a lot of aggravation from
the Old Bill. In Southend I've been nicked twice for things I never
done. My mate kicked in a rockabilly and I got put in a cell for 24
hours for that . . . and here they just stop you on the street, RO
you. Give it all out on the radio. See if they've got warrants out for
your arrest.

'I've been beaten up by the Old Bill. There was me and another
guy, me mate, he ran away. They took me home, found a starting
pistol. Then they got me in the back of the car. Twisting my neck
and punching my mouth. Bastards they are . . . and you get a lot
of DS [drug squad] at gigs. Round here the DS are easy to spot,
just old geezers. But at gigs some of 'em are really young. I was at
Dingwalls [also in Camden Town] the other night, and suddenly
the DS was all round us.'

Mark, the letters of his name tattooed on his four fingers, flicks a
hand over his crop, asks me if I want a cup of tea? Skinhead crops

come in four categories, from grade one to grade four. Mark's is grade one, the shortest. He has to get it cut every three weeks.

Over the tea Mark says he has no time for mods ('just a load of wimps'), Teds, rockabillies or Asians. Why Asians? 'I don't like Pakis and I don't know any skinheads who do. Pakis just don't mix. You'll see one of them,' he points to the Peter Tosh poster, 'with a white man. Never see a Paki with one. Paki-bashing is all part of the cult anyway.'

There is an Asian band in south London called Alien Kulture who take gangs of Asian youth with them wherever they play. Mark had said he thought 'niggers are okay, I like the music.' But he just shakes his head about Alien Kulture: 'I don't think they'll last. I don't think they'll last five minutes. A Paki band? I never heard of such a thing.'

Tonight Mark is going to see Madness, the all-white ska band, at the Lyceum. Madness are the darlings of the British Movement and National Front skins: somebody's going to get hurt tonight. Mark himself says he isn't into fascism, and he isn't into violence. 'I don't fight unless someone provokes me.' But what is it then that provokes skins to punch, kick, nut and razor? 'It's just the cult. Skins are trouble, aggro, Paki-bashing, the lot. The cult is trouble.'

Choose your cult and live inside it. Skinhead is trouble. Make trouble. The cult is big in London, Birmingham, Liverpool, Manchester. In Glasgow and Belfast, punk is still the biggest youth movement. In the country as a whole, the 'heavy metal' revival is in the ascendant (loud rock from the likes of Saxon, Iron Maiden, Def Leppard). No one is really too sure what is happening in the youth culture. Fascist skins, left-wing skins, and yet more skins who just like the clothes and the music? A psychedelia revival, a rhythm-and-blues revival? Black skins and white rude boys? Asian rock bands?

I take a train up to Bradford. Bad Manners are playing at the university. Bad Manners are from Stoke Newington. All white apart from the drummer, they say they got to know ska sounds hanging out in local black clubs. The lead singer, Doug, has been a skinhead since the first time round, in 1968. 'I'm the leader,' he says, elongating the vowels to fake dumbness. 'I'm the one who encourages all the violence at the gigs. I think you haven't had a good gig unless you've had a good *punch-up*.' He smacks his ample fist into his palm and laughs.

The accent, like the clothing, is constructed from the cartoon worker, the Jak navvie. Skinhead style takes the bourgeois caricature of its class (dumb and violent) and makes it yet more extreme. Shave off the hair to emphasise brainlessness and criminality, make the head ugly and lumpen. Wear boots to emphasise drudgery and violence. A donkey jacket, like the one that Doug wears on stage, completes the look.

Active in a housing co-op in Stoke Newington, Doug is smart all right, he knows all about the parody and he has no time for racist gig-wreckers, but what can he do except make jokes about it? Trapped by his chosen style, the farthest he can go is to say, 'Well, anyone who votes NF, they're not too clever.'

The band are changing and tuning up in a lecture room. The tables are littered with empty bottles of Stella Artois, the remains of pasties. 'I'm tough, I'm rough,' shouts out one of the band, sub-Clint Eastwood. 'I'm mean, I'm clean,' screams someone else.

The boys from Stoke Newington, living on £25 a week and touring the country, are having a good time. After an American-football-style huddle they rush out to play. No violence, of course, at a college gig. Bradford seems a lot further than 200 miles from London where, the next day, I have an appointment with the National Front.

I ring the bell and the front door is opened cagily by a fat man with greased back hair and an army-surplus jumper. Joe Pearce, the organiser for the Young National Front, and editor of their magazine, *Bulldog*, shows up. He looks every inch like a college boy, which he was till he was forced to abandon his course on polymer technology at the South Bank poly. His medium-length brown hair is well groomed. He wears a green car-coat and beige flares. He says he's told the NF skins to meet us down at the pub. We leave Excalibur House, the National Front's Shoreditch headquarters.

Proud of the Front's impact on the youth culture, Joe Pearce boasts of widespread support among heavy metal fans and mods, as well as skins. 'Like the mod movement in the East End is NF. There's a link between the glory boys and the NF, the gang that used to follow Secret Affair and now follows the Cockney Rejects.

They're the ones that have mod tattoed on the inside of their lip.'

The first skin to arrive is Gary Munford from Ealing YNF. He was first a skinhead in 1970, when he was twelve. Since then, he's been a suedehead and a soul-boy. 'I used to go down the discos, wear pegs and American bowling shirts. It was such a posy scene. I was spending about £30 a week on clothes. And then there was all the niggers at the discos and white slags hanging about with them.'

The few black people in this bar start finishing off their drinks. Another crophead sits down at the table. He's wearing an army-camouflage flying jacket. I ask him what he does for a living? 'Demolition,' he says, with a mechanical chuckle. His name is Alex Barbour.

The recent National Front march in Lewisham was 80 per cent skinhead. What's happened to the older support? 'More important you have the young support. Look at the police running away, like they did at Bristol. Older people aren't prepared to take that violence. Young people have got the bottle to go out there and . . .' Gary Munford clenches his fist, adorned with punching rings.

'If there's going to be a ruck, skins'll be the first ones in, they'll steam in. Except I do disagree with them going down to Brighton and Southend and beating shit out of each other, when they could be beating shit out of more constructive people, mentioning no names.' His friends laugh.

Tony Duck and Rita Hope, from the Haringey YNF branch, finally turn up. He is an unemployed electrician, and she works at Swan and Edgar on Piccadilly. He thinks a lot of recent skin converts are 'just a bunch of wallies who've learnt how to chant *Sieg Heil* at gigs. They're the sort of people who'll grow their hair and start going round with blacks again.' Tony says that, in his branch, there are two fully paid-up black members. 'It's because they really want to go home.'

Gary Munford says his girl friend is in the Front. 'She's been on marches with me. But a lot of the time the blokes tell the birds not to come. There's gonna be a riot.'

'Half of us can look after ourselves just as good as you lot anyway,' says Rita Hope. Even here, in the backwoods of the NF, some cracked reflection of a women's movement: a woman's right to ruck.

Jeering at this notion of physical equality, Gary Munford recalls a time he arrived at a march with 14 skins, to find 200 Anti-Nazis blocking their path: 'We got all the girls behind us, said keep walking, then just ran at them shouting, "White youth unite." They all just turned and ran. Whatever anyone says, our blokes have got more bottle.'

'The birds of the reds are worst,' says Rita Hope.

There is a vicious feel to those East End streets, where all the white boys are skins, which is absent in Somers Town: the small triangle between St Pancras, Euston and Camden. There is no reason to go through Somers Town, unless you happen to live in one of those blocks of council flats that comprise the neighbour-hood. At around a quarter to four, boys are pouring out of the local school, Sir Williams Collins, an all-boy comprehensive. The blacks walk home with the blacks, the whites with the whites.

Two white skins, Andy Sophocleous and Steve Rawlinson, both 13, say that out of 165 boys in their year, about 70 are skins. They reckon the school is all right: 'Same as all schools really. Some parts you like, and some you don't.' What is it they don't? 'Some of the teachers. Some of 'em are grumpy. Don't let you have any fun in the class. Kids work best if you can have a laugh, too.'

Andy is carrying a school-supplied acoustic guitar. 'I want to be in a band when I'm a bit older.' I ask him what his parents said about him becoming a skin? 'Well,' he pauses. 'I walked in after my first crop, and my Dad goes, "Oh, what? You think you're a trouble-maker now?" And our teacher, Mr Malinson, he sort of goes to me and him,' pointing to Steve, '"If I saw you two on the street, if I was a cop, I'd pick you up before two normal kids." For sus, like. People can get the wrong idea because of the hair.'

'My Mum don't like it,' Steve says. 'Thinks you're going out just for trouble. . . . Best to be normal if you think about it. Then you don't get beaten up by no one.' Steve and Andy aim to keep out of trouble. That's why they don't go to gigs. 'There's trouble on the train. They won't let you on 'cos they think you'll vandalise everything. On buses they can make you sit downstairs.'

Moved on, stopped, questioned, denied entrance – skinheads, these boys reckon, have a lot to put up with. 'Yeah, they get a hard time, especially from the police, and quite a few teachers. One teacher suspended a skin. He had a swastika shaved into his

head. I think that's bad as well,' Andy says. 'I think he should
have gone home. He would have got into a lot of trouble with the
coloured kids, anyway. He would've got beaten up. The school's
roughly half and half, a few more whites . . .' They're getting a bit
fidgety. It's 4.20 and the football is on, live from Rome, at 4.30.

Down through Somers Town, over the Euston Road (a terri-
torial divide for the gangs round here), and again on into King's
Cross. Just down the road from Midhope House, where Mark
Dumsday lives, is a youth club called the Tonbridge Club. Open 6
to 10, six days a week, it's the hang-out for local kids too young or
too poor to go drinking and dancing. They come here to play table
tennis, snooker and pinball, listen to records. Most of the boys
here, too, are skinheads. One of them, Michael, tells me he's up
in court next week for not going to school. He's 15. Why did he
get a crop? 'Dunno. Just like the music, reggae and ska. And I'm
into me own band, play bass. Get the name of the band down. It's
called Youth Cult.'

Another skin, Eric McQueen, takes Bob Marley off the turn-
table and puts on the Sex Pistols single, *Anarchy in the UK*. Eric is
living in a hostel for juvenile delinquents in Westbourne Grove.
'Well, it started at primary school, see,' he says. 'I used to fight all
the time. I went to a hostel in Chapel Market and then they put
me in Stratford House, a remand home, for six months. From
there I went to a community home. Spent a year there, and then I
got a job. I've had seven jobs since I left school, in shops,
factories, decorating, everything.'

And what's the idea of this place he's in now? 'Sort your life
out,' he smiles. 'It's all right. Ain't got many rules, except you got
to be in by 12 on Saturdays.' Eric is 18. He has only had his crop,
which is dyed blond, for two months.

Eric tells a couple of young girls who've sidled up that he gets
about £8 a day from his social worker. They look impressed. I ask
him how he got the scar on his left ear? 'Some nutter.'

Hugh Byrne, who's also 18, has a crop which is starting to grow
out. He's out of work. 'He's a good artist,' says one of the girls
standing by a bar which sells Kit-Kats and Coke. 'Skinhead is just
the thing round this area,' Hugh says, with the air of someone
bored with the whole idea. 'Used to be a lot of mods round here
too, 'cos the star of *Quadrophenia*, Philip Daniels, used to live
round here. Half the skins round here used to be punks or mods.'

One local skin gang, about 40 strong, have recently given it all up, Hugh says. 'They've all changed to normal 'cos they were always getting picked on and that. I used to get picked up by the Old Bill a lot.' Is that why he's letting his hair grow? 'No. Not really. It's only been two months. I can't be bothered to get it cut.'

Post-skins, like Hugh, and his friend, Tony French, all describe themselves as having gone 'normal' once they've let their hair grow out. Tony French, who now looks like a King's Road smoothie, used to be involved in all the gang feuds round here. 'No reason,' he says. 'Something to do.'

Reasons? Anyone interested in reasons (for skins, for punks, for Rastas) should take a walk through the meaner city streets, then turn on the TV. 'We want a riot.' You must have heard the skinhead chants. 'We are evil.' The straight world, the Rastas call it Babylon, is threatened with style: a sneer, a strut, a beat that has soul. . . .

The teenagers at the Tonbridge Club start drifting off home at around nine. Youth Cult are playing *London Calling* down in the basement.

26 June 1980

2
Hustlers, teenyboppers and other sinners

Ken Pryce

Strode is standing tall at the counter of the main bar, impeccably well-dressed as usual, sipping a bottle of beer. Strode is a hustler: and so rather than sip his beer from a glass, he drinks straight from the bottle. This is St Paul's – Bristol's Shanty Town.

Tonight he is in a brownish-grey, three-piece suit, shiny brown shoes to match, a light-brown embroidered silk shirt and a broad trendy tie, also to match. Several rings glitter from his well-manicured fingers. Strode always has the same smell: clean, fresh and expensive – the unmistakable smell of Brut Fabergé, a cologne popular amongst hustlers because it smells 'loud and expensive'.

Strode was standing up and drinking alone. I went over to join him, said hello, and bought him a drink. Immediately after I paid for the drink, he bought me another drink. I knew he wouldn't allow me to buy *him* another. It was all a matter of status for Strode. It was his way of showing he had the money to back up his appearance. More generally his motto was: 'Nobody should have anything over me.'

Strode is known for his distance and reserve and overbearing attitude. According to Wally, a London hustler, just out of prison, 'Strode tink him is a white man.' But Strode explained about himself that 'I'm a funny man, everybody here will tell you. I know all these guys here,' flashing a bejewelled finger, 'but I don't talk to them. Only few guys I talk to. But they have to respect me, because I say hello to them.'

I said to him: 'Where is your girl friend tonight?' 'Which one?' he replied. 'When you ask me a question like that, you have to specify which one:

'The long-hair piece you see with me sometimes, Jennifer, is my real woman. But I have two other women who like me, and give me money. There is one woman I live with for four years, and she walk out – eleven months now. I had a "doze" [gonorrhea], right? And I told her. I had to tell her or else she would catch it, and it would keep bouncing back. But she didn't like it, when I tell her. She thinks I run round with too many woman. Okay, so she didn't catch no doze. She leave.

'If a woman could just understand me, everything would be all right; but they can't. So I just use women. Now Sue hustle for me. She hustle, she give me money. She knows I don't like her but she still give me money . . . hoping. She lives in hopes.'

If you talk to Strode long enough, he will tell you that though he hasn't got the 'brain for education' he has got lots of common sense: 'You can't beat me when it comes to common sense.'

One other important trait that he knows he has, he says, is that he always tries to speak proper English. He says he doesn't bother with the Jamaican patois much, as it is no help to him here in England. One infers that this is another of Strode's common-sense traits. Typically Strode substantiates his reasoning with numerous examples from his day-to-day experiences, in which women always play a great part. 'Women' means 'white women' in his vocabulary, even when he drops the adjective 'white'.

Bang-Belly is another well-known figure in Shanty Town. Now around 30, he has been in Bristol since childhood and has spent most of that time in the St Paul's area.

Bang-Belly is a professional ponce. That has always been his favourite hustle. But, like Strode and all the other ponces, Bang-Belly is also a stud. This is because poncing is only partly an economic activity: it is also a kick. Bang-Belly enjoys 'throwing his cock': he is a 'cock-man'.

In physical appearance he is not half as 'beautiful' as Strode – though like all the regulars, he dresses well and is always clean. He is much smaller than Strode, but recently he has developed a paunch and this has earned him his nickname. Unlike Strode, Bang-Belly speaks nothing but patois, and in this he is a typical hustler. Since it is the only language he knows well, he uses it freely and unselfconsciously.

Iron-leg, too, is regarded as a character. This is because his contemporaries feel that somehow he is 'crazy'. Iron-leg is loud, irritable and abrupt, to the point where his reactions are almost completely unpredictable. The typical attitude towards him is that you don't know when he'll explode or, if provoked, what kind of violence he will resort to. My own experience of Iron-leg confirms this. Even if you are a total stranger, he will strike up a conversation with you, leaving you with the impression that you are his friend. Then, after that, he will regard you with hostility, as if he had never seen you before. I, too, find that I cannot predict what he will do next.

I once sat beside him at the Club. He was sitting with his favourite prostitute. Out of the blue he chose to speak to me, complaining that the disc-jockeying at the Club was deteriorating, going from bad to worse: too much reggae, he said. I nodded in agreement. But before I could complete my sentence, he had already sworn about three times and was off in a huff, dragging his girl friend behind him. This is the kind of behaviour on which his reputation rests.

Yet, despite his craziness, Iron-leg is one of the steadiest hustlers in the business. Year in, year out, he has the same girls working for him. He is also a steady gambler and is much liked, because he is big-hearted and spends freely. But he does not move around buddy-buddy fashion with 'the other guys', the regulars like himself. He is too cantankerous to let himself be subdued by the norms of any group.

Iron-leg may be a kicks boy (a pleasure-oriented hustler), but he is no sweet boy (an impeccably dressed beautiful 'cat', like Strode). In other words, he is no dandy. Not particularly attractive in appearance, he takes no special interest in dressing up in expensive suits and he does not own a car (all are musts for the successful hustler). Iron-leg is perhaps something of a country person. He always wears a working man's hat, and lacks the style and cool urbane grace of Strode. But, like Strode, he specialises in white women, though he is not admired half as much by them, nor can he change them as often. His technique is to hold a girl for as long as possible.

Once, in the Cafe, from behind a plate of rice 'n' peas (a

Jamaican dish: red beans and rice boiled up together and served with meat or chicken), Iron-leg told me what he thought about England, in his usual out-of-the-blue fashion.

'If coloured people never come to this country, a-wonder what this place would be like?' he blurted out. I volunteered something about employment, but Iron-leg wasn't interested in that. He knew England from the angle of sex and prostitution, and his views reflected this. 'There would be much more lesbians and queers,' was the reply he gave to his own question.

From his table, he peered out on to the busy Grosvenor Road, and saw the stream of traffic and the many women drivers.

'All those top women you see out there, they don't shake when they fuck their husbands. That is why white man come here looking for prostitutes, and they married wid wife and children. Yet they leave their wives, and come down here to go with prostitutes. And sometimes they don't even do anything. They just want to see the girls' private parts and wank!'

What are the factors responsible for the hustlers' estrangement from legal work?

The definitions they are most sensitive to relate to the West Indian male's conception of manhood and masculinity, his fear of the 'whip', and his distaste at having a white as 'bossman' over him. All these attitudes should be understandable in terms of the historical roots of slavery in the West Indies. There is a tendency to ignore the *subjective* feelings of members of the West Indian minority in Britain.

The hustler dreads having to work as a menial; abhors having to take orders from a 'cheeky white man', indifferent to him as an individual; and resents the fact that these experiences hurt his pride as 'a man'. The terms, 'slave labour' and 'shit work', are used interchangeably to mean monotonous work which the hustlers all say they can never put up with. The attitude they adopt is: 'Who wants to do de white man's work anyway? Let dem keep it! I will die before I stoop to any white man!'

Harry Saunders was sent to prison for his attempt at trying to pull off what is considered in Shanty Town the greatest hustle – stealing a mailbag with several thousand pounds in it. One day he and I were engaged in a long conversation in which he spoke of his 'great awakening' in prison. He is a deeply religious man, and the awakening he described was a religious experience. I was interested to know how, with all this spiritual rebirth, he still wasn't able to hold down a job for very long. Saunders had just lost his last job as an unskilled worker in a factory. Was it true that he had knocked down the foreman?

'Well,' he replied, 'this is showing how a man's soul is in conflict with the coarser elements of life: because here is a white man pushing me about in a way – and this is the thing I hate most. I don't like weaklings for a start, and I don't like to be pushed by people who feel . . . because consciously I say to myself: "Well I'm not a weakling and if I let myself be pushed, then I am behaving like a weakling." I'm one of dem Negroes who is always conscious of the whip, you see, that sort of thing. Perhaps it comes from reading too much history of slavery.

'I mean, I know I can drive a lorry. I drive lorries for a living, and I was pushing a little trolley [at the time of the flare-up between him and the foreman] and I decided: "Right I won't pull the thing. I'll push it so I can see where I'm going," and this man [the foreman] came behind me and say: "E . . . e . . . em, em, you ought to pull it, don't push it," and I turn round and says: "Well, it more convenient for me, pushing it. . . ." This man turned round, and said to me: "Well, I'm the foreman and I'm telling you to pull it . . ."

'At the same time, I know this woman has this little baby coming [his common-law wife was pregnant by him]. . . . Now because of these things, I will kill! . . . I don't like to be worried. . . . Perhaps if I didn't have problems, I wouldn't hit the man. I'd probably just go and get my card, and walk out.

'But what's facing me now?!! I have this woman who's bringing this baby at the time, and rent to pay, and all this sort of thing, and this man is saying to me: "If you don't like it, you know what you can do: you can get your card!" I said: "Is that all I can do?!!" [demonstrating how he was poised to knock the man down]. He said: "You can go and get it." "Well," I said, "Well, you go and fucking get it!" [shouting in front of me, to demonstrate the rage he was in]. And when I hit him, I see blood; and I said, "Right," and I decided to go the whole hog.'

Some of the men in Shanty Town believe that because it is so hopelessly difficult either to derive intrinsic satisfaction from work, or reap high remunerative rewards, there is no purpose in conforming to the model worker ideal of getting up early, clock-

ing in on time every morning, doing overtime, and remaining a
loyal employee.

Once this decision is taken, legal work then comes to be seen as
a kind of ordeal, a kind of unprofitable restraint that restricts the
full enjoyment of life. One Shanty Town denizen, who was not
himself a hustler, expressed this attitude well when he said: 'I
must enjoy life now, and not when I am too old either. I believe in
the other life, but I want to spend my money in this one.'

People in Shanty Town become the victims of their own un-
restrained irascibility. In their day-to-day interaction they inflict
much damage on themselves and on each other, in much the
same way that the environment brutalises them socially and
economically.

However, hustlers and their associates are not completely
unaware of what is happening to them. This is suggested by some
of the concepts in their vocabulary. For instance, one of the most
common sayings in Shanty Town – indeed, in the entire black
community – is that black people are what they are, emotionally
speaking, because of 'pressure' (ie, the unfortunate circumstances of their lives).

The people of Shanty Town, rightly, attribute their hot temper
and irascibility to this economic and social pressure. Because of
this, they need to 'give off steam' – another common Shanty
Town expression.

Shanty Towners argue that the quality most needed to survive
is strength. A person who shows himself to be impervious to the
disapproval of others is 'strang'; a self-supporting and indepen-
dent-minded woman is 'strang'; Strode, because of his exaggerated arrogance and success, is 'strang'.

'Giving off' means to express oneself. But, at any given time,
there is a tension between giving off and 'playing it cool' – which
is a form of stoicism, a way of repressing one's feelings as a
defence mechanism against the punishing realities, the pressures, of everyday life.

The release of pressure in Shanty Town attains its fullest and
most characteristically, orgiastic form of expression in the phenomenon of the blues dance. A blues dance is where people go
to dance, smoke marijuana and listen to 'sounds'. It is a public
dance, held every Friday and Saturday night, which is open to all
those West Indians who want to dance, get high, or let off some

steam. The blues dance is commonly referred to as 'the blues', 'house party' or 'kicks party', and is generally held in a basement flat. One is usually not required to pay to go in. But one is obliged to pay quite exorbitant prices for food and drink, which are sold illegally.

People who frequent the blues dance are generally hustlers, 'teenyboppers', in-betweeners, prostitutes, and other black residents in Shanty Town peripheral to the disreputable lifestyle. Fear of the police, abhorrence of marijuana, contempt for prostitutes, and distaste for fights and violence, are what keep the typical proletarian respectable West Indian away. But the excitement stemming from the blues dance's potential for danger is part of the attraction for the disreputable crowd.

The blues dance should be compared – and contrasted – with the black church. Both are highly stylised ethnic institutions, with their roots deep in the black community. Both provide a cathartic outlet for their participants. Both are items of culture from the West Indian background that have been retained to help adaptation to the metropolitan setting.

Both, too, are highly emotional and musical. But whereas the black church exists to ethicise the individual and make a 'saint' out of him, the blues dance is an institution for sinners, representing a kind of profane, grassroots secularity among Shanty Town West Indians.

The element of deviancy and illegality is an essential part of 'the blues'. Its most ethnic aspect, however, is the music and the participants' attitude to it. Only two kinds of music, soul and reggae, are ever played. But reggae is fast outstripping soul as the dominant form.

The 'sound' of the music is all-important. In hustler parlance, blues-dance music does not play; it 'thumps' and 'punches' – a reference to its heavy, explosive beat.

*   *   *

I used the term 'teenybopper'. It refers, first and foremost, to a West Indian youth in his teens or very early twenties, who is male, homeless, unemployed and who, in the language of liberals and social workers, is 'at risk' in the community – that is, a young West Indian who is either already a delinquent, or in danger of becoming one.

But the teenybopper is much more besides. In the vernacular of Jamaicans he is a 'rudie' or a 'rude boy'. He aspires to the Rastafarian rude-boy way of life – an English extension of the Afro-centric Rastafarian attitude that originated in Jamaica. This has injected into the lifestyle of teenyboppers a strong cult element, characterised by a concern with 'blackness' and 'liberation'. It has added a new political dimension to their activities.

Teenyboppers are only partly British, and are sometimes referred to as the 'misplaced generation'. They were born in the West Indies but grew up in Britain. They are the representatives of the bulge in the much talked-about young West Indian age groups, and are the outcome of the process whereby parents migrated in the 1950s individually – as opposed to migrating in family groups – and later sent for their children.

In my interviews with teenyboppers, a number of the boys described the strangeness they experienced on arrival in Bristol from the West Indies. One teenybopper said about his father that . . . 'When I see him at the airport, I didn't even know who he was; is my Mom tell me he is my Dad.' Another teenybopper described the difficulty he had recognising his mother at the airport:

'My cousins were the ones I recognised because they came to the airport with my sisters. I recognised them, but I couldn't recognise my mother, because it was when I was six or seven that my mother leave for England. And I couldn't really recognise her. Her face ring a bell like, as the white people dem would say, you know, but I couldn't really place the face.'

Today the teenybop explosion is one of the biggest social problems in Britain. It is the result of inferior education in working-class schools in the West Indies, as well as of the racist practices prevalent in British schools. With further discrimination in employment and rejection by the parental home, young West Indian boys drop out to become teenyboppers.

The teenybopper response involves, to some extent, a rejection of white society. This, of course, sooner or later brings them into conflict with the law. The adult hustlers relate to the Negro hipster in America; but the younger teenyboppers take their cue from the Rastafarians, Black Power militants and the Rasta message in reggae. Like hustlers, they place a high premium on black music and black dance styles.

The goal of 'freedom' is continually emphasised by reggae singers, who reassure their listeners that revolution is on their side and that there is a glorious future to come. But underlying this quest for freedom is the philosophy of 'peace and love' which is fundamental to the creed of Rastafari, despite its racialist overtones:

> Man and woman, girl and boy
> Let us try and give a helping hand
> This I know and I am sure
> With love, we could all understand,

I suggested to one teenybopper that he should take his singing more seriously: that if he rehearsed more, he would probably be more successful. His reply was that the reason he hadn't been more successful was that he just didn't have the right contacts. I asked him why Jasper, the best known teenybopper singer in Shanty Town, with all his braggadocio, hadn't made it to the top. His answer was that Jasper was 'a dreamer'. Later I asked Jasper himself what was preventing him from hitting the big time, and his immediate reply was: 'No contacts.'

The case of Jasper demonstrates the many kinds of identification with reggae found among teenyboppers. He has built his whole identity on it. The people of Shanty Town accept him as a singer, though they realise as well as he that he'll probably never make it. But if, in the long run, he really doesn't succeed, he can find ample rationalisation in the way the music business is run both here and in Jamaica, and in the legendary ups-and-downs of others who have gone before him. There is comfort in reggae even for people like Jasper:

> Boy life really rough
> Boy life really rough and tough
> But me nah give up
> Me still a-fight for me rights
> Because I know one day deliverance will come.

*   *   *

Delroy was an 'in-betweener', living a life partway between the 'respectables' and the Shanty Towners. He has since left Bristol in order to start a new career in the West Indies.

Delroy's last letter to me ran like this:

'Home I am, England you are? Oh, just let me light a cigarette, wipe my face and pick my toes. . . .

'I know you are dying to hear what is really taking place in Jamaica, Ken, havoc!! Help!! The government first, then the rudies.

'The government taxes everything any anything. They claim to themselves that they are putting pressure on the rich. What a load of fucking idiots we have in the House! Imagine adding 50 per cent, 75 per cent onto things that the majority have to buy! Who feel the pinch? The rich man? No! He saw no problem. The middle class? Nc! They can work it out. The poor man? Yes. There is where your squeeze is felt. The poor man never had anything and will never have anything. Why? Everything is sky-high. That is why the revolution always starts from the pressurised poor. . . . Slavery is here again. . . .

'Now about the rude boys. . . . Man, the rude boys kill for fun. They regularly kill their own kind, the innocent, they kill for fun. Why? Nothing to occupy them, so they get rid of their frustrations on any one. Kill has become a way of life. They do not go to the hills where all the rich are, but the poor and the weak, they find them easy picking. They devour them.

'Brother, the only thing these guys understand is violence, that's why I say public execution. . . . Summing up, I cannot really blame some of them, with the low wages that are paid and the high cost of living, no wonder they are so frustrated. But you mustn't let this kind of news scare you. The country needs guys like you. You remember the old English saying: "A faint heart never fuck fair lady". . . .

'Regards to all the guys in Shanty Town. Liberation will come when we blacks really know what we want. So I will close with this one word which I honestly mean for all people.

'LOVE. Delroy.'

29 March 1979

3
'The most abused and pilloried community in the world'

Ian Walker

He is 42, but looks much older. He sits in the front room chain-smoking, head turning from the television to the window whenever a car or a pedestrian passes by this two-up two-down terrace in east Belfast. Bill Baxter is in the paramilitary Ulster Defence Association. He's done time in Crumlin Road jail for gun-running, and there have been three attempts on his life.

His wife, Judith, a Catholic from the Falls Road, is in the kitchen making bacon and eggs for tea. Their son, aged 10, is out collecting firewood for the Protestant bonfires that will be lit the night before 12 July, the day of the Orange procession.

Bill is a semi-skilled engineer at Harland-Wolff shipyard. He was a shop steward up till a year ago. But he's taken the last three weeks off to work in the UDA headquarters on the Newtownards Road. The Ulster news is over. He turns off the television.

It was some years ago that he received the framed scroll, black and white except for an orange blob at the bottom corner, which hangs on the wall. When he became master of his Orange Lodge he was still living in Suffolk, a Protestant enclave off Andersonstown in west Belfast. Before internment in 1971, about 5,000 Protestants were living on that estate. Now there are about 500.

'Can you tell me what this means, *troops out*?' he says, jumping up from his seat and brushing the cigarette ash from his old brown suit. 'Did people ever want the troops out in two world wars? Ulster lost 50,000 men in the battle of the Somme. Five out of seven generals in the last war were Ulstermen.'

His face is all lined and taut with despair, till he wipes the grey hair out of his eyes, relaxes the muscles, and tells a story which,

he says, probably isn't true, but seems to get truer as the years go
by:

'The story is that the Pope, as Italy sort of gets more communist, wants eventually to come here to Ireland . . . I don't
know. I'm not a good Protestant to be truthful with you. I'm more
anti-communistic.'

Judith walks in with the bacon and egg. She is 39. Her hair falls
long down her back like a schoolgirl's. Her face, like Bill's, shows
signs of the travails. It is thin and pinched.

She grew up behind a police barracks on the Lower Falls, and
learned to shoot by watching the local cop giving firearm training
to his sons. She's worked in factories, a draper's, a shoe shop.
After her family went to London, for a spell, to work in a hotel,
she was a chambermaid. She met Bill in a cinema queue on the
Falls Road.

No one told Judith, when she was a teenager, that her mother
was dying of cancer. She later discovered her father had been
having an affair with another woman throughout her mother's
illness. As soon as she died, the father re-married. He now lives
in west Belfast with his two teenage children. Judith hasn't seen
him in twelve years.

'I was never that good a Catholic, so I wasn't,' she says,
pouring out the tea. After her mother died, she ran away with Bill
to London. They got married in Stoke Newington registry office.

Robert walks in. He only got one chair for the bonfire. This
afternoon he brought home his school report: he came seven-
teenth out of a class of 32. Bill says that there are other things that
are important, apart from academic ability.

The Protestant working class has been used to its boys taking
up apprenticeships at 16. Education, before the current recession
anyway, wasn't a priority.

When Robert, their only child, has finished playing his latest
single – *Embarrassment* by Madness – Bill rises from his chair. He
has a single he wants to play, too, by Johnny Johnson.

To the tune of *Amazing Grace*, and with a choir of schoolgirls
doing the chorus, it is a spoken lament for the abolition of
Stormont, the disarming of the police, and other Westminster
betrayals, together with a call for Ulstermen to fight back.

'This sort of sums up how I feel about things,' Bill says, sucking
the smoke past his few remaining yellow teeth.

The Baxter dog, a dalmatian which is kept outside for protection 24 hours a day, starts barking. Bill always answers the door. He gets up, his face screwed up, pulling at his clothes, coughing. 'He doesn't know who it is at the door,' says Judith.

The stranger knows someone Bill knows. He is let in to use the telephone. When he's gone, Bill washes his face in the kitchen sink. There's no wash basin in the house, just a shower that Bill built out into the backyard.

His hair combed, Bill is waiting now for Louis to show up. 'Did you know Louis was coloured?' he says. 'Out of between thirty and forty thousand members of the UDA, there's just two that's coloured – Louis and one other.'

Born in St Lucia, Louis came to Belfast when he was six, he says, as we drive down to a bar called the Oakley. He used to hang out with Prods and Fenians, and played in a Catholic football team till he was 14. 'But in Belfast you can't sit on the fence.' At 16, Louis was interned in Long Kesh for 18 months. He parks the car in a narrow alley and walks into the bar.

Photographs of bulldogs, and one of the Queen, hang on the walls. There are eight men drinking (one of them in the Royal Ulster Constabulary), and one woman serving, now that the whisky-drinking barman has gone to the other side of the counter. She pours the barman another. 'The only problem with Ulster,' he says in a drunken slur, 'is the Roman Catholic church. . . . There are one million Protestants being forced into a corner. The sooner we get rid of the army the better.'

He goes on to describe how the Prods will finish off the Taigs (the Catholics), no trouble. Bill goes off for a game of pool. Underneath the UDA coat of arms by the bar is the motto QUIS SEPARABIT.

George Best used to live just round the corner from this bar. 'Great tradition of footballers in east Belfast,' says Louis, who used to play for the Manchester United youth team in his holidays, and went on to represent Northern Ireland schoolboys. He later developed a lung disease which has made him fat. He is now, at 23, a quantity surveyor for the council.

Back in the car, Louis drives past swastikas and National Front graffiti on the corrugated iron fringing some waste ground. His destination is a pub called the King Richard, which has stone alcoves, murals of palm trees and, in one corner, a Dean Martin crooner. The publican here, who runs bars all over east Belfast, is reputed to be a millionaire. He owns a pet lion.

'He's a good man,' Bill says. 'If you come in here with your electric bill, he'll pay it for you, if he knows you, like. If I come round here collecting for loyalist prisoners, he'll write me a cheque for a hundred pound.'

Louis raises his hand in greeting to the man who's just walked in – Jim, who's only been out of prison for six months. Jim says he can't find work, because of his prison record. This began when he was 17, jailed for hijacking cars in the Ulster Workers' Council general strike of May 1974, which destroyed power-sharing. The second time Jim was put away, the charge was attempted murder.

'I was stopped by the peelers [the RUC] when I was carrying guns,' he says. He tried to shoot his way out.

He is now 24. He keeps pretending he has a gun inside his black car-coat, plunging his hand in there and pulling it back out, gun-shaped, and firing it off with his own sound effects, like a small boy.

'It's the only country in the world where you get locked up for fighting for your Crown,' he says, turning to spit on the floor.

When he was younger, Jim used to run around in a tartan gang, fighting other Prod tartan gangs, and sometimes going 200-strong up the Catholic Lower Falls district. 'We used to fight anyone,' he says, and then looks at Louis, 'including niggers.'

Louis smiles and says, yes, they've been on opposing sides of a fight many a time. But that it's all forgotten now.

Driving to the Ulster Arms, Louis points along a narrow street. Half the terraces down there are boarded up. The whole street is being demolished to make way for a supermarket.

Bill sits in the back. 'We know we can't go back to the old days,' he says; 'to Stormont, when the Catholics were tramped on. . . . In the UDA we're talking about getting rid of the Republicans, and then just all the ordinary Catholics and Protestants living together.' He rakes a hand through his hair. Protestants have their backs to the wall.

On the dim-lit street, an old man can just be made out, staggering away from the Ulster Arms. 'Did you hear?' he shouts to Louis and Bill: 'Billy Archibald's dead.'

Archibald used to be one of the main men in the UDA. He died this afternoon of a heart attack. 'It'll be a big funeral,' Bill says, staring past his vodka and Coke.

'It won't be like Bobby Sands,' Louis says. 'Because we don't believe in our people losing a day's pay for a funeral. Things are bad enough as they are.'

The pub is quiet. Two other men sit in a corner watching *A Town Like Alice* on the television. The Ulster Arms was bombed ten years ago. 'No one's got any money any more,' Louis says.

The only growth industries in Northern Ireland are security and policing: there were 4,556 men and women in the RUC in 1974, 6,659 in 1979. The Protestants still march through their town on 12 July. But every year, there are fewer and fewer bands.

'Prods are a very private people,' Louis says over his last vodka. 'They aren't like the Catholics. And they never forget; they are like elephants. They never sink down roots, either. If Ulster becomes part of the Republic, then they'll fight hard, to the end, and then probably they'll go off to some other island or country and settle there, until the same thing happens again: they'll fight and leave.'

He drains his glass. Bill follows him out. The Ulstermen return to their wives.

After Judith has made Bill tea and sandwiches, she sits down, and starts talking about Robert. She remembers a time when Robert and a friend found a gun in the river, and took it along to the police interrogation centre on Landas Road.

'The boy who went along with him, his father was doing 25 years for murder. And me, with my record. So you can imagine how we felt when they came back and said,' Bill says, looking at Judith. Both of them laugh at the memory.

Next morning, Judith is in the front room reading the *Star*. She's already looked at the *Sun*. The death of Billy Archibald, an old friend, has made her think of those old days. She can't concentrate on the newspapers.

After Bill was arrested, with a machine-gun in his suitcase at Aldergrove airport in 1971, the police came round to the house, and found an arsenal of six handguns. It was lucky, Judith says, that she wasn't carrying her own gun when they came round. She'd put it in the sideboard.

She claims she was the first woman in Belfast to be 'lifted'. In the police station, she invented a story about Robert, a baby then, needing medicine every hour. It meant that when she called her friend, on the hour, she could try and get news of Bill. In the end, it was through a detective, who was in the UDA, that she discovered Bill was up on eight charges.

His lawyer predicted that Bill would get ten years. But six of the eight counts were thrown out of court, and he got away with six months. After Ian Paisley had got her out of the police station, she moved house. She went first to Sandy Row, where Bill was raised. But she was being watched by someone, from a car that was always parked down the street, and the neighbours panicked. So she moved into a squat in Ballybean, where Billy Archibald and his sons guarded her round the clock.

When she went to visit Bill in Crumlin Road jail one day, he told her that he'd received a death threat, and that she would have to make arrangements for the three of them to disappear. She did. The Baxters fled to London the day Bill finished his sentence.

'I was never much bothered about Catholics and Protestants,' she says. 'It was just when they [the IRA] threatened to shoot my son, I sort of got involved.' That was when they were all still living in Suffolk. She told Bill then she wanted to start carrying a gun. He said she didn't know how to use one, but Judith explained that she'd watched a policeman, from her backyard, teaching his sons to shoot. She'd had six miscarriages, she says, and she wasn't going to stand by and watch her son killed.

'I don't much care if they do come and kill me now,' she says, sitting on the sofa, rolling another cigarette. 'At least I've raised Robert up to a decent age. Nothing much bothers me now.'

The only member of her own family she still sees is a brother in London. 'I'm getting the children ready for mass and my sister-in-law says, "What about you?" I say, "Don't worry about me." Some people think I'm strange. But I don't worry about much.'

She laughs. When she's in Belfast she does the toast, Belfast-style, just on one side. When she's in London she does the toast both sides. 'You just adapt to wherever you are.'

The next-door-neighbour, a good friend, walks in and then does a U-turn when she sees Judith isn't alone. Prods are a very private people. This neighbour is, in Judith's phrase for ascetic, 'good livin''. She is also a devout member of Paisley's Martyrs' Memorial Free Presbyterian Church, on the Ravenhill Road, five minutes away.

It was on the Ravenhill Road, in 1946, that Paisley began his ministry. And in 1951 it became the headquarters of the first Free Presbyterian Church. He started that church with 66 members. Its first year's income was £360. By 1969, he had a congregation of 3,400, and the church's annual income was £60,826.

Yesterday, Judith says, her neighbour told her that Paisley had gone to the European parliament. 'She said, "The big man's away in Europe this week. . . . And you're to pray for him." I said, "I will *not* pray for him." And she said, "Oh, you shouldn't say that." So I had to say, "Oh, maybe while I'm praying for myself, I'll do one for him too."'

Robert returns from school with a friend. Judith asks if his mother knows he's not going straight home? He says his mother never worries about him. Judith looks disapproving. She says she always makes Robert check in straight after school, so that she knows he's safe.

The friend has a SKINHEAD MADNESS badge on the arm of his black jacket. In his school, he says, there are three Teds and three mods. The rest are all rude boys and skinheads.

'What's our Robert, then?' Judith asks.

'Rude boy,' he says.

'I can never keep up,' Judith says. The skinhead and the rude boy go out to collect firewood.

Bill must have had a bad day at the UDA. He rubs at all the loose skin folded round his lantern jaw, pacing the front room, fulminating against the Provisionals and the press, the priests and the traitorous English, people like Pat Arrowsmith, Lord Longford, Vanessa Redgrave. 'To my way of thinking, they're all just anarchists.'

His condition doesn't improve over tea, which tonight is chops and roast potatoes and kidney beans. The IRA, Bill is convinced, do their recruiting through the Gaelic Sports Association. 'You go to one of their games,' he says. 'You look up. You'll see the tricolour there. Not the Union Jack.'

The raging goes on. It is desperate, rearguard, the laager consciousness incarnate. *No one understands us.* Perhaps it is also the redneck running scared in the southern Bible Belt. Paisley got an honorary degree from the Bob Jones University, South Carolina. Judith is trying to watch *Crossroads.*

Television news makes things worse: dustbin lids beaten for

Prince Charles in New York; eight Republican prisoners who've escaped from Crumlin Road jail are safe in hiding south of the border. Bill watches the enemy winning another phase of the propaganda war. His eyes go wild.

'They abolished our parliament and disarmed our police. I've been paying taxes to Britain for 25 years. What happens if they just pull the troops out of Ulster?'

The official line of the UDA, as set out by its political arm, the New Ulster Political Research Group, is that there *should* be a phased withdrawal of troops, with the aim of setting up an independent Ulster state. But that official line has no resonance down here, in the loyalist heartlands. Bill needs a drink.

He walks out, this cold and rainy summer, past the London bar, a hang-out of the Ulster Volunteer Force, another Protestant paramilitary group. A boy is out trying to sweep the rubbish down the pavement, away from his front door; but the wind just keeps blowing it back.

Past a sweetshop that used to be owned by an RUC reservist, who was shot dead one night locking up, and on past a Free Presbyterian Sunday school, Bill walks down towards the mouth of the river Lagan.

The owner of the Oakley bar, Wilfie, has a kind of GI haircut. In the second war, about 2,000 GIs were stationed in temporary barracks nearby, at the old Bushmills distillery. Wilfie worked for eight years as a boilermaker and two years at Harland-Wolff. 'Then,' he says, 'I robbed a bank and opened a pub.'

Wilfie now lives in a five-bedroomed detached house in east Belfast. He built a small bungalow on to the house for his mother, who went there from her slum clearance parlour house. But she couldn't abide the central heating, and she missed her fire. She stayed in the bungalow a week, then returned to the ghetto.

Wilfie stands about five foot eight, his big hands clenched either side of his Bacardi and Coke. 'If there's one thing I hate more than a Provo, it's an Englishman,' he says. 'This is the most abused and pilloried community in the world. . . . I'm standing here in a forty pound suit, getting drunk, but I'm staying. I get drunk, hung over, dry out, get drunk again. It's okay. But I'm fucking staying here.'

Wilfie is one of the top men in the local UDA. He calls himself an atheist and a hoodlum. 'But everyone's a hoodlum, and the higher up you get, the bigger hoodlums they are,' he says. 'I'm finding that out.'

He ran summer camps for local children for seven years, but finally got fed up with all the hassle from the 'powers that be'. It had to be 50–50, inter-denominational. It had to be kids of certain ages. It had to be either boys or girls. 'What kind of holiday is that?'

'Haughey. Paisley, Fitt. Devlin. Hume.' He spits out their names. 'The powers that be. . . . It'll be solved eventually by the people on the ground, Prods and Taigs, getting together.'

Prods and Taigs – there's no real difference, he says. Same houses, same culture. He comes himself from a family of ten. 'Good as the Taigs can manage,' he says, making a quick circle with his finger at the barmaid, who lines up the fourth round in 40 minutes.

'You spend all night talking and plotting. How you're going to smash everything, assassinate everyone, the lot. You go to bed feeling like King Kong.' Wilfie tightens his neck muscles, and beats his fists on his chest. 'Then you wake up in the morning. And you wonder what the fuck that was all about last night?'

Bill walks up to say that the army have swamped the Short Strand, the nearby Catholic enclave, that there are two Saracens and two pigs (armoured cars) down there, and that everyone's house is getting searched. Only soldiers wearing uniforms, Wilfie says, can get into the ghettoes.

'Can you imagine any SAS man getting into the Short Strand? He'd be spotted a mile off. I can see immediately any stranger who comes into this area. How do they get people into those areas? The answer is they don't. That's the truth. That Captain Nairac [the SAS undercover man who was killed by the IRA in 1977], everyone knew who he was, first fucking minute he came into the bar. They said he had perfected a Belfast accent.' Wilfie laughs. 'Every night they were all looking at the bulge to find out what kind of gun he was carrying tonight.'

On both sides of the peace lines in Belfast they tell the same stories about Nairac. They see him as a symbol of British arrogance.

The Oakley was blown up a few years ago by the Provos, Bill says. 'Wilfie built it up with his bare hands.' Bill splays out his work-calloused hands, and holds them up to his face, showing the tattoes on both forearms.

'I'll have a glass of stout, Bill,' says an old man called Tom, who just has ten minutes before a tenants' meeting to discuss the next phase of the rehabilitation plans for the old 'parlour houses' (two up, two down) in this area. Most of his life Tom was a dustbin-man; but for the last few years, he's been doing paperwork for the Royal Ancient Institute of Buffaloes, which he says is a non-sectarian organisation.

Tom remembers the old Lagan village: the white cottages, the old timber yard, the bakery where you could get loaves a bit cheaper than they were in the shops. He remembers, too, Paisley coming round these parts in the fifties. 'He didn't have the arse in his trousers.'

Shouting across the bar is Wilfie: 'We don't know fucking anything. We're all idiots. Here's to idiots.' He raises his glass. A land surveyor who's supposed to be the spitting image of Stewart Granger holds his glass up for the toast.

This surveyor, a good friend of Wilfie's, was in the Young Communist League twelve years ago. He voted for Paisley in the last general election. He says he wouldn't mind living in a united Ireland if it meant he'd be better off.

A young drunk, with a dirty bandage unravelling round his right hand, leans forward and retches up right at the bar. 'Go to the toilet if you want to be sick,' the barmaid says, handing him a mop.

After last orders, at 11.30, Bill walks back home. Before going to bed he plays again the single by Johnny Johnson, the pathetic lament for the Orange state.

Up in Robert's tiny bedroom, two pennants hang on the bionic-man wallpaper. 'Arsenal 1971, double winners', says one; 'Ulster 1690', the other. Out of his window, beyond the backyard, the view is of a convent. Barbed wire runs along its walls.

'Do you find it interesting here in Belfast?' Robert asks, next morning.

'Yes.'

'Aye. Plenty of things to do.'

His mother is downstairs, listening to the radio. The widow of an RUC man is being interviewed. She's started a new org-anisation called Widow's Mite.

Over at the UDA headquarters on the Newtownards Road, Judith's best friend from the old days in Suffolk, a 42-year-old woman called Laura, is rushing round organising the food and drink for Archibald's funeral this afternoon. She wears a black leather jacket and black PVC trousers.

Laura went to live in the Suffolk enclave in 1967, because the council had said that she and her husband would get a house within the year if they were prepared to go to west Belfast. For four years there was no trouble with the Catholics round about.

'The people were really cracker, you know. Everything was great. Until the day they introduced internment,' she says. 'And then people stopped speaking to me.'

Laura used to feed the soldiers soup, and let them sleep in her back garden after the night patrols. One night she was kidnapped at gunpoint outside the newsagent's, and left in the mud at the bottom of a hill. Another night she came home to find 49 families piling belongings on to open lorries. There had been a rumour that the Provos were coming up.

'It was raining. And they were all going so quietly, like the Jews in the war. I always wondered from the war and that, why the Jews didn't stay and fight, you know. And now here we were, they were, doing the same thing. I just sat and cried as hard as it was raining.'

She says that, before the troubles started, she had supported the civil rights marches. She had never had anything to do with Orange orders, any of that; but she couldn't understand any more what was going on.

'Suffolk was just like what was happening in Ulster,' she says. 'We were supposed to be the majority. What was happening? I mean I'm Irish. I'm not one of those who says, "Oh, no, I'm from Ulster." I am Irish, but in a way I'm British, too. The education was British. The television, the things you were into, were British. The royal family. Britain is part of our culture.'

Laura left Suffolk in 1978. She went to live in Scotland for a while, but got homesick. She lives now in east Belfast, where her mother always wanted her to live. It's very quiet. 'Dead as a dodo,' she says.

Before tea tonight Bill gets his stamp collection out of the attic. He reckons he must have spent more than £1,000 on stamps over the years. He specialises in British stamps. He says it was only two months ago that Eire had its first stamp with a Protestant on it, Harry Ferguson, the man who developed the modern-style tractor.

Judith is upstairs getting ready for parents' night at the school. Robert is hunting the streets for firewood. Bill paces the front room, lights up his fortieth cigarette of the day, and says that though most of the men who've tried to kill him are now dead, there's still a bullet with his name on it.

He stands now in the corner of the room, by the bronze-effect wallpaper. 'Come doomsday', he says, he'll fight.

29 July 1981

4
A visit to Patrick on the blanket

Eileen Fairweather

This is the first time that I've arrived at Teresa Sullivan's house and she hasn't instantly greeted me with food and tea. She apologises: 'It's good to see you, Eileen, but I'm not myself. I haven't slept these last two nights for thinking about tomorrow's visit to the Kesh.'

I've known Teresa for several years now. Her ghetto home is the kind that raiding squaddies, new to Northern Ireland, look over in discomfort. With its small, neat rooms, inexpensive but homely furnishings, it's probably too like the council homes from which they come for them to pull it apart with ease. Nor does Teresa fit any of the 'Republican women' stereotypes portrayed in their regimental magazines: the Fenian whore, rapeable terror-ist ('When you said you'd show me your rubber bullet, I never thought you meant *that*', sighs the captive woman in one army cartoon), or hard-bitten gun-toting granny. Rather discon-certingly, Teresa seems like an ideal 'good mum' anywhere. Her eldest child, Patrick, however, is in the H block of Long Kesh prison. (This is the name the Catholics of Northern Ireland still use. The British government has re-named it the Maze.) A half-hour visit is Patrick's once-a-month sole release from solitary confinement.

He is one of the Republican prisoners taking part in the dirty protest. These men have gone 'on the blanket' – wearing nothing else – rather than accept the uniform and status of criminals. They have also refused to slop out their cells, which are therefore soiled with excrement.

Patrick's war began when he was 10. In 1969, the Sullivans lived in a mainly Protestant area. They were given 15 minutes to walk out, or be burned out. The Sullivans left. Three weeks later, Teresa's brother risked sleeping in the house because he, too, had been turned out of his home. In the morning, he answered a knock at the door and was shot dead.

Against individual Protestants, Teresa bears no grudge. It's only the uniformed supporters of Unionist power that she resents. She recalls how, in Coleraine, the mainly Orange town in which the Sullivans were re-housed, 'the RUC harassed my son from the moment we arrived, from when he was ten years of age – by stopping him coming home from school, asking him why we left Belfast. Then they'd laugh and try to tell him that these things couldn't happen. And then as he got older they just made it impossible for him. Each time he went into town he'd be stopped, questioned, arrested. The first time he was lifted, he was twelve.'

Patrick wanted to be a teacher; but his education ended when, at 16, he was interned. He was held for nine months. A year after he was released, and four days after his eighteenth birthday, he was once again arrested. This time he was charged.

In a trial which lasted one and a half days, Patrick was sentenced to 14 years' imprisonment for alleged membership of the IRA, and possession of an Armalite rifle. No weapon was ever found on him or in his home, none was produced in court. Indeed, the police offered no evidence at all. They simply said that Patrick had verbally confessed to them during his three-day interrogation.

Patrick is just one of the staggering percentage (the law department at Queen's University, Belfast, estimate it to be 80 per cent) who are convicted in the special 'Diplock' no-jury courts on the basis of statements alone – statements made by the police, or signed by prisoners, sometimes after days of questioning and even, allegedly, torture.

The Human Rights Court at Strasbourg, Amnesty International, the government's own Bennet inquiry, the Northern Ireland Association of Police Surgeons, the NI Association of Medical Forensic Officers – all have condemned the illegal and brutal treatment of suspects in custody and in the courts. Nothing, however, seems to change.

At 22, Patrick has spent the last four years mostly in solitary confinement and naked, save for a blanket. Sentenced very soon after the abolition of political status, he was one of the first prisoners to go on the blanket.

It is through Patrick that Teresa now pays the price of mother love: 'For you're haunted by it, day and night, thinking of what torture those kids are going through.' Teresa belongs to the Relatives' Action Committee, and has taken part in more pickets and demonstrations in support of political status than she cares to remember.

Teresa has been demonstrating for years now – sometimes wearing only a blanket like her son – yet political status seems no nearer. Teresa firmly believes that her child is a prisoner of war, and supports his protest. But because he is her child, she feels 'half wrecked through seeing the state he's in; at 22 he looks like an old, old man.' Guiltily she tells me that at Christmas she asked Patrick to come off the blanket. 'I never asked him before, but I can't see how he'll survive it.' Teresa thinks her son is dying. When we do sit down, it is not for the usual relaxed chat, but to make up a 'parcel' – small bits and pieces for Patrick which we will try to smuggle into the prison in our vaginas.

Given that the prisoners are deprived of everything save food and drink, some smuggling by visitors is inevitable. Our contraband is pathetically humble: half an ounce of tobacco, a few cigarette papers and broken-off matchheads, the inner tube of a tiny biro, four migraine tablets, a letter from a friend, and a few pages from the writings of James Connolly. Both are written out, in tiny writing, onto toilet paper.

Patrick doesn't smoke, but he's asked Teresa to bring in the tobacco for those who do. The one time he and other prisoners make contact is when they're unlocked for Sunday mass; if he can hold onto the tobacco throughout cell and body searches until then, he will smuggle it on. The biro re-fill is the most precious gift of all, for it will allow Patrick to write toilet paper letters and say the things that can't be said on a visit surrounded by warders. The prisoners are allowed just three sheets of toilet paper a day, but they regularly use them to send out accounts of life 'behind the wire'.

Teresa tells me they're allowed one outgoing and one incoming letter a month. But since April 1978, they have refused to use the prison mail service. This, with their monthly visit, was their sole remaining 'privilege'. The prisoners ceased to write through official channels once they realised that the information in their letters was being not only censored, but also actively used against them. A man who wrote home about feeling ill or depressed would find himself picked out by warders for special taunting and pressure to break his protest.

I have a letter which Patrick wrote to his father, shortly before Mr Sullivan underwent major heart surgery in 1977. The letter is purely personal, expressing Patrick's hopes for his father: 'I've said the prayer to St Joseph for you every day and every night, Dad. Please God it won't be long until you are home.' The postmark on the envelope shows that the prison mailed it six days later, four days after the father's operation, and one hour after he died.

Patrick had applied for compassionate parole, but was refused. After a 40-day hunger strike, prisoners were, until 1976, sometimes allowed to attend family funerals, or visit someone critically ill. I don't think any Republican prisoner has ever jeopardised another's chances by using compassionate parole as an opportunity to escape. But the privilege was withdrawn.

The day before Patrick's father entered hospital, during 1977, he visited Patrick in Long Kesh. Teresa recounts how her husband 'told him, as we were leaving, "Never break your protest, son, no matter what happens to me." I think my husband knew he was going to die. After two weeks in hospital, the doctor sent a letter to the governor of Long Kesh, requesting Patrick be allowed to see his father before the operation, as the doctor knew then it would be touch and go.' After further representation by the prison welfare board, the governor agreed. Teresa received this news two days before the operation, while she was at the hospital.

'I was told to go to the ward,' she says, 'and tell my husband that Patrick would be with him in one hour. I shall never forget the delight in my husband's face when I brought him the good news.

'The hour passed and Patrick didn't come. About ten minutes later, the ward sister came in to tell us she had had a call from Long Kesh, saying it was all a mistake. Patrick wasn't getting out to see his father, after all. This was very hard for us to take, especially my husband, who was in an awful state. He said to me then, "I'll never see my son again." After his operation, he never even regained consciousness.

'It wasn't until after my husband's death, when I went to visit Patrick, that he told me that the screws had let him dress, and he was in the van all ready for the hospital when they told him, "When you come back, you must wear the uniform and come off the blanket protest." Patrick knew he could not even pretend to agree. If he'd said he'd come off the blanket, so he could get the visit, and then gone back on it afterwards, they'd have had even more excuse to beat him up. So he just said, "No, I am not a criminal, I am a political prisoner and I will never wear that uniform."

'It was then he was taken out of the van, and put back into his cell. So he never did get to see his dad. My husband died on a Monday, at 3.45 pm. I was with him.

'My daughter rang the jail to tell them. Again, it wasn't until I seen Patrick that he told me a prison officer came to him about four o'clock and said, "Your da is getting better." Then he came back again, saying, "I gave the wrong message. Your da's snuffed it." Then another one came in and said, "Your da's okay. We keep getting you mixed up with another boy." This went on for about four hours.

'For a long time after his dad's death, Patrick was tortured [that is, excessively harassed] by the prison staff. They told him it was his fault he died. They wouldn't let him sleep. They kept kicking on his door. They left razor blades in his cell, and kept asking Patrick when he was going to kill himself. They also told him I had taken a breakdown, and was outside the prison screaming for him. They said, "Your ma's too demented to even write."

'Of course, that was all lies. The letters I wrote – the boys was still accepting letters then – they never gave to him. When I finally got a visit, Patrick broke down and cried, and the screws pulled me away from him. He was 18½ at the time.'

Later, during our visit, Teresa whispered to Patrick that she'd not forgotten to smuggle in migraine tablets. His face lit up like a kid who's got what he most wanted for Christmas. The gloss-white paint in the ten foot by six foot cells intensifies the glare of the electric lights, which are often left on night and day. It is four years since Patrick saw natural light, or breathed fresh air. So, like most of the prisoners, he is plagued by migraines so severe that he vomits and sometimes passes out from the pain. If he asks the warders for medication, he will either be ignored or they will begin kicking their boots against his cell door. Every sound is magnified.

But Patrick wrote in one letter, 'Physical hardship, bodily pain, are things a human being can get used to. You don't like it, but you learn to endure. It's the mental punishment that hurts most of all. In these blocks we are locked up 24 hours a day, with only our own thoughts for company. Sorry – there are of course the maggots and flies.'

It is because Patrick so desperately needs some mental stimulation that his sister has now laboriously transcribed 15 pages of James Connolly onto six sheets of Bronco Best. Through smuggled extracts, Patrick has managed, over the past four years, to read nearly half of Connolly's *Labour in Irish History*. When he's finished reading them, he eats the paper. Otherwise, the next search of his cell and body might result in a find and a beating.

Self-education has long been a solace for Republican prisoners. In the evening, when there are fewer warders on duty to overhear, the prisoners teach each other Irish. The windows to most cells are broken through the force of the high-pressure hoses, spraying disinfectant, which were regularly turned on the prisoners in their cells during the dirty protest.

The broken windows mean that the prisoners suffer in the cold and rain. But they also allow them to communicate with each other, by shouting from cell to cell. Alternatively, the prisoners send messages along the pipes of the heating system, or yell until hoarse to be heard through the thick metal doors. In this way they hold after-hours Irish classes, debates, political discussions, singsongs, concerts and quizzes. Of course, if they are caught entertaining themselves, that too is punishable. Two men who made chess boards out of the cardboard tube of a toilet roll, and chess men out of screwed-up pieces of toilet paper, were sentenced to the punishment cells for 'damaging government property'.

On the morning of our visit to Patrick, Teresa wakes me up early. She instructs me on how to pretend I'm her daughter, whose name is on the Visiting Order. Even if we had applied in good time for a pass for me, she's not sure that I, as a journalist and friend of the family, would have got one. I have been exchanging smuggled toilet-paper letters with her son for three years.

She hands me the 'parcel' I've to smuggle in. She's made up two, one for each of us to carry inside ourselves. They're long and thin, and wrapped in cling-film. Somehow, during the visit, Patrick has to insert them into his rectum.

The prison is nine miles outside Belfast, deep in the country-side. It is not served by a regular bus route. Green Cross, the Republican prisoners' welfare organisation, provides a twice-daily mini-bus service. When we reach a row of dismal, vandal-ised shops, we find the bus already waiting. Gradually it fills up – mothers, tired, worn and haggard even in their prison 'best'; wives clutching babies; young girls, mostly girl friends, I sup-pose, sexy in their split-thigh linen suits. The two men on the bus seem strangely out of place. Visiting prisoners is unthinkingly accepted as another part of women's emotional housework.

In my lap sits Mark, Teresa's six-year-old grandson. He has the golden hair and blue eyes of a nativity angel; but when he sees soldiers on a foot patrol, his perpetual smile vanishes. White-faced, he stands in the garden making V-signs and shouting, 'Bastards! Bastards!' I asked him once why he shouted at the soldiers. 'They come in the night and took my Patrick away,' he said. Mark was 2 at the time, and asleep in Patrick's bed. (Mark's teenage brother, Kevin is also with us.)

Once the bus stops behind the metal gates, corrugated iron and barbed wire fences of the Kesh, we make for the Quaker-run tea room, and the first of the day's many waits. After 15 minutes, we are called across to hand over our bags and visiting passes. We go to the toilet and insert our 'parcels', then we wait to be called in for the search. Pregnant women are made to lift their skirts and take down their tights. Menstruating women are often asked to remove sanitary towels. Nappies have to be unwrapped from babies. Refuse, and you don't get your visit.

In a tiny cubicle two female warders frisk me from head to foot. But they only ask me to remove one of my boots. I rejoin Teresa in another waiting room. 'It's those boys I'm thinking of,' she says, 'and the search *they're* being put through at the minute.' How do you console someone whose naked son is undergoing an anal search?

In one smuggled letter to me, Patrick described this 'degrading and humiliating search, during which the most private and intimate parts of our naked bodies are examined by screws. This search is known as the "mirror search". At the start of the search procedure, the towels we are wearing are removed, and we are forced to stand naked, legs spread wide apart, above a mirror which lies face-up on the floor. Two screws then grab hold of each arm and kick us in the back of the legs behind the knees bringing us down into a squatting position over the mirror (this position has been aptly named [after the then Northern Ireland Secretary, Humphrey Atkins] Humphrey's Hump), another screw then lifts the mirror up off the floor and brings it closer into contact with our private parts.

'When this part of the search has been completed, we are left standing naked on the bare floor while a screw goes over our bodies both front and back, with a metal detector. Next our mouths, ears, and hair are thoroughly searched, before the towel is finally returned. A long thin torch is sometimes used during this search to probe into a person's anus, and on occasions a pair of tongs has been used.

'The screws present at the search often pass insulting remarks about our bodies and characters, and excessive physical force resulting in bad bruising is often used. The physical scars and bruising left after the brutal beatings which are a regular feature of life in H block will heal, but will the mental scars left as a result of these degrading body searches heal as easily?'

Before visits, during the four years of the dirty protest, prisoners were also forcibly bathed. That meant being immersed in disinfectant and scrubbed with the sort of brushes used on decks.

At last our names are called. Along with about ten others, we leave the waiting room for the mini-bus that will transport us through the prison grounds. About five minutes and two metal gates later, we arrive at the H block visting area.

We are decanted into yet another waiting room. It's tiny, stiflingly hot and there aren't enough chairs. Screws watch through a glass partition as, one by one, the women slip off to the toilet. Teresa waits a while, then nudges me, and we go off to lock ourselves in and retrieve our hidden parcels.

Patrick's name is called, and the number of the cubicle we're to see him in. The visiting hall is long and narrow, divided on either side into small stalls which contain a table and chairs. Warders, dozens of them, pace up and down the gangway, monitoring what goes on: who says what, which hands touch, and what possibly may pass between them. The jangle of their keys, and the tread of their feet, seem louder than any voice. Most conversations between visitors and prisoners seem to be conducted in whispers. At either end of the room, a warder sits in a very high, umpire-type chair, the better to ensure that absolutely everything can be seen.

The cubicles are partitioned on three sides. But through the entrance to them, you can just get a glimpse of those inside. As we pass up the gangway, I see a man holding his wife; they don't speak, they don't kiss, they simply look at each other. The woman smiles. I look at the gaunt man with his thin, greasy hair that reaches way past his shoulders. His skin is so white it almost seems translucent. Rather unnecessarily, Teresa whispers to me that he's a blanket man.

We see more of these emaciated figures on the way to our cubicle, and I can't control the feeling of shock. Despite all I'd heard and read about the men's condition, I suppose part of me had dismissed it as the exaggeration of propaganda. Yet how else could men look after years without any exercise or fresh air, and (as punishment for being on protest) at least three days in each fortnight spent on a starvation diet?

The government itself did not attempt to deny that these are the facts of the men's imprisonment; they simply denied the consequences. The consequences, to me, are at last as obvious as they should always have been. I'm frightened, now, of meeting Patrick. I've seen his photo – that sturdy, good-looking teenager's face – and know he won't look anything like that.

At least, the eyes are familiar. Otherwise, the prisoner escorted to our box by four warders seems ten years older than 22.

Teresa, Kevin, little Mark, and I, all take turns to quickly hug. Before we sit down, Teresa whispers to Patrick: 'You know who this is, don't you? It's Eileen, from England.' As he realises who I am, a smile spreads across Patrick's face. He offers me his hand. It's clammy, ice-cold, grey with engrained dirt; the thin fingers quiver. The coldness of his hands doesn't surprise me. In one letter, Patrick wrote: 'The heating system here seems to work in direct reverse to the seasons of the year. In summer, the pipes are turned on full blast and the cells are like sweat-boxes. . . . During the winter, the pipes are either off or on so low that they are of little use, and then we freeze. Do you think we could put it down to some kind of psychological torture?'

Right now, it is winter. Patrick tells me that 'the boards' (as the punishment cells are known) are even colder. But he sees that Teresa's face has tightened at the mention of the boards. So he tries to joke away her worry: 'Ach, Mum, the boards aren't so bad. At least you get a change of cell and to stretch your legs on the way.'

But Patrick doesn't really want to talk about the Kesh. It's news of the outside world he's hungry for. For one so cut-off, he asks me surprisingly acute questions about current affairs. Why, he asks me, did the Russians invade Afghanistan? What is Khomeini really doing in Iran? Is it true that three million have died in Cambodia? But the questions I find most difficult to answer are those about Britain. Is Ireland a political issue? Do the people care, or even know, about the H blocks?

A look of pain crosses Patrick's face. I realise that he must have just inserted the first 'parcel'. I hadn't even noticed it change hands.

There are now four screws around our cubicle, and Teresa eyes them anxiously. We all feel tense. We have remembered where we are. Teresa asks Patrick about Christmas. He looks away, and makes a joke, if a feeble one, about his Christmas breakfast egg. Teresa isn't so easily fooled. Before she can stop herself, the appeal blurts out: 'Son, I wish to God you'd give the protest up.'

Patrick doesn't look at her as, slowly, he says, 'Mum – please – don't ever ask me that again.' His voice softens, 'Mum, how can I survive this if you're not behind me?' Now it's Teresa's turn to feel hurt and angry, 'Of course I'm behind you. Where do you think I was on New Year's Eve night? Standing in a blanket, son, in the wet and rain, holding a placard for you. It's just that. . . .' But she doesn't continue.

Despite this tension, Teresa and Patrick are clasping hands. Then I remember what they have to do. But the screws behind Patrick have ended their brief chat, and are watching us closely again. Teresa withdraws her hand, the parcel still concealed in her fist. In frustration, she turns to little Mark, 'Go over to your Uncle Patrick,' she urges. Obviously, she wants Mark to act as a screen. This time I do notice as the parcel changes hands.

Another warder joins those already leaning over the partition to our cubicle. 'Oh, Jesus,' breathes Teresa, 'it's Jamie Byrne.' This screw, Teresa whispers to me, is notorious for beating the boys: 'the worst bastard here.'

Why is he standing over us? What has he seen? What does he want? For a while we carry on talking. Then Byrne leans over and says our time is up. 'No, it's not,' protests Teresa, 'We've ten minutes yet.' 'Your time's up. Out,' he says, unmoved.

As Patrick embraces Kevin, I hear him whisper into his ear. Later, Kevin tells me that the prisoners have finally set a date for going on hunger strike. But we're not to tell his mother. 'She'd crack up, you know,' Patrick said.

On the way out of the hall, Teresa turns. I don't know what instinct makes her do so, or what perhaps she's seen. But suddenly she runs back up the gangway, and moves out of bounds so that she can see down the corridor where Patrick's just been led. A screw goes after her, but I get there first. Patrick is being half pushed, half kicked, his arm twisted back to the shoulder in an arm lock. A door is opened, and Patrick is shoved in, the screw who follows him briefly looks at us: it is Jamie Byrne. As other screws lead us away, Teresa mutters, 'Patrick's away for a beating now. Oh, God, they must have seen us,' over and over again.

Outside in the yard, other women wait for the prison bus. But Teresa doesn't join them. Instead, we go out of the cold to sit in a Portakabin waiting room. Two screws come up to the door and call us out.

No one else is called into the bus. The group of women who are waiting silently watch as we are herded in. For the first time, I have to admit how right Teresa is to worry: yes, Patrick is getting beaten; yes, the screws found his aspirin, the James Connolly and tobacco; and, yes, we too are now in trouble. Three warders sit beside us. No one talks. Kevin takes a coughing fit. Later, I find out that he was swallowing a letter Patrick gave him.

The bus stops, and we're taken out. There are about ten warders there to meet us. 'Mrs Sullivan,' says one of them, 'your son's been found with a letter. Which of you passed it to him?' He speaks softly, politely, as though wanting us to know that the performance of his duty pains him. Teresa is clearly frightened. But her voice stays steady as she looks him in the eye and says,

'None of us passed nothing. How could we with all yous there?' 'You're lying,' says another screw. This one is not bothered at all about seeming sympathetic. He evidently enjoys carrying out orders. He jabs his finger at Kevin. 'I seen you,' he snaps, 'and you were caught at this before. You're coming with me to be searched.' At this, Teresa steps in front of Kevin, shouting, 'You're not taking him anywhere. Leave him alone. He's only a child.'

When Kevin was 13, a letter was found on him, after he'd been stripped and beaten. A doctor testified to Kevin's bruises and Teresa made a complaint. As a result, the Sullivans were banned from visiting for three months.

The screw makes as though to pull Teresa away from Kevin, then obviously thinks better of it. He contents himself with a verbal attack: 'Well, your other child,' he says, 'is getting a beating right now, because of you. Don't tell me you passed no letter. One was found on him all right. You're a stupid woman, breaking the rules.'

When he repeats that Patrick is being beaten, and because of her, Teresa goes to run at him. But I and a warder reach out together to hold her back. The softly spoken warder tries to calm her down, tells her not to worry; he will ring up and make sure Patrick is all right – well, hasn't he always tried to help her?

But Teresa shoves him away, crying: 'Leave me alone. You heard what he said. They're beating my child. So you've been all right to me. I know that. But look at that pig. Look at the smirk on him. You bastard, bastard!' she screams at the taunting screw. He simply laughs, and shouts to a British soldier who is restraining a howling Alsatian: 'Let him go. That's right. Let's turn the dogs on the natives.'

At this Teresa breaks free, grabs the only weapon she can see – a bin lid lying in the corner – and runs for him. He steps behind a gate and locks it, looks at her with cold hatred and contempt. 'Victory to the blanket men!' she shouts through the bars. 'You bastards, you'll never break them.' Tears are running down her face. Her small figure is quivering uncontrollably. Kevin and I get to her just in time as she blacks out, falls, and the bin lid clatters down.

*   *   *

Patrick, in fact, came off the dirty protest in March, when the Republicans called this protest off. But he is still on the blanket. In every prisoner and every relative, Britain has sown the seeds of yet more bitterness, and therefore potential violence. They are the people who feel they have nothing to lose; people who live without hope.

7 May 1981

5
Anarchy in the UK

Ian Walker

At the end of Angel Alley in Whitechapel, the name of Kropotkin is written in whitewashed capitals. In a small room on the first floor of this building, eight men are collating the latest issue of *Freedom*, the anarchist paper founded by Kropotkin himself. An adjoining room is stacked with back numbers of *Freedom*, going back to 1866, in brown envelopes. There are pictures of heroes on the walls, and a poster: 'All exercise of authority perverts. All subordination to authority humiliates.'

An A in a circle, spraypainted on walls in city streets, is the nearest most citizens come into contact with anarchism. The media spectacle that the anarchists themselves find comic and tragic, has no room in its schedules for the ideas and actions of the anarchists. But they have chosen to live on the margins, in a kind of political exile, and that is the way it must be. The support group set up on behalf of the five anarchists now facing conspiracy charges at the Old Bailey is called, appropriately, Persons Unknown. Marxists say that anarchists don't live in the real world. But a lighthouse is as real as a supermarket.

Some of those who shop in the supermarket of ideas are attracted to anarchy, but most aren't. It does not have the academic respectability of Marxism. (Students, after all, answer questions on alienation under examination conditions.) Yet the anarchists have always had an influence, even in Britain, out of all proportion to their numbers. William Morris, Shelley, Oscar Wilde, Edward Carpenter, Herbert Read, Augustus John, were

53

all anarchists of sorts. Over the last 15 years, anarchist ideas and
methods of organisation have had an impact particularly on the
'alternative society' of lifestyle politicos, on the women's movement, on squatting and other forms of community activism, on
punk.

I have been speaking to different kinds of anarchists. Orthodox
ones like members of the *Freedom* and *Black Flag* editorial groups.
Unorthodox ones like a punk band called Crass, and an electrician who produces a libertarian motorcycling magazine, *On Yer
Bike*, in his spare time. I went along to a meeting organised by a
libertarian group called Solidarity, and to the Persons Unknown
trial.

The weight of ideology and history hangs as mustily in the
atmosphere at the Old Bailey as it does, in a different way, at
Freedom's HQ.

'I said, "Are you denying you're an anarchist?" "No!" he said.'
A policeman is giving evidence. He has a working-class accent –
unlike the barrister questioning him, who possesses the voice
which seems to fit the oak and wigs and the motto on the crest
which says DIEU ET MON DROIT.

Two of the defendants, Iris Mills and Ronan Bennett, were
active in *Black Flag*, I am told by the two members of *Black Flag* I
meet in a pub. This is the 'organ of the anarchist Black Cross'. It is
a paper set up by Stuart Christie after his release from a Spanish
jail, where he was serving time for an alleged attempt on Franco's
life. Christie is now up in the Orkneys, running a publishing
house called the Cienfuegos Press.

Rob is 28, and Kate 31. They speak with pride of two anarchist
veterans still active in *Black Flag*: Albert Meltzer and Miguel
Garcia. Garcia fought in the Spanish civil war (always called the
Spanish Revolution by anarchists) and was imprisoned for 20
years. '*Black Flag* has got people throughout the world, helping
political prisoners where they can,' says Kate, who has not lost
her Australian accent. She is a friend of Iris Mills. 'I met Iris in
Australia. She stayed in the same house. That's how I first got
involved in anarchism.'

Ronan Bennett was in Long Kesh, awaiting trial, when he first
came across *Black Flag*, which is sent out free to prisoners who
request it. 'He wrote to *Black Flag*,' Kate says, 'and Iris wrote
back to him about anarchism. That is how they first made

contact.' Mills and Bennet were subsequently charged with 'conspiring with persons known and unknown.'

Rob and Kate seem unaffected by recent movements in libertarian politics. Kate brushes aside feminist critiques of language: 'I think it's a load of shit myself. I call people "chairman".' They cling to the anarchist eternities.

Marxists and Trotskyists are every bit as much their enemy as capitalists. 'Even groups like the IWW [International Workers of the World] in Oldham,' Rob says. 'They're trying to revive syndicalism, but we couldn't work with them due to the corruption of international socialism.'

They proceed to list the atrocities committed by socialists against anarchists: the suppression of the Kronstadt revolt and the execution of anarchists after the October revolution, Communist Party manipulation of the war in Spain. Here in this saloon bar, too: the weight of history. Showing in Kate's face as she rages about these events which occurred before her birth.

I ask Kate how she feels about the current political situation. She says she feels very depressed. We all go our separate ways.

Another night, another pub, and another anarchist view of life from Michael, who says he gets less outraged and more cynical as he gets older. He is only 29, but has been through a number of things, including the Harrogate Anarchist Group, the Stoke Newington 8 defence committee and the Organisation of Revolutionary Anarchists. Michael has been up at the Old Bailey himself, charged with 'conspiracy to effect a public mischief'; but these days he has withdrawn from what he calls 'official anarchist politics'. He now works for *On Yer Bike*, is an electrician for a housing co-op in north London, and an active trade unionist.

Michael started out in politics in 1968 with the Young Communist League. 'They were still living in the cold war,' he says. 'Read your Lenin, be a good boy, live cleanly.' But it was not just the YCL's asceticism which turned Michael off. 'I also came to believe that being a socialist entailed notions of equality which all hierarchical structures contradicted. That's what led me to anarchism.'

Michael rolls his own cigarettes, has one ear-ring and a skinhead haircut. He says he got his hair cropped because he was working on a co-op that was full of 'squatters-army types', with hair down to their shoulders. 'They think I'm strange. Last job I

had was a straight job; those people thought I was strange, too.
Blokes I used to work with, when they stuck up tit-and-bum pics I
used to tear them down.'

He says that most ordinary life is about observing conventions,
and he enjoys flouting them. 'I ignore hierarchies. Say you get
some cretin of a supervisor who wants to be called Mr Blah – you
call him "Squire".'

The capitalist, in Marxist cartoons, is a fat man with a fat cigar;
the workers are puppets in his pudgy fingers. The anarchist has
more sense of the comic absurdity of those who crave wealth and
power. The anarchist, too, has confidence in his/her personal
ability to resist the diktats of the leaders. 'Ain't no fucker going to
grind *me* down.' The anarchist must be an egoist of sorts.

Two of the people Michael has tagged 'squatters-army types'
come into the pub, sit at our table. One has hair down to his waist.
The other speaks very slowly, this slowness a result of ECT
treatment he received in a mental hospital. 'I worked down t' pit,
in Wakefield, for six month,' he says. 'Fucking murder, man. I'm
not doing that again.'

Six punks walk into the pub, and the landlord refuses to serve
them. One of the women, bleached hair and black leathers,
jumps up and down singing, 'We're too dirty. We're too dirty.'
They leave and are followed out by another dozen who quickly
quaff their drinks and walk out in solidarity. Michael takes the
piss out of the man with long hair. 'Didn't refuse you a drink did
they? See, it's respectable now.'

For Michael, anarchy is 'a way of living your life'. He lives in a
squat, is not married, and says he never will get married. The
feminist message that 'the personal is political' has led Michael,
like many anarchists, to experiment with life: anarchists are to be
found these days around whole-food co-ops, housing co-ops and
squatting groups, libertarian cafes, anti-nuke protest, animal
liberation, community newspapers, women's aid centres.

Hundreds of thousands of words produced for publication by
this libertarian movement have been typeset by Ramsey, a
worker at the Bread 'n Roses co-op in Camden Town which, he
says, is 'the premier left typesetter'. But Ramsey, after a long
involvement in anarchism, has now turned his back on it. 'It's the
politics of individual paranoia.'

He now believes what most Marxists believe, that anarchism is an idealist philosophy. 'It's rooted in ideas of wouldn't it be nice if. . . . Instead of saying, this is the present, this is how we got here, this is how things change, the whole materialist approach. On the continent, anarchy is a more collectivist, class-based politics. Here anarchy was to do with the youth revolution, and the consumer society of the fifties and sixties.'

The most imaginative of the critics of consumerism, as Ramsey prints it, were the Situationists (who were a catalyst for the events of May '68 in France). 'They turned Marx on his head. Instead of saying that consciousness was determined at the point of production, the Situationists said it occurred at the point of consumption: this is the consumer society, the society of spectacles, spectacular commodity production. But there's not many Situationists left. It fizzled out when the boom ended, and there was no longer any scope for talking about never-ending commodity production.'

Nicolas Walter, whose grandfather was a middle-class dropout who met Kropotkin at an 'at home', disagrees with the idea that the Situationists are burned out: 'I think we're much more Situationist now. This new book on poverty [Peter Townsend's] shows how definitions of poverty have changed to include anyone who doesn't have a television. Give them the dole and put lots of crap on the telly. . . . And that lovely American cartoon showing a bombed-out landscape and a man walking across it with a TV set trying to plug it in. Of course, the Situationists themselves were part of the spectacle. Especially in France in '68, there were TV cameras all over the place.'

Respected authority on anarchy (?), Nicolas Walter is now editor of the *New Humanist* and still a prolific writer for anarchist newspapers and magazines. He was introduced to the *Freedom* group by his grandfather. 'I haven't changed my mind in 20 years. I'm just more pessimistic now.'

What are the highlights of his anarchist career?

'Spies For Peace in 1963. And the Brighton church demonstration in 1966, when I was one of the members of the group which carried out the interruption of the church service before the Labour Party annual conference. Also, the reproduction of James Kirkup's poem, "The love that dares to speak its name", when Mary Whitehouse prosecuted *Gay News* in 1976. I reckon I circulated more copies than anyone – even though I think it is a silly

poem – on the old libertarian ground that anything anyone wants
to ban should be circulated.'

Anarchy in the UK was a Top Ten hit for the Sex Pistols in 1977. It
introduced the word 'anarchy' to a new generation. It became
fashionable again, for a time, to say you were an anarchist, to spit
in the face of the normaloids. But most punk bands who attached
themselves to anarchy were merely boarding the gravy train.
That is why I went over to a cottage in Essex to talk to one punk
band, Crass, who seemed to have thought more seriously about
their anarchism.

A man in black with dyed blond hair – his name is Pete – pours
tea for an old farm worker in the living room. Someone upstairs
has *Dr Roberts*, by the Beatles, at high volume. We're waiting for
the rest of the band to come back from wherever it is they are; and
when the farm worker has gone, Pete explains the various
activities they have going here at Dial House. One of the women,
he says, is away in New York, printing the latest issue of their
magazine, *International Anthem*. Two other publications produced here are called *The Eclectic* and *Existencil Press*. A film maker
lives and works in the cottage.

There is, too, what Pete calls a 'graffiti operation'. He says they
have taken over a section of the Underground. 'We don't just rip
the posters down or spray them. We use stencils, neatly, to
qualify them. Especially sexist posters, war posters and the sort of
posters for sterile things like *Milton Keynes*.' He spits those two
words out.

'A few of us going round and spraying with stencils reaches
more people than the band ever could. It gives people the feeling
that something is going on; that there's a possibility of something
happening; that things aren't all sewn up. You're bombarded
with media which you don't ask for when you go from A to B and
a lot of it is insulting and corrupt.'

'But what have you got against Milton Keynes? What's wrong
with it?' I asked.

'I was actually working on the plans for the place. I started
discovering what a complete shithole the place is. Cardboard
houses, no facilities. It's just a work camp, totally sterile, offers
nothing.'

It was Steve who was playing the Beatles. He comes downstairs, runs his fingers through his Vaseline-spiked hair as he tells

me he ran away from home seven years ago, and has lived in this cottage for two years. A woman who drifts in says that her name is Eve and that she sings in the band.

We talk about the various gigs that Crass have done – for Persons Unknown, the *Leveller*, *Peace News*, Birmingham Women's Aid – and the violence that has plagued their gigs of late. The band, it seems, has developed a following among British Movement skinheads. But Crass blame this on Rock Against Racism which, they allege, has polarised youth. 'If you're not in RAR then you're a Nazi. Now we're sandwiched between left-wing violence and right-wing violence.'

The rest of Crass show up: Andy, Phil and a man called Penny Rimbaud. Two children appear at the door and look around with interest. 'Racism and mohair suits,' says Steve, who has not said much up to now. 'That's the difference in punk music. Two years ago, you had Johnny Rotten standing on stage saying, "I am a lazy sod." So where's it all gone?'

What's wrong with mohair suits, and anyway why is everyone in this room clothed in black? 'Lots of reasons,' Pete says. 'Convenience. Anonymity. I'm doing the washing at the moment; it's very convenient.'

We're drinking tea in this room which is filled with books, and I'm wondering which writers have influenced . . . 'Zen and all its offsprings,' interrupts Penny. 'Existentialism.'

'Zen and punk,' smiles Andy.

'The American beat movement,' continues Penny. 'Kerouac or Ginsberg.' Pete says he hasn't read Kerouac or Ginsberg. Andy goes off to make another pot of tea and when he comes back announces that, 'Anarchy to me means living my own life, having respect for other people, respecting their right to do what they want to do.'

This is a long way from *Black Flag*, *Freedom* and anarcho-syndicalism. I doubt if Andy has read many books on anarchism, but he speaks of the kind of anarchy which has always been at the heart of rock'n'roll. It's my party. Do anything you want to do. I can go anywhere, cha-chang, way I choose. I can live anyhow, cha-chang, win or lose. Anyway, anyhow, anywhere I choose. . . . Take your desires for reality and make your reality your desires was, I think, one of the slogans of the Situationists.

One man who has remained true to himself through war

resistance, two prison sentences, public-speaking campaigns on a long trail of causes, is Justin. Now, at 63, he is still active in *Freedom*. I met him over the road from the British Museum.

'For me it all started with the Spanish revolution, grew with war resistance. And then you realise that war grows out of certain things in capitalist society. So you have to oppose the whole bloody lot. Nothing that's happened since has made me change my view.' Justin is bearded, wears a black peaked cap, and a cord jacket. He drinks whisky.

'A lot of intellectuals supported the movement in those days. People like Herbert Read, Alex Comfort, Ethel Mannin, all rallied round marvellously when *Freedom* was attacked in 1945 by the Special Branch. We were charged with disaffection of the forces; mustn't tell the soldiers the truth about war.' He got nine months, and served six.

'When I came out, the Special Branch tried to do me again for refusing to serve in the forces, tried to make me take a medical. I refused that and got a further six months, of which I did only six weeks because quite powerful papers like the *New Statesman* started to huff and puff.'

Justin remembers the days in the 1950s when he used to speak three times a week: once at Tower Hill, once at Hyde Park Corner and once at Manet Street in Soho. He remembers demonstrating at the Shaftesbury theatre when a dance troupe came over from Francoist Spain and he remembers occupying the Cuban embassy. 'We just wanted to show everyone we were as opposed to the communist regime in Cuba as we were to the Americans in Vietnam. Plus the fact that Castro, as soon as he'd got into power, had begun to lock up all dissident leftists. Same old story: use all the anarchists and libertarians to make the revolution; then get rid of them.'

He remembers a libertarian literary quarterly called *Now*, edited by George Woodcock and contributed to by George Orwell, who also wrote occasionally for *Freedom* when he came back from the Spanish civil war. 'Orwell didn't really agree with the anarchists,' says Justin. 'But when we were attacked, by God, he came out and supported us; spoke at Conway Hall in 1944, a meeting on free speech. I chaired it. He was a straight man, straight as a bloody die. He respected the anarchists, because of what he'd seen in Spain.'

He remembers Spies For Peace too, and the campaign for the abolition of the death penalty ('The anarchists kicked off that campaign and I'm particularly proud of that').

Justin remembers enough things to fill a book, which is why he's going to write one, when he retires in three years' time. But most fondly of all, it seems, he remembers the Malatesta Club in Soho, which was run by the London Anarchist Group from 1954–8, seven nights a week. Habitués used to write songs and poetry and perform them at the club, which also had a resident jazz band. 'I used to make up songs – sort of sing and shout, to a drum. Couldn't play anything, used to hammer away on the drum . . . it was really something, all run completely voluntarily.'

The anarchists' coffee house (it never had a licence) was called the Malatesta because he was the only anarchist writer the group could agree on. 'Some were Kropotkinists and some were Bakuninists, but we all agreed Malatesta was a good guy.'

'There's a man used to be in the anarchist movement in wartime.' Justin is pointing at a man who's just walked in, a woman on his arm. 'Hello,' says Justin to this old comrade, who smiles back briefly but doesn't pause to chat.

I ask Justin if he's ever doubted his views? 'Towards the end of the war, when we saw the pictures of the Nazi camps, we wondered whether, after all, we had been right to oppose the war. But then the war ended with an atrocity from our side, Hiroshima. You can't choose between any of those bastards.'

Sitting over a pint next to a man who has fought good causes for a good few years – against bombs and hanging, against spies and censorship, torture – you feel humble, and you wonder if you'll have anything to say for yourself when you're 60 and in a pub with someone 30-odd years younger? But there is one last question: does he still, deep *deep* down, believe that some of what he has fought for and dreamed about will ever come true?

'You've got to think your ideals have got a chance before you'll give your life to it.'

Two days later in the Drill Hall, just off Tottenham Court Road, the question under discussion is not so much about whether the ideals have a chance, but more what *are* the ideals? The meeting was organised by Solidarity, a libertarian group who draw on themes first developed by the 'Socialisme ou Barbarie' group in France. About 50 people are sitting on the floor, listening to a man called Akiva Orr, who says he is an 'ex-Israeli'. He has no notes and uses his hands theatrically as he speaks. His cigarette, too, he holds as if he is on the stage.

'The emphasis has shifted from the exterior to the interior, that's it. Suddenly there's an awareness that life, reality, meaning, dadadada, it's all in there.' His finger a gun to his head. 'Used to be a time when meaning was all up there,' he points to the ceiling. 'Or out there,' he gestures to the streets below the windows. 'Now it's shifting, it's in here. . . . There's a jungle out there,' he pauses for dramatic effect. 'I mean in here,' putting his hand to head again.

'All I can say is that we've got to develop answers in this battle for the interpretation about what is real. *We are the meaning-making animals.*'

Someone sprawled on the floor drawls that he needs a coffee break. On the stairs leading down to the cafe a woman wearing a yellow T-shirt which says I AM A HUMOURLESS FEMINIST tells someone that her father-in-law is a judge.

Outside these windows, people are buying new stereos on the Tottenham Court Road; people are standing on football terraces; watching the TV; cleaning the car; knocking up shelves, watering the plants – whatever the hell it is people do in an attempt to relax on a Saturday afternoon. 'The central human question,' says a man in a black leather jacket, 'is how to be happy without hurting people.'

The various critiques are over. Time for Akiva's reply. He has great style, and he knows it. He has his audience in his hands. 'We could expend a lot of time and energy discussing Marx. We want to discuss *ourselves*,' he says, his hands pointing elaborately at his chest. 'What do you want to smash when you say you want to smash capitalism? The police stations? Parliament?'

'Yeah,' someone shouts from the floor.

'You must smash structures which are abstract, too,' Akiva continues. 'You won't find them. They aren't lying around. You have to construct them. Fuck the historical process. I want to construct a model which is enjoyable for *me*.' He lowers his voice now to say, 'But it's not an easy task.'

The anarchist who wanted to smash up the police stations interrupts again. He is, someone tells me, a postman. There is a heated exchange between him and Akiva: the young activist versus the older intellectual. 'I have a friend,' says Akiva. 'He spent the first half of his life constructing socialism in Czechoslovakia, the second half of his life dismantling that structure he spent the first half of his life building. The system has smuggled itself into your mind. Your own system will be a mutant of that system you set out to smash.'

Discussion over. Some will stay in the Drill Hall for the social tonight. There will be real ale. I go out to watch *Alien*, and remember a drawing by an artist called Cliff Harper. It shows a spaceship landing in London. The Houses of Parliament have toppled from the impact of the laser beam attack. A woman holding a ray gun steps out of the spaceship. 'Take me to your anarchists,' she says.

22 November 1979

The trial of anarchists at the Old Bailey, before Judge King-Hamilton, ran from September to December 1979. The case became a 'cause-célèbre' when it was learnt that the police vetted potential jurors politically. Despite the vetting, all those who pleaded not guilty (including Iris Mills and Ronan Bennett) were acquitted.

6
In ethnic England

Paul Barker

A man sits on the imitation marble kerb of the pool in the Arndale Centre. An artificial plastic rain glitters behind him and a small fountain sprays genuine water. It is not yet ten o'clock this Saturday morning in Bradford, but already there are two Benson and Hedges packets in the pool, and three matchsticks floating.

The man is wearing a good John Collier suit, and a flat cap. He has a square Bradford face, self-assured but a bit sad. He has put down his tartan holdall, and leans his chin forward onto the top of his walking stick, to rest it. It is a white stick.

Bradford is where the Arndale company began, before it went on to conquer every city north of the Trent. But Arndale is now part of a London property business. As you come from the railway station, the middle of Bradford is a desert of ring roads and municipal grass. Only the police station and the new black-glass building for the *Telegraph and Argus* have any boldness to them.

The Gothic town hall, with its tall campanile modelled on Siena, has survived civic improvement, and it Westminister-chimes on the hour and every quarter. Here in the centre, there is a Galts for toys, a Lilley & Skinners for shoes, a branch of Rackhams for polite teas, and a Cinecenta for pornography (today: *Hollywood Blue* and *The Life of Xaviera Hollander*). Most of the banks have held on to Victorian premises, each more glamorous than the last. An extraordinary semi-ecclesiastical structure at the end of Hustlergate has been spraypainted YE OLDE GLUE-SNIFFING HALL.

Given the birthrate, a fifth of the population of Bradford will soon be Asian. Three young Asian boys pedal past on smart new bikes as I walk up to the Arndale Centre; but most of the faces here today, so far, are white. Outside the Arndale, a huckster sells Rubik's cube puzzles cheap: 'Known all over the world. As used by fifty different nations.' On the other side of the doorway, a woman is selling underpants and bras out of a suitcase.

There is a cautious little garden by the Arndale's indoor pool: 17 plants potted out into peat. Mother-in-law's tongue, philodendron, a small yucca.

A plump man in a brass-buttoned blazer waits by a set of stands. He is a salesman for Barratt Developments. There are chrysanthemums below the stands, and on them the layouts of Barratt estates and pictures of Barratt house-styles. The prices go from £12,000 to £130,000. The dearest version is called the Harewood, but you can take your choice from a whole clutch of dream-names. The Windermere, the Alderney, the Barden (a bungalow), the Gainsborough, the Padstow, the Eskdale, the Redwood, the Elm. Men around 30 stop to read, and walk away with brochures.

Trade is brisker at the booth for the Bradford lottery. The saleswoman has a purple cash box and a yellow hair-do. She is like an electronic Gypsy Rose Lee: her booth is wired to the roof for light. It is barely a yard square, but it has gold curtains inside. '£OTTERY. In prizes, every week. £3,000 guaranteed.'

An Asian teenager buys a ticket, and takes it over to his family. There seem to be husband, wife, son and two daughters. The husband has a silky shirt and a very prosperous air. He has just been buying another shirt. The family discuss the lottery ticket. The son looks certain to be doing well at school.

˒ The crowd of shoppers is beginning to thicken. You realise that bags and baskets have now become a major means of self-expression. A woman carries a big round willow basket: it looks so new she must have just bought it. An elderly husband and wife have brought enough bags to try to hold everything they mean to buy. A determined-looking young woman has a bag labelled 'Darjeeling. Florida. Rome.' No one worries any more about taking a rival's trade-bag into another shop. Two boys go past with plastic Saxone bags. One speaks. It's a girl.

By Brentford Nylons, the three men sitting on a bench, who

look like old photographs of farm labourers, are immigrants. Flat caps, cheap trousers, cheap shoes. They are sitting, with shrewd eyes, watching and talking. There is a smell of chips.

Children, or rather their parents, pay 15p a time to go on a plastic roundabout, with the big face of a laughing policeman above it. The Arndale security men walk by, in dark-blue uniforms but hatless: looking more like laundrymen than police. The children smile or cry as the machine goes round.

Up the escalator, things become more basic. Four women sitting on a bench couldn't be anywhere but West Yorkshire. Their faces are clamped tight like a Gammidge cartoon. They are eating ice cream.

In this part of the Arndale, there is 'Kirkgate Market', with its rows of bargain stalls. Many of them are run by Asian families – smiling and pressing bargains on you, like Petticoat Lane. Cheap skirts, cheap blouses, cheap jackets. The hard sell.

A Pakistani girl in pigtails is shopping with her mother in a skirt shop. Her sweater says REBEL. She is carrying a nylon tote-bag; her mother has a mock-leather holdall. She is nine inches taller than her mother. They both look preoccupied, as if they have just had a row. She sees me looking at them, and she makes sheep's eyes at me in a very old-fashioned way, like a dance-hall.

An archetypal Yorkshire shop has a frontage solid with sweets to weigh out from jars. Dairy fudge, strawberry sherbet, paregoric tablets, Bottomley's lime fruits, Doncaster butterscotch.

On the household stall, there are cheap tin trays with imitation Dutch seascapes on them. For £1.32 you can get a stainless steel 'pickle set' (where but Bradford combines such gastronomy with such cutlery?): it's a small dish with six two-pronged forks for the onions.

Outside the Victoria Wine Company, a West Yorkshire police poster is headed MURDER. It is nothing to do with the Yorkshire Ripper – though Bradford was the heart of his territory:

'Mrs Gertrude Gray (72) was savagely attacked in the doorway of her home at 53 Heath Hall Avenue, Bierley, shortly after midnight on the morning of Sunday 24 February 1980.'

She was stabbed, and died in hospital. There is a blurred photograph – perhaps from a senior citizens' outing or a daughter's wedding. She looks both cheerful and tough. She must have lived long enough to give the description herself. The attacker, it

says, was in his early twenties or thirties. Tall (which, in Bradford, means '5 foot 10', it turns out), slim build, broad shoulders,
neck-length hair, dark knee-length coat, dark trousers and shoes.

I feel helplessly angry that such things happen, and cross the
road into yet another market. This is the old, covered kind. In the
Arndale, air-conditioning whirred. Here there is an overpowering smell of meat. Rawson Market is fruit and veg, fishmongers,
and butchers. I see my first West Indians of the day: three or four
black wives are buying steak. At counter after counter young men
in bloodied white coats have the aggressive stare of all butcher
boys.

At the Arndale, you are conscious of dreams and displays;
here, of people and smells and food.

The fish stalls offer peeled prawns, haddock, kippers, 'fish
bits', rabbit portions, coley, conger eel, salmon steaks; all on
marble slabs. One shop sells 'sausage, mash and onion gravy',
ready in a dish with a filmy cover, for 50p. Pie Tom tells us he has
been 'established over a century'.

There is even a tripe shop. A Yorkshireman, who must have
acquired the taste as a child about 60 years ago, eats a mixture of
titbits from a plate with a small plastic fork. Tripe 54p a pound.
Udder 24p a quarter. Bottles of neat's foot oil, for sprains, bruises,
rheumatism. A rather defensive sign says: 'It might be TRIPE to
you, but it's BREAD AND BUTTER to us!'

Here, you might think Bradford had stood still since 1881. But if
you walk out and up towards Manningham Lane, you will soon
see you couldn't be more wrong. Bradford 1981 is a strange new
world. Perhaps both brown and white Bradford people (there are
few blacks) are foreigners in it.

Manningham Lane begins with a big hole. A sign tells you to
make inquiries from another London property company. There
are two large night clubs, Gatsbys and Tiffanys, but what used to
be a theatre (and later the Royal Cinema) is shut. Fly-posting by
the big hole advertises a roller disco at Tiffanys, a meeting of
Bradford claimants' union, Pudsey agricultural show, and Rock
Against Racism. There is barbed wire on top of the hoarding. The
sun comes out and makes the wire sparkle.

Motorbikes continuously buzz along the road, and a few heavy
lorries. Past the Connaught Rooms, Eldon Place, Victoria Street: a
once-respectable inner suburb, now down on its luck. The indus-

trialists named their streets after aristocrats or the Queen. It turned out that, solid though they thought they were, the industrialists were the transient ones. In these streets with the aristocratic names, the pop world has taken over. Young men in bright gear cluster with their bikes outside a store that sells gleaming Hondas, Suzukis, Yamahas. They are all white. On the opposite side of Manningham Lane, a Pakistani stares at some equally shiny second-hand cars.

In this stretch, the road has become like an American 'strip'. All the take-away services are here. Next to the Saree Centre, there are two sex shops; near Tiffanys, a pizzeria and a tandoori house. Branches of the Lombard Bank, the National Bank of Pakistan and the Sonali (Bangladeshi) Bank are all in the same block.

Being on a succession of low hills, Bradford never seems as big as it is. You can often see the green of field or moor beyond, or there are empty strips between different neighbourhoods. Behind Tiffanys (which is, behind its garish front, only a kind of brick shed), the ground slopes down to the railway. A diesel to Keighley clicks by. Here is sheer slum. It is like walking into turn-of-the-century Whitechapel. It has the same grubby vigour, too.

Cornwall Place (did this street once belong to the Duchy?) is paved with unkempt setts. The gantry lights of Bradford City football stadium rear up at the end of the street. There must be unpleasant confrontations here sometimes after a match: these streets are almost entirely Asian.

All the back yards have rows of washing, much of it children's clothes. Windows are dusty, curtains half-drawn. It is dinnertime and a stream of children go up to the fish and chip shop on the corner. Another shop seems to sell nothing much apart from batteries. A handbill advertises Kung Fu films. A building with a stone cross and bell above it (a Catholic mission once?) is now the Edwardian Club.

Peter and Iona Opie should be here. The back alleys between the houses are marvellous for children to play in. Hopscotch is chalked out on the york-stone pavement. A small boy tries to organise his brothers and sisters. In an empty tract where houses have been demolished, two girls watch while three boys fight each other with sticks among the tall cowdocks. The weeds come up to their shoulders. 'You bastard,' one boy shouts. The rest of what he says isn't English. A mother comes out and tries to get the children to come inside. The girls go in. The boys don't.

A West Indian learner-driver does a three-point turn by a board that advertises the Tawakkulia Mosque. Below the board, a boy is playing with a scrap of brightly coloured rug. He keeps falling onto his knees on it. Is he practising to be a mullah?

From the yard behind Tiffanys, a lorry sets out; it is going to drive through the streets to let Bradford know that tonight there is a special American Night at the club. It is festooned with streamers and balloons. A group on the back are playing heavily amplified country-and-western. Some are dressed as Puritans, some as cowboys, one or two are made up as Indians.

When they hear this extraordinary noise in the drab streets, the children's faces light up, and they scramble off after the din. They follow the lorry right up onto Manningham Lane. It pauses there, and the children all stand and stare in wonder. To these 5-, 6- and 7-year-olds it is the Pied Piper. As the lorry moves off, down into the town centre, the children reluctantly go back into their own territory. One small white girl in a silk dress is so grubby that I mistake her for brown: but that *is* the colour of her young sister, clutching her hand, dummy in mouth.

There is a playground in the middle of the streets. It is full of children. I cannot remember when I last saw so many children playing out – *being children*. They are a very attractive sight.

Mothers and aunts stand at street doors in the sun. Adolescents sometimes appear, trying hard to look nonchalant and uninterested in anyone apart from themselves.

By one doorway, four extremely rough-looking white men stand talking in a desultory way with a white woman who looks like a tart. Unfinished 'slum clearance' has left all these houses surrounded by heaps of litter and old mattresses. Before clearance began, it must have been a respectable working-class and lower-middle-class district. One back garden has a flurry of roses. There is a white man, in his seventies, sitting under the roses, reading a newspaper. Keeping himself to himself. Such a man must feel that his own country has been taken away from him.

The proudest building hereabouts is up on Manningham Lane itself. This is the neo-Jacobean stone pile of Belle Vue Higher Boys' School, put up by Bradford school board in 1895. This information is carved into the stone, with Bradford's city motto:

LABOR VINCIT OMNIA. Now there is a painted wooden sign nearer ground level: 'Manningham Middle School.' It looks like a cut-price sticker.

As you go along Manningham Lane, the streets start to spruce up. Dentists' and doctors' plates appear. Down one street there is a large house that turns out to be the Hungarian Cultural and Social Centre. Saturday is wedding day. A group is gathering on the front steps and in the garden for a photograph. This is (just) the right side of the tracks. Everyone smiles. As well as the official photographer, they all seem to have their own Instamatic. The bridesmaids are in royal blue. The bride's sister is heavily hand-some in the Hungarian manner, with dark glossy hair. I can't hear anyone speaking other than Yorkshire.

Back on the main road, an estate agent advertises a 'superb barn conversion down on the Wirrall' for £100,000. A typewritten notice on the house next door tells us that Mr Mohammed Zabir wants to change it into nine bedsitters. (Write to the Director of Development Services if you object.) The next door-but-one house already has nine doorbells; then there are three; then eight. I wonder how long the doctors, dentists, and even the estate agent, will last.

Every Victorian city has this same structure. If you walk through the ex-bourgeois swathes of Toxteth, you come to Princes Park. At the end of Manningham Lane, there is Lister Park.

As you go in, the park feels like the oasis it was meant to be – despite the noise of the traffic going along Manningham Lane. You can smell the grass and the trees, feel a breeze on your face, hear birds. The statue of old Sam Lister faces you, bold and proud – even if across rather too much tarmac.

But in the postwar gents by the gateway, all the divides between the urinals have been smashed. The walls are spraypainted in black: BULLITT, GAY IS BEAUTIFUL and NF. This and the park are like three-dimensional models of Ego and Id. And even in much of the park, Id is winning.

Across the tarmac from the gents, on a bench in front of Samuel Cunliff-Lister's statue, two winos – a man and a woman – drink cider from a bottle. A man in a flat cap walks his white dog on a lead, and lets it shit on the mown grass. Of the two huge litterbins, one has been overturned, and all the debris has been spilled out. A young man in a black jacket, Hell's Angel style, goes into the gents. I wonder if he's adding to the spraypaint.

Those who're using the park as Lister intended are Asian. Two young men sit on a bench across from the winos, and look at them distastefully, as the respectable have always looked at the roughs. A group of Pakistani boys are playing cricket under the trees. Families, brown and cheerful, are *promenading* in the formal gardens in front of an Edwardian-baroque museum. Some are photographing each other.

A rather intellectual-looking group is being photographed against the bright white statue of Diana, reaching for her quiver among the begonias. Another, noisier family is being snapped right up against the grand entrance of the museum. The mother claps with pure pleasure.

The foundation stone of the museum – Cartwright Hall – was laid in 1900 by Lord Masham (ie, Cunliffe-Lister). It was opened in 1904 by the Prince of Wales, the future George V. The high summer of empire.

Through the doors, they have put back into the main display the white marble Victorian statues that originally stood there. They are like a Plasticine version of the classics. But they are comforting, and somehow impressive. An Asian family, who've come inside, stop and admire them greatly; and take more snaps of themselves standing by them.

*   *   *

I want to walk back into Bradford along Lumb Lane, the other great ethnic highroad. But I walk first towards the enormous bulk of the Listers' source of wealth: Manningham Mills, walled round like a prison and topped with a 250 foot Italianate chimney. This on the hill, and the town hall in the valley, were what Bradford once was about. Now Bradford is a district of West Yorkshire metropolitan county; and the Cunliffe-Listers having finally, in 1955, in the last gasp of hereditary peerages, made it to an earldom (of Swinton), sit tight in the smarter county of rural North Yorkshire.

On the way to the Mills I pass some of the houses where better-off immigrant families live, around St Luke's church. The church is very overgrown and deserted. There seem to be Asian children on bicycles everywhere, bright and well-scrubbed, as spick and span as their bikes.

There is a huge coat of arms over the door of 'No. 1 Lodge' at the Mills. FIDEM PARIT INTEGRITAS: Integrity confirms trust. Where there is an angle in the outer walls, a cast-iron 'modesty plate' has been slotted in, to stop drunks peeing there. The Mills, of course, are why the Asians came. They would work the night shift, when the ethnic whites had mostly decided to make their own version of Earl Swinton's switch. They grabbed the white-collar jobs of the Macmillan-Wilson boom – for their children especially – and they moved into further-flung council houses, or took out mortgages rather than pay rent.

The man from whom I asked the way to Manningham Lane, in the town centre, sounded Hungarian. The man by the Mills who tells me the way to Lumb Lane, has the high cheekbones of a Slav. The displaced of a war and a failed revolution bridged the time-gap between the Yorkshireman's distaste for mill work and the Pakistani's willingness to take it on.

I start down the hill, past an outcrop of small shops. In the pet shop, a tabby dozes on top of a fish tank. Outside a secondhand shop is an array of fridges and veneer tables; the window says, 'Deceased Homes Cleared Immediately'. There's an Indian restaurant and a halal butcher. The window of 'M. Rafiq Furnitures' is smashed, and the whole place looks very dusty and closed. In an antique shop, two very large Pakistani matrons bargain over two silver fruit dishes with the white woman in charge.

Three black teenagers in Rasta hats hang about outside an Indian corner shop. Their style is much tougher than that of any Asian I have seen today. One of them mimics the action of a catapult towards the window, while another goes into the shop.

A middle-aged Asian walks down an alley between the backs of two rows of houses. He is holding a broken alarm clock, and goes into yet another corner shop, where they repair things like this. (How many whites now get alarm clocks mended?) Children are playing in this alley, too – in and out of the garden gates. Some boys use a stick as a cricket bat. Others play with some old plastic lorries. They speak their own language, but some English words stick out – the language of the school yard: 'C'mon' and 'I don' care'. Two girls sit on a homemade go-cart while another pulls it. The older children are in charge of the younger ones.

Behind one house, beyond a tidy gate, there is another rose garden, with another white man in it, tending the flowers. It is the whites who seem displaced around here. *Their* world has gone. You can see why some might vote for fascist candidates. But most, I imagine, are conservative Labour or working-class Tories. They grew up among the short time and deprivations of the thirties, probably had the best time of their lives in the army during the war, came back to raise a family in Attlee's austerity years. Then, after that, their world began to change, unstoppably, around them. They were stranded. It is impossible not to sympathise.

On Lumb Lane itself, there is a Conservative Club. It is the first building I see here. There is dereliction all around. Houses boarded up; streets half pulled down. At Southfield Square, there is a board saying that it is to be made good again by the council and the Department of the Environment. But how long has it been how it is? Two little girls, very self-possessed, in bright blouses and trousers, walk through the long grass of the square. They are talking in what sounds like Urdu-with-a-Yorkshire-accent.

The one building on the square that seems to be functioning is the house labelled TABLIGH AL ISLAM and CENTRAL JAMIA MOSQUE. Men in white caps go in at the rate of about one a minute. (They all seem to come out on the other side: as if it were a conveyor belt.)

A bit further down the lane, there is a site for a new mosque. But, rather suddenly, I find myself among blacks. I see the reason. There is a club here. The door is open. A man walks into it, cigarette in one hand, beer can in the other. Through the door and the haze of smoke, you can see a pool table; a man leans elegantly with a cue. A teenager stares out from the dimness into the sunny street. The men are wearing what Damon Runyon would have called fedoras. It is very different from the Central Jamia Mosque.

Some of these streets are like the worst of America – or Toxteth. The pubs are emptying, but only whites are coming out of them. Blacks are walking up from the town centre, past row after row of Indian and Pakistani shops. The Muslim Commercial Bank, Pakistan Airlines, Mirza Electronics, Z. & N. (Moh'd) Patel, newsagents, Saddique Hosiery and Footwear. These are all next to one another. A little way along is the Sweet Centre, its window piled high with sugary coloured tit-bits.

Peel Square is more of a terrace than a square. It has the date 1851 and a loyal crown. It is now Asian: the empire has come home. The house doors are all painted in bright colours – though the panels and the frames often present odd mixtures. They remind me of the Sweet Centre. There's green with puce, and peach with crimson. At one door, a mother watches her children, with her dark headgear drawn half across her face. At one end of the terrace there is a Pakistani store; at the other, a clothing works. An Asian woman watches from an upper window as two white teenagers, and then a West Indian jump onto the wall on their way down into town.

Manningham Mills are now big and heavy on the hill behind.

The white teenagers stop by the window of Roots, which sells West Indian music and clothes. There's an 'African hair stylist' alongside.

From the street you can see out across the other hills of Bradford again, to the moors beyond. In the museum there was an exhibition of painting by local Royal Academician, Bertram Priestman. In the early years of this century, he painted Bradford from the moors – a smoky core of industry against the wilderness. Now the wilderness is *in* Bradford, and you look *out*.

Lumb Lane has now brought me back to the edge of the centre. At a picture framer's there is another murder poster. This time the police have put out a drawing of the man they want. The victim was stabbed to death at a quarter past midnight on 26 May. The drawing looks very much like the description on the other poster.

Back in Rawson market, it is the time of day when things are being sold off cheap. The butchers are starting to wash down their green artificial parsley. One butcher shouts: 'Anyone now for pork steaks. Let's have a crowd round at these prices. One pound 15.' He has a large crowd already. At the next stall, a very smart black woman is buying sirloin.

The Arndale Centre has also got that end-of-afternoon feeling. A small child howls with tiredness. A black boy and a white girl chat each other up. They drink Pepsi, and push cigarette ends down among the potted plants. The girl selling peaches at Littlewoods yawns unashamedly.

The hands of a woman selling newspapers are grey from

handling coins. On the front page of the *Telegraph and Argus* there is a protest by the mother of Peter Sutcliffe's last victim about a waxwork of him being put on display in Bridlington, 'dressed in a velvet jacket and standing in a model of the Old Bailey dock, with an array of screwdrivers, hammers, chisels, a saw and a piece of rope.'

*   *   *

The railway station and the bus station are now a single unit: a Travel Centre. The futuristic roof makes it look like part of Cape Canaveral. The EIIR letter box, in traditional red, looks very out of place (or, rather, out of its time) in the lobby.

There are several Asians here. But far more blacks. Bright-looking black girls are catching trains out, and arriving.

There is a set of public lavatories down below, by the bus section. A group of black boys are hanging around outside them. Some elderly whites, waiting for their buses, watch them with apprehension. It has the feel of bus stations in America. I wonder what has been created here that is better than before. Not even 'efficient centralisation': there is still a long list of buses that don't use the centre.

As I go into the lobby, two well-dressed black girls come out. Several boys follow them out. They have studded leather jackets, with the names of rock heroes sprayed on the backs. They are carrying small plastic water pistols, and they're squirting one another with them. It's like Kubrick's *A Clockwork Orange*.

I think there may be trouble between these whites and the black girls. But then I see that one of the boys is black. I hadn't been looking forward to having to decide to act with civic courage.

I go to catch my train into a part of the Pennines where, as a child, I never saw a Jew and now will not see a Pakistani or a West Indian. On the train, a young white girl soldier and a young RAF policeman in civvies talk interminably about saluting. They hate their officers, especially when they don't return a salute properly.

15 October 1981

7
The Irish English

Paul Harrison

The wave of bomb attacks has spawned a new generation of anti-Irish jokes in Birmingham, told as readily by the Irish themselves as by the English. One goes: 'There are two IRA men planting a couple of bombs. One says, "We'd better hurry up now this one's about to go off." The other replies, "Sure there's nothing to worry about, we've got another one here."' One of Birmingham's bomb scares was caused by an Englishman walking through a glass door at the Bank of Ireland office.

The Irish have only just started exporting their war to Britain – but one thing they've been exporting for more than two centuries is themselves. No one knows exactly how many Irish there are in the United Kingdom (outside Northern Ireland), but they are by a long head the largest foreign-born group. The 1971 census gave just over a million Irish-born, which is certainly an understatement. Estimates of the numbers of immediate Irish decent go up to four million – there are six million practising Catholics. Outside London, with 250,000 Irish-born (on census figures), the largest gathering is in the West Midlands conurbation, with 57,000. But there are thought to be 100,000 Irish and their immediate descendants in Birmingham alone. Most of them came over after the war and have been here from 10 to 20 years. They are not so conspicuous as the Asians and West Indians, until they open their mouths – their children can only be distinguished by their names. The true Brummie, the saying goes, wears a shamrock in his turban.

The Irish are still found in heavy concentrations in one or two

areas of Birmingham, particularly Smallheath and Sparkhill, to
the east and south of the city centre along the Coventry and
Stratford roads. These concentrations were partly a matter of
necessity and partly of choice. In the days when you could still
see 'No Irish' signs up at bed and breakfast places, new single
arrivals tended to go where relatives were and lodge with
them. Until about ten years ago, as many as half the Irish
families owning houses might have lodgers. But gradually
these would marry and move out. They would choose houses
near Catholic churches and schools, creating a second focus of
concentration.

English Martyrs Church in Sparkhill probably has the largest
Irish congregation outside London. You have to arrive 15 minutes
before the mass to get a seat – services are so packed that overflow
masses have to be held in the parish hall and in a school hall
nearby. At the end of the road Cunningham's newsagent's
devotes half its window space to the material expressions of faith:
rosaries in wood and pastel shades of mother of pearl; paintings
of the Virgin, Saint Christopher or the holy family; plastic statu-
ettes of saints; and a natty line in gilded plastic replicas of St
Peter's that light up, showing transparencies of the Pope.

Evelyn Road, where English Martyrs stands, is nearly all
owner-occupied by Irish. Brigid and Martin McGreal, now both
66, settled there in 1952 with their four sons. Now the eldest lives
next door to them with his Irish wife and four daughters. The
differences between the three generations illustrate the cultural
change among Irish immigrants. Brigid and Martin first came
over in 1934, but went back to Ireland for health reasons during
the war. Till 1952, Martin worked in the peat industry in County
Offaly. 'By that time the eldest were getting restless, and we
could see they'd soon be off to England,' says Brigid. 'We decided
to move as well so we wouldn't be left on our own.' Martin got a
building job, then later became a caretaker at the church school
over the road. They made friends with the Birmingham lady next
door, who sold her house to the eldest son. Now they've had the
wall at the back knocked down, making two gardens into one.
Brigid, who has arthritis, doesn't do much that is specifically Irish
in her spare time: 'I just have the family and I thank God for them
every day.'

Paradoxically, it is the generation that came over as children that seek to preserve their Irishness more than either adult migrants or children born in Britain. Eldest son Jerry's four daughters all learn Irish Ceilidh dancing. 'They've got jarfuls of medals for it,' says Brigid. 'It's wholesome, you know where they are and what they're doing. But I suppose they'll be after liking pop music and discos when they're older. They all do.' They also learn Irish traditional music on the piano, accordion and tin whistle. Jerry drives a heavy goods vehicle for Lucas, and they go to staff dances as well as Irish dances. For a long time he and his wife Anne, whom he met over here, took in Anne's three brothers as lodgers to help pay off the mortgage. But as the brothers moved out to their own homes one by one, they did not take any more in.

Patrick, Brigid's other son still in Birmingham, is an ardent follower of Gaelic football and hurling. Both games draw crowds in Glebe Farm Park. Every social club has its own team. Because matches are on a Sunday, Irishmen don't have to choose between that and soccer, and the majority follow both sports. 'But Gaelic football loses its sparkle for many,' says Patrick, 'because it doesn't have the personalities or the television programmes.' He admits he probably wouldn't be half so keen on things Irish if he were still in Ireland.

Patrick married an English girl, Christine. Because his first job was in a shop, he came across more English people than many Irishmen do. He met Christine at a party. 'Ninety per cent of those brought up here marry English people – but with those who came over here as adults, 90 per cent marry Irish.'

Patrick is a detective with Birmingham CID, whose chief is an Irishman. He has been involved in one or two heated arguments since the bombs started going off, but is quite sure there have been no incidents of victimisation of Irish people because of them. 'What gets me most is the anti-paddy jokes. The English flog to death the thick mick bit – it's diabolical. Everyone feels it's their duty to tell you the latest one. The English are basically very open-minded and liberal, but when they've got their backs up against the wall, they're bigoted. One bloke said to me the other day "I hate the micks and I hate the coons" – but when I told him I was Irish [Patrick has a Brummie accent] he was apologetic.'

Another Irish-dominated road is Bolton Road, Smallheath. The dilapidated houses, built in the 1880s, are rented and due to come down in the next few years. Even here, Asian families are beginning to creep in – the local shop is the Royal Bengal grocer's. Irish families are moving out from Bolton Road all over the city – the houses they vacate are gutted and sealed off with corrugated iron – or lie open with mouldering heaps of rubbish. Here far more of the breadwinners are unskilled labourers or in the building trade.

Susan Brady, aged 20, and Brigid Flynn (about 14), illustrate the cultural differences that just a few years can make. Susan, whose parents came from the Falls Road in Belfast 18 years ago, thinks of herself as completely Irish. She's only just packed in Ceilidh dancing. A few doors down Bolton Road, Brigid didn't like Ceilidh dancing and wasn't forced to do it. Her best friend is a Brummie and she likes pop music.

Some of those who left Bolton Road have gone back to Ireland. After two centuries of exporting people, Ireland is now attracting them back with a booming economy, ten or more columns of jobs in the Irish papers (on sale in Stratford Road on the day of publication). Many return to exploit skills acquired in England that are now in demand back home. A few go back to bring their children up in a saner moral climate (though the Irish I spoke to say things are even more permissive over there). Others have saved up to buy a home or a business.

Some have been back, stayed for a while, and returned to Britain again. Christine Smyth, from Bolton Road, went back six years ago with her husband, but found she could not stick life in a small Northern Ireland village. After two and a half years they were back again. Tom Bermingham came to England 19 years ago after an argument with his foreman – 'I told him where he could stick his job and he did.' Now he works at a BL factory in the body shop, which is 80 per cent Irish and 40 per cent Dublin Irish: 'The English are all right – when they're in a minority.' Tom knows he could not live in Ireland now because he's lost all his roots there. 'I went back to Dublin recently and toured the pubs looking for old friends. I had about two whiskies in each. By the end of the evening I was stone drunk and hadn't met a single person I knew.' Tom is now chairman of St Anne's community centre in Highgate – one of the parish centres that are becoming a main focus for Irish social life.

Only the second generation of Irish in Britain mix a great deal

with the English outside working hours. The rest keep mainly to
their own haunts – dance halls, Irish pubs, clubs with traditional
folk music. Dances are still taken seriously as a courting ground
by Irish men and women in their twenties. Patrick McGreal
explains: 'The Irish male usually works with other males, so he
looks to his leisure to meet girls. The men all sit on one side and
the women on the other. When the band starts up there's a mass
movement across the room. You don't see girls dancing together
like the English do. A man gets very offended if a girl refuses to
dance. He might even complain to the master of ceremonies.'
Teenage boys and girls, though, mix together with much less
formality.

Irish social life in Birmingham is tending to diversify along
social class lines – as it already has done in London between the
upper-class Irish Club, the professional Irish Universities Club,
and the Irish Centre in Camden Town. The two main Birmingham dance halls both feature Irish bands on Fridays and Saturdays, but the building workers and shopgirls go more often to the
Shamrock, and teachers, nurses and social workers go off to the
Mayfair.

Parish community centres are booming. Theoretically, they are
open to all Catholics. In practice, most are Irish. At St Anne's, for
example, some 80 per cent of the members are Irish. Two years
ago, when they opened their new buildings with a gym, a steak
bar, a hall for dances and functions, and two bars, they had one or
two hundred members – now there are 900. Even on a Tuesday
night, when I was there, they were packed in for ballads and a
quiz.

The oldest-established Irish social club in Birmingham, the
Irish Development Association, has an extension of drinking
hours till 2 am. Some disgruntled Irish professional people term it
a 'glorified after-hours boozer'. But it plays a more important role
than that for its 1,500 members. It started up in 1958, and moved
into the Irish Centre, a converted civic restaurant, in 1967.

All the members belong to one of the 32 Irish county associations – there is a provision for a thirty-third association for
people from the Midlands. Each appoints one member to the
governing council. The county associations have three main
functions. Socially, they cater for nostalgia by maintaining links
with the home area, inviting prominent local personalities over,

such as the bishop or the football team. They organise charitable functions to raise funds for adopted institutions in Birmingham or Ireland. And they have a benevolent role for widows, pensioners and the sick – although more serious cases of need are dealt with by the separate, church-sponsored Irish Welfare Association.

The Irish Centre is very conscious of its mission to represent the Irish in Birmingham, and council members are very concerned to counter the blarney-and-booze image. Anyone may be expelled who is guilty of conduct 'unworthy of a gentleman' or who 'fails to uphold the honour of Ireland', or is made bankrupt or expelled from his professional association. Although the Irish vote is not organised as in America, party politicians are discreetly aware that a strong Irish vote can swing whole constituencies (there are 25 on this side of the Irish Sea where their vote is more than 6 per cent). High-ups of both parties, including Harold Wilson, have graced the Birmingham centre with a visit.

The roll call of the association's 33 founder members shows how diversified Irish occupations had become even by 1964, when it was incorporated: five building workers, six factory workers, seven engineering trades, two other workers (a bus driver and a glassblower), ten white-collar or professional (three accountants, a librarian, a teacher, an estate agent, a public health inspector, a clerk and a priest), and three self-employed (a shop owner, a building contractor and a company director). Nevertheless, in selected London boroughs in 1966 (the Birmingham figures are not available), 81 per cent of Irish males were manual workers as against 65 per cent of English and Welsh. That still left 13.2 per cent white collar (English 22 per cent), 3.6 per cent employers (8.3 per cent) and 1 per cent professional (English 3.1 per cent). The Irish are becoming more prominent in other ways. There are now nine Irish councillors on the Birmingham city council. The auxiliary bishop is a Dublin man, and the first Irish JP was recently appointed. There is a weekly Irish column in the Birmingham *Evening Mail*. Irish contractors dominate the Midland building industry.

But they have been much slower than the Asians in setting up other kinds of enterprise. Even along Stratford Road, the main artery through Sparkhill, Asian names crowd out the Irish ones. Takhar enterprises, Anwar supermarket, Rafiki food store, Saree

House, Chief of India restaurant (offering Indian, Parsee, Malayan, English and Irish dishes) – against a scattered few Irish names: Muldoon Autos, Sweeney Rentals. Asian banks outnumber the two new Irish bank branches in Sparkhill. But then, proportionate to population, Asian enterprises would probably far outweigh those of the English working class and their immediate offspring. And the Irish who came over 10 and 20 years ago were overwhelmingly working-class.

As the balance of migration has swung back towards Ireland, the type of migrant is changing, too. Where, before, migration was a sheer necessity, now it is a matter of choice. With a flourishing Irish economy, only the extremes of the qualification scale now look to England – the completely unskilled, among whom there is an increasing proportion of social casualties; and the qualified professionals (teachers, social workers, nurses, doctors) for whom career prospects in Britain are broader. There is a third type, as Irish-based business sees an expanding market among the Irish in Britain – Irish banks and insurance companies. What the actual figures for emigration now are, even the Eire government does not know: but from a postwar peak of 42,400 emigrants in 1956–61 (most of these to England), net emigration fell to 10,781 in 1966–71.

The majority of Irish have settled in well. But at the lower end of the social scale, there are the minority who maintain the image of the 'flailing paddy' – the single labourer who moves about the country from site to site and does more than his share of drinking and fighting. You can see them at seven in the morning outside the monolithic Highgate Hotel in Birmingham – a 500-bed hostel differing from a doss house only in the price (65p for a bed) and the fact that there are single rooms, hardly big enough to hold a bed. Subcontractors roll up in vans, pick their men and take them off to sites all over the Midlands at £4 to £7 per twelve hour shift, with no insurance and no tax. The older ones who can't get work lie all day in Highgate Park next to the 'hotel'. I was talking to one Irishman who was obviously an alcoholic when another came up and told me to take no notice of him: 'He goes off to the national assistance, taking the money out of our mouths he is.' 'And good luck to me if I do,' says the one. 'I'll bash your fucking teeth down your throat one of these days,' says the other. I asked him why he didn't work during the day. 'Could you work after a night under those trees there?' he said, and then touched me for the price of a bottle of cider.

But, for the overall picture of the Irish in Britain, the stereotype of the fighting navvy is laughably inaccurate. There are divisions which become increasingly complex as time goes on. There are pronounced generation gaps between first-generation migrants and their children, and between these and the grandchildren. The gaps are no wider than among the English, but their form is different. And there are sizeable clefts widening between working-class Irish, those who have now made it, and the new professionals: they all preserve their Irishness, but they are beginning to do so separately. There is increasing political and economic integration with the English – but only a beginning of social or geographical integration. It is a pity that the wave of bomb attacks has made most of those I spoke to feel less at home here, and more like aliens.

20 September 1973

8
The Jews of Cheetham Hill

Ian Walker

Tombstones and synagogues are daubed quite regularly, she said, sitting in the cafe in Cheetham Parade which looks out on to the benches at the centre of this ugly, purpose-built shopping centre around which the old Jews of the neighbourhood gather to pass the time of day.

Estelle is 32, a third-generation Manchester Jew. Her grandparents came from eastern Europe at the turn of the century. Her father was a *schmeerer*, Yiddish slang for the work of smearing rubber solution on to fabric in the waterproof garment industry which, before the war, was a big source of employment for Manchester Jews.

A supply teacher of mathematics, Estelle lives with her parents in Cheetham Hill which, with Whitefield and Prestwich, houses a suburban Jewish middle class whose ancestors came mostly from Poland, Rumania and Russia between the late nineteenth century and the middle of this century. Sephardic Jews, who came from Spain and Portugal in the eighteenth and early nineteenth centuries, live in the south Manchester suburbs.

There are an estimated 35,000 Jews in Manchester. Like the Jewish populations of Leeds (18,000) and Glasgow (13,500) and London (280,000), Manchester's has changed identity – blue collar to white, terraces to semis – without solving the problem of identity. In Manchester the waterproof garment industry is more or less dead, and the Jewish Working Men's Club closed down in the 1960s. But anti-semites aren't impressed by upward mobility.

And among the *goyim* – the non-Jews – anti-semitism runs

deep. There are seven definitions of 'jew' in the Collins English Dictionary, that most updated collection of British meanings. They range, in the dictionary's typology, from 'offensive and obsolete' (*to jew*: to drive a hard bargain) to just plain 'offensive' (*jew*: a miserly person). Estelle doesn't believe in any gods, but she lives with those definitions.

Her brother, she said, is different. A computer programmer, he has turned his back on his Jewishness; he decided it is irrelevant. That is his strategy. Estelle, who immerses herself in the Jewish political and cultural life of Cheetham, has another. Others, still, turn to religious orthodoxy or hardline Zionism. Some settle in Israel.

Estelle drained her coffee. Outside, the tarmac was sweating in the sun, sticking to the soles of the old men and women who stood and talked. Sitting on the bench, under a poster for cider, a woman read her romantic novel. On the next bench two men discussed Begin.

'Well,' one said, with a strong Mancunian delivery. 'I think he's a good, straightforward man.' His friend, who was wearing a blue suit and a brown trilby, wasn't too sure, but anyway he was more interested in talking about the problems of finding a second wife.

'I want a woman who is nice to look at, with money, high principles, who is kind and clean. My friend says you aren't looking for a woman. You want five women,' he said, holding open his hands.

Estelle walked home along Upper Park Road. This tree-lined lane fronts prewar and postwar semis, 1940s mock-Tudor palaces, 1960s bungalows, new redbrick blocks of flats. Shiny V, W and X-registration saloons sat on the driveways.

Estelle's semi was in a more downmarket zone. The living room was strewn with clothes. Her mother makes some money doing alterations for the neighbours. It supplements her father's pension and Estelle's irregular earnings from teaching. Jews tend to leave one family only when they are about to start one of their own. The youth do not disappear to bedsits and flats, nor do the old live alone.

Her mother went outside to make a cup of tea. Estelle said that her father was also an atheist. The *menorah* (seven-branched candelabra) on the piano, she explained, was there simply because it was on the piano when it was given to them by a neighbour.

That night Estelle and two of her friends, Sheila and Mike, met in a new nightclub called Quentins. Sheila, an unemployed teacher, is a divorcee with two children. Mike, a pharmacist, is also single. 'It's a sort of tragi-comic situation for Jews in our position, who would like to marry another Jew,' said Estelle. 'Because it's a very small number of people who are in the right age group. You go round and round in ever-diminishing circles. There's fewer people every time.'

The disc jockey played compilation 45s. There were only about a dozen people in the place, a slow Monday. Sheila said that her grandfather had walked all the way right from Russia to France, before getting the boat across to England. Mike grinned at her, disbelieving. Sheila continued with the story.

He used to walk at night, she said, to avoid detection. When he arrived at British customs, he had a sign hung round his neck and on the sign was written his name, age and place of birth. He spoke Yiddish. Sheila, like a lot of third-generation Jews, said that although she can't speak Yiddish herself, she finds she can understand it.

Mike is short and bearded. Like Estelle, he drinks Coke. Sheila has made a sweet sherry last an hour. 'It's because the Jews were always driven out by drunken bigots. That's why we don't drink much,' said Sheila.

Estelle disagreed. She said that it is because Jewish children were routinely given wine during celebrations. Alcohol is not the forbidden fruit it is for non-Jewish children. Judaism is a home and family-based religion.

'None of us is religious,' said Sheila, and then looking hard at her two friends around the table. 'But we know what we are, don't we?'

After Sheila broke up with her husband, she started going out with a non-Jew, a Welshman; and he used to shrug when she wanted to talk about being a Jew. 'He wouldn't talk about it. He wouldn't understand how important it was for me. I remember once, he'd been driving me around, and I said that's the third National Front poster I've seen tonight. He said, "Don't be ridiculous. You're making it up, imagining it." But I had seen three,' she said.

Sheila went out with the Welshman for four years. She never told her parents about it. Once her boyfriend took Sheila home to meet his parents at Christmas.

'As soon as I walked in, his mother cried,' said Sheila. 'I thought she was crying for joy, for seeing her son after such a long time. But no. It was because he'd brought a Jew home for Christmas.'

A man in a lounge suit, who looked like a nightclub manager, came up and apologised for the candle going out. The DJ was playing a song by Spandau Ballet: 'Don't need this pressure on, don't need this pressure on. . . .' Do you ever feel schizophrenic, I said, carrying a Jewish identity through the scenery and sounds of British culture, like this trashy nightclub, for example?

'I've sat in a Chinese restaurant with reform Jews,' replied Estelle. 'They were eating chow mein and complaining about assimilation.'

Sheila said that she liked eating bacon, but she would only buy it at Tescos, where she could hide it under some vegetables or something. Jews had, on occasion, spotted her picking up the perma-sealed packs. She said she felt terrible.

None of these three kept the *kashrut*, a kosher kitchen; but Sheila said she observes some of the rituals because she thinks they are very beautiful, and also because she has fond memories of them from her childhood: the atmosphere created by the candles on the Sabbath.

'Judaism is a highly absorbent religion,' said Rabbi Silverman next morning at the reform synagogue in Jackson's Row, in central Manchester. 'Orthodox rabbis at one time used to wear dog collars. And there was a new title created, the Chief of Rabbis, which corresponded to the Archbishop of Canterbury, something of an English invention. In marriage we have a best man, which isn't a Jewish thing, and the father leading the daughter down the aisle.'

There is also a Jewish prayer for the Queen, said Rabbi Silverman, who is young and wears a lounge suit and a skull cap.

A Londoner, he has been in Manchester for three years. This was his first appointment after leaving rabbinical college. The synagogue has 1,300 individual members, and there are 800 households on his mailing list. The congregation is predominantly middle-class.

He described himself as 'ceremonially traditional, but radical in theology, aggressively so.' Though he denied there was any antagonism between the reform and orthodox wings of rabbinism, he acknowledged there was a problem there sometimes.

The reform movement is regularly accused by the orthodox of diluting Judaism, of copping out, of encouraging *assimilation* – the word that spikes most Jewish discourse about themselves, though there is no evidence that young Jews are becoming less Jewish, or 'marrying out' more frequently, than their forbears.

'People marrying out are weakening the Jewish fold,' said the rabbi. 'Jewish survival has always been dependent upon people leading a full Jewish life within their home as well as the synagogue.' He added that there was also a fair amount of 'marrying in' – people who take on the faith when they marry a Jew – which strengthened the Jewish fold.

On the way out I talked to the secretary, a woman of 26. She is still single. She would prefer to marry someone of her own kind, she said. 'But if I met a non-Jew I really hit it off with, I might. You never know. But probably because of the ghetto-like conditions in which we live, I just don't mix with non-Jewish people. And with me working here. . . .'

She also said: 'I mix in mostly Jewish circles. Because it's what I want.'

I went back to Cheetham Hill, and walked into the kibbutz club. On the noticeboard one poster advertised the Women's Campaign for Soviet Jewry, which is trying to establish family links between British and Soviet Jewry, to make it easier for the latter to emigrate. The poster had lists of names against towns, starting with Abramovich of Moscow.

Upstairs in his office was Baruch Kalmon who left Liverpool in 1961, when he was 24, to settle in Israel. He is now 44. His home is a kibbutz called Matzuva, a couple of miles from the Lebanese border. But he has been living in Cheetham Hill for the last 18 months, working in Britain for the kibbutz movement.

A short-sleeved shirt, tight, displayed his muscular frame. He folded his fists on the table, looked at me hard in the eye. There is still a trace of Scouse in his accent: 'I think Cheetham Hill is a community that has a problem of identity.'

Baruch is one of 30,000 British Jews who have resolved that problem by emigration to Israel. He is not religious himself – 'I observe the Sabbath and that's it' – and he sounded weary of the *Angst* exhibited by Jews in the diaspora. But he had more respect for orthodox than reform Jews. The way he put it, the orthodox had more bottle.

'I don't think you can be Jewish in name only,' he said, 'and that's why I respect the orthodox. They're toeing the line. And that's why the other people, the reform, have a problem. The other alternative is the renaissance of the Jewish people in their own land. And I've done it, a living example. So I'm not soapbox, you know?'

Baruch's wife is Dutch, a survivor of the holocaust, and he has just returned from a tour of Holland and West Germany with 76 Jewish young people from Manchester, London and Glasgow. The idea was to bring the holocaust home to them, he said. In Holland a non-Jewish survivor from Auschwitz came over to speak and, in West Germany, the young Jews were told: 'You are here today as free Jewish citizens of the UK in a Germany where, 40 years ago, you'd have been locked away on sight.'

A lot were in tears, he said, after the Auschwitz survivor had spoken.

Downstairs is a private nursery. The children were eating their lunch – shepherd's pie. I walked again up this leafy lane, Upper Park Road. It seemed, even more than before, too conspicuously normal, as if a whole subculture had become disguised in the clothes, houses and cars of the English bourgeoisie.

Heathlands is a Jewish old people's home, opened in 1971. It stands in five acres of grounds, and at 3.30 that afternoon the residents were out in the gardens, taking tea.

Mr and Mrs Brazil had only been there a week, but it's a lovely place all right, she said, adding that her husband – staring blankly across the lawns – was a touch senile. She is 79.

Her parents came from Warsaw. She was born in Manchester. Her father, she said, was a ladies' tailor. Her husband's father was a gents' tailor. She thinks the current generation have turned away from religion:

'When we were little girls we weren't allowed on the buses on a Saturday, and we had someone in to light the fire. Used to come in and put wood on the fire and light the kettle. It has changed, all that. Now everything is made easy for everyone, and still people moan. My father, he used to work through the night, every

Thursday through to Friday. He died a young man, he was only 52, but he was a gentlemen.'

Away from the main tea-time clamour on the terrace, three men sat under a parasol on the lawn. They all thought that Jews in Manchester were far more religious these days.

'In my day,' said Henry, who worked as a *schmeerer* and has hard Mancunian vowels, 'the Jewish lads wasn't religious as they are today.'

The reason for that was poverty, said Abraham, who did all kinds of jobs but ended up being a taxi driver. 'Worked eight days a week to get a living. No time for religion. These days, more time, more money, smaller families. Only people these days who have big families are the ultra orthodox: they like a lot of sons,' he said.

Sam also worked as a *schmeerer*, from the age of 14 to 16. But he said that work was scarce; they'd only be employed in the factory for up to six months a year. The rest of the time they'd go out 'clapping': knocking on doors, trying to buy things which they'd sell on the markets. Or else, he said, they'd run a book, try to make a bob or two.

'That's how Gus Denning started. Biggest bookmaker in the country,' said Sam. 'He still owes me ten bob.' Sam has lived for spells in New York and Boston. For 40 years he ran a gents' outfitters.

'There's our Reverend, with the black hat on,' said one of them, pointing to a man stepping into a saloon parked outside the terrace. There is a small synagogue at Heathlands. 'You need no less than ten men for a service,' said Henry, pulling down his flat cap. 'Very hard to find ten men who are willing to do it. Seventy per cent are women here.' Women don't count to a quorum.

'You're not forced to go,' added Abraham. 'We're not what you call fully orthodox. Very hard to be an orthodox Jew. Very hard.'

Sam stared down at the terrace, looking for a man called Simon Stone who is 100. He would have liked me to have met him. Great character, he said. 'He likes a pint.'

There is no bar at Heathlands, just a confectioner's. The inmates get their pension taken off them, and every fortnight they are given £10.90 spending money. If you don't smoke, there's not much to spend money on here, said Henry. He sold up his house after his last family died, and wrote the cheque, for £9,000, to Heathlands.

A man in an old grey suit and flat cap, Lionel, shuffled across the lawn. Lionel was a bookie's clerk for 25 years. Now, at 86, he's almost completely blind.

'Oh, I've been well looked after,' Lionel said. 'All good lads, especially at Manchester. You can't lick 'em.' He said he once took Chico Marx to the races.

A couple of the inmates had told me that at Heathlands there were some survivors from the concentration camps. I remembered getting a lift in Israel with a man who had a number tattooed on the back of his hand. The holocaust made it impossible for a non-Jew in Israel to be critical of Zionism. The same was true of Sheila: anti-Zionism, for her, is just a modern form of anti-semitism.

In a wine bar on Bury New Road I met another of Estelle's circle, Alan Ross, chairman of the Jewish Community Relations Group, one of about 150 voluntary Jewish organisations in Manchester. He sat down with Beryl Werber, secretary of the group. Loud disco played through the speakers.

A tall, shy man, Alan works as a superviser in the Unilever factory. Born and bred in nearby Crumpsall, he has been active in community work for the last ten years. He's now 36. Beryl, who is 34, runs a shoe shop in Salford. The community relations group, said Alan, tries to build bridges between the Jews and other Manchester minorities. So far they'd held joint events with the local Ukrainians, Moslems and West Indians.

But it was an uphill struggle, Alan said. People were too suspicious, too insular. 'There's a lot of people scared of their children going to non-Jewish discos and clubs,' he said. 'Last year I met someone from the West Indian community, a community leader, and she was married to a Jewish bloke. It was ideal, to me. They'd met in Jamaica. Heart-rending in a way, wasn't it?' He turned his head towards Beryl, who nodded.

Alan once organised a dance for different minorities in Manchester. 'People didn't come, with it being a dance. Thought they might meet people of a different religion,' he said, sighing. 'Plus it was an awful night. Hadn't stopped raining all day.'

They both sipped their *rosé*. By 9.30 pm the wine bar was packed, mostly with Jews in their teens and early twenties, with money to spend midweek. 'Did you see the film, *Babylon*?' Alan asked, suddenly. 'It was fortunate that in Manchester it played in a porno cinema. So most of them there was expecting some soft porn or something. But it's a good job not many white people saw it. It would have given them a terrible idea about blacks. The whole film was about disco equipment, and who could play music the loudest. I mean, what a terrible impression to give of the black community.'

'It was very violent, too,' said Beryl.

Alan said how pleased he was that the local police would be sending representatives along to the group's festival at the Ukrainian Centre this month. Alan believes that the riots in Manchester in the summer were a disgrace, and that the fascists must have had a hand in it.

Sheila arrived at the wine bar with Estelle, who said that a friend of hers had seen National Front leaflets being distributed during the riots, which was proof positive. Brick-throwing and Nazis seem, for Estelle and her friends, to be an irresistible connection. Rabbi Silverman had told me that Jews in the suburbs were scared now, thinking that the rioters would maybe come up round their way.

Riot. It summons up Germany in the 1930s, disorder in the streets, banging on the door. It provokes a sort of sickness. Sheila said that that is one of the reasons why Jews tend not to publicise racist attacks on their people and property: they are fearful it will encourage more, imitative, violence.

She knows of one incident in north Manchester where a Jewish youth club leader was beaten up by the National Front. She said that the Jewish boys stood and watched. She wished they had fought back, like the Asians in Southall.

Later that night, towards closing time, with most people disappearing to the cars outside, Sheila got involved in an argument with an Irish friend of hers, who was born a Catholic, then was an atheist for 18 years, till recently he became converted to the Pentecostal Church. Sheila believed, first, that there was an international, terrorist, anti-semitic plot and, second, that no act of terrorism was ever justified.

The Irishman replied there was no conspiracy, and that terrorism was just a pejorative, used to describe the violence of the enemy. It was, therefore, a complicated moral question. The disco tape clicked off. Everyone went home.

Martin Bobker, whom I spoke to next afternoon in his garden, was orphaned at 16, worked as a butcher's boy, then for a French polisher, before becoming a *schmeerer*. After the Second World War, he was able to re-train as a teacher. He is now, at 70, head of Cheetwood primary school.

He joined the Communist Party when he was 21, the day after Hitler came to power in 1933. 'The definition of a Jew is the definition that is acceptable to other people. Hitler didn't give a bugger about orthodox or reform,' he said. 'I agreed with Leo Abse when he said, "What makes me a Jew is anti-semitism." Marx also said that the Jewish people had been preserved, not in spite of anti-semitism, but because of anti-semitism.'

Martin grew up in High Town, just below Cheetham Hill. He remembers the anti-Jewish gangs that used to maraud around Strangeways in the mid-1920s, and it was these people who later joined Mosley's blackshirts. Mosley had his local headquarters in London Road, by the railway station, but his barracks were in Salford. It was a direct route through Bury New Road. Young Jews had to form their own gangs to defend the area.

'The blackshirts bullied and terrorised everyone, until these lads got together. Put a stop to it,' he said, seated on the sloping back lawn of his semi in Whitefield.

In the 1930s, most of the young Jews in the Strangeways and Cheetham area were identified in one way or another with the Young Communist League, he said. Some of his friends went to fight in Spain. Martin was too young to go. He stayed behind and organised events for the YCL, including camps on behalf of the British Workers Sports Federation.

'I organised some good camps,' he said. 'Peace camps. Anti-fascist camps. Unity camps, which we held jointly with the Labour League of Youth.'

Martin left the Communist Party in 1953 to join the Labour Party. He is chairman of his local ward, and vice-chairman of the Middleton and Whitefield constituency. His own life, *schmeerer* to headmaster, is a mirror of the class movement of the Jews. He said it first really hit him, how much things had changed, when the Jewish Lads Brigade (a branch of the Boys Brigade) invited him to speak, in 1960, about a neo-Nazi movement which had risen up in West Germany.

'I was talking to them like I had done prewar – I mean, I used to stand up on chairs outside factories and address the Jewish workers. And I suddenly realised not one of them worked in a factory. They didn't know what I was talking about.'

The only Jewish workers left in Manchester, he said, are a few old men. And whereas, before the war, no Jew would vote right of Labour, now there are large numbers of Tory Jews. The other force which has shoved Jews to the right has been, he said, the growth of Zionism.

'With the establishment of Israel,' he said, 'the Zionist influence was complete, on the Board of Deputies of British Jews, and in the local representative councils. And with the advent of people from eastern Europe coming over to take up jobs, people who were very learned in Jewish traditional life, there was a tremendous development of ultra-orthodox elements.'

Martin feels it is possible that some of the actions of the state of Israel could lead to the development of anti-semitism. In any case, Israel could not solve the problems of Jews in the diaspora, he said. 'Zionism has deflected people from trying to find solutions in the countries in which they are settled.'

He took me into the house, made a cup of coffee, and then pulled some old folders, pamphlets and cuttings, in plastic bags, out of a drawer. He scattered his political past all over the table, and put on his glasses.

There he was at a peace conference, a good-looking man of 25. That was the censored issue of the *Daily Worker*, on 5 September 1942. Those were the files he kept on the Rosenberg case. There was the magazine he edited while he was at Freckleton training college, from 1949 to 1950. And there were two letters he wrote to the papers: one about his opposition to German re-armament, in 1963, and one about the price of kosher meat.

He grabbed another cutting: the Jewish Lads Brigade tried to organise a mixed dance with Flixton youth club in July 1958, an event which was stopped by the communal council. And another: COUNCILLOR SAT SHTUM (said nothing), SAYS AJEX MAN. The Ajex (Association of Jewish Ex-Servicemen) man was Martin. The event this time, the Notting Hill race riots in 1958.

Martin's eldest son is a research chemist, his youngest a doctor of mathematics. His daughter is a deputy head. 'They haven't done badly really. In spite of all my nefarious activities,' he said, taking off his glasses.

                                                            1 October 1981

9
The tents at the gate of the city

Michael Williams

'Decide who you are,' wrote Jonathan Raban in his book, *Soft City*, 'and the city will assume a fixed form around you.' Toxteth is a bit like that. It doesn't even exist as a place – locally it's Liverpool 8, or even better, the Rialto, Princes Park, Granby or the Dingle. If you really know your stuff, you simply call it the Southend.

If you're a Liverpool poet (and the fame that Adrian Henri and Roger McGough brought Toxteth in the 1960s may still outlast that of the riots), it's a crumbling bohemian paradise for romantics, writers, painters, students and lovers. If you're a Pevsner, it's Scott's Gothic cathedral (Europe's third largest) and the Georgian terraces built for the carriage- (and slave-) owning classes.

If you're a poor white Protestant, living in the back-to-backs down by the Mersey, the view is dominated by the South Docks, once everybody's employer, now weed-choked and derelict.

If you're black, you probably live a bit further from the riverfront. You're probably locally born and educated, and speak the common language of Liverpool. Yet you know, without reading the statistics, that living in Toxteth means you're more likely to be unemployed, picked up by the police, less likely to get a proper place to live, or even a taxi to take you home. The irony of living in a former slave-owner's home is wasted, if the rent is extortionate and the council won't re-house you.

Margaret Simey's view, as the new chairman of the police committee, is from the top of the Merseyside county council offices, a megalopoloid new tower on the waterfront, opposite the place where the big liners used to berth when they still came up the Mersey. As a veteran campaigner for social justice and a Toxteth councillor for 18 years, she's more at home in the streets of the Southend, where she lives. But the vista across the business end of the city to the cathedrals and disused dock warehouses in the south makes her point. Toxteth, she says, is a 'fourth world' now – a place where ordinary political and moral structures have lost their meaning:

'In school, they tell you to work hard, but there's no work. The churches tell you to be good, but where's the incentive for being good? The city has become like a citadel with high walls. For the people in Toxteth it's like being in the tents outside. Within the gates, the council, the police, the judiciary, make the rules, but the outsiders are excluded. Magistrates and policemen don't live in Liverpool 8. The people there can only respond by making their own subculture.'

On this Thursday after the storming of the citadel, Liverpool is on the defensive. All the way up Leece Street and Hardman Street on the way out of town, the shops are boarded up, just in case. It looks like a Greek town at siesta time, except it's coming on to drizzle. In the alley by the Philharmonic Hall is a line of coaches that might be a holiday tour. Rugby, Heckmondwike, Caernarvon, Portmadoc, Wakefield, they say on the back. It's only when you notice the riot shields being loaded on board, and the policemen inside, that you realise what they're there for.

'It makes you ashamed,' says a woman in the bus queue outside Littlewoods. 'I read in the *Echo* the other day,' says a man selling newspapers at Moorfields station, 'that one of these black fellas, big he was, knocked on a door and pulled all the rings off a woman's hand – 92 she was, I think.'

At the Community Relations Council, up the road in Mount Pleasant, everyone says they're exhausted. 'I've got a French television crew just come in. What shall I do with them?' At the *Daily Post* offices, the Liverpool 8 Defence Committee hand out pamphlets saying they're asking blacks to boycott white press reporters.

But Liverpool has a well-rehearsed knack of coping with the hurt. When they tore the heart out of the city in the sixties – decanting people to the new estates like Cantril Farm and Netherley – they wrote songs about it. They still sing them in the pubs round Everton, even though most of the old inhabitants have gone.

The playwright, Alan Bleasdale, who like many Liverpudlians who've made it down south, prefers to live in the city, says he's heard the first of the Toxteth jokes already. One doing the rounds goes: 'Willie Whitelaw is in the official car on the way to do his inspection of Upper Parly Street and Lodge Lane. He looks out of the window and says, "Terrible, terrible." "We haven't got there yet," the driver replies. "You're looking at what the Corpy built last week."'

Things do seem to get back to normal. Schoolgirls in uniforms and white ankle-socks walk past the old Rialto cinema, which still smells of ashes and water, to get to Blackburne House school. Up in Lodge Lane, thick with gas and electricity vans, the Alis, Mohammeds and Giovannis – untouched by the looters – put out meat and vegetables for the day's business.

There's an old Scouse saying, 'It's a long lane widout a lump of dog's muck in it', and many realistic Liverpudlians had seen the trouble coming for a long time. 'Like ants,' Margaret Simey says, 'we brought the sticks bit by bit to the bonfire.' In the Playhouse the artistic director, Chris Bond, talks about a local writer, Ken Murray, who predicted the burning in a play three years ago. A policeman is stripped naked by the crowd at the bottom of Upper Parliament Street and thrown back into the police lines. Then the fire goes up. Bond would have put it on – except that there wasn't the cash for such a large cast of battling policemen.

There's another bit of local wisdom that runs: 'The existence of the good old days depends on a bad old memory.' And there's a lot about the current troubles that isn't new. At the Christian Centre, in Princes Road, Pastor David Valentine waits for people to bring back the spoils of the looting – which nearly everyone seems to agree was done by the whites from the Dingle while the blacks had the police busy down by the Rialto.

It would be surprising if he got much back. In Liverpool there's a different morality about putting something in your pocket: it derives from the casual labour system that the city operated for so long. As Margaret Simey says: 'If a man was laid off in the docks, and he didn't know when he'd be hired again, he might snitch a bunch of bananas. It was accepted.' The point is neatly made in the old dockers' joke about the man called Dulux because he gets it all in one coat.

A man describes how someone he knew got a washing machine from a shop window and was chased by the police with it up the stairs of a Mill Street high-rise because the lift wasn't working. In a bookshop behind St George's Hall, you can buy a paperback biography (*Back Crack Boy*, by Joseph McKeown) that tells the same story but from the Birkenhead unemployment riots of 1932: 'It's the Jacks, came the drunken yell. The house became a kaleidoscope of activity as we tried to hide the loot. Everywhere bulged with ill-gotten gains, as we sought hiding places behind the Sacred Heart picture, in the lavatory.'

Racial conflict isn't new to Liverpool. In the university sociology department – built on the site of one of Toxteth's old shopping streets, which might well have been looted if the university hadn't looted it first – Ian Law talks about his research into the history of racialism in the city. By Victorian times, he says, despite the familiarity with blacks through the port and the slave trade, racialism was in full swing.

In 1862 Henry Mayhew wrote, on a visit to the city: 'It is only common fairness to say that Negroes seldom slack at work – their only trouble is to obtain it.' Dickens got the same picture when he toured the Liverpool slums for *The Uncommercial Traveller* in 1866, and noticed how the blacks suffered 'slights' from the local people.

It was when these slights turned to violence that the first race riots happened, in 1919. Often encouraged by the local police, groups of men toured the Southend, attacking blacks and their homes. One night a black seaman called Charles Wootton (now a local folk hero) hit back with an axe, injuring eight people. The mob threw him in the South Docks.

The 1948 Toxteth riots followed a similar pattern. The issue here was partly about jobs, but white groups attacked black clubs and houses, leading to 50 arrests. In 1972 there were more riots – this time over housing – on the Falkner estate built on the edge of the university in the first phase of Toxteth's renewal.

There may seem to be many of the old racial ingredients in the 1981 riots, but there's one crucial difference. This time, it's not black versus white, but poor black and poor white against white authority. The equation has taken on a new element from a different but equally deep-seated aspect of Liverpool culture.

Hatred of the police has always been strong in the city. In 1911, police and troops fired on strikers who were demonstrating against falling wages. Two strikers were killed. But there's another anti-authoritarian tradition that springs not just from Liverpool's black immigrants, but from other groups who came to the city with experience of oppression or poverty – the Irish, the Jews, and particularly the Welsh, whose Nonconformism was vigorously anti-Anglican and anti-establishment. People still remember a song that goes:

> Down Richmond Row they pay no rent,
> When the landlord comes, they say the
>   rent is spent –
> Hit 'im on the 'ead wid a poker,
> Lay 'im out on the sofa.

The point about white authority is underlined by Alex Bennett, a black community worker. 'It was obvious why people went for the police, but there were exact reasons why each of those buildings was hit' – the bank for obvious reasons, the Racquets Club because the judges use it, Swainbank's furniture store because people felt he was ripping off the community. He says it's a newspaper lie that anyone touched the hospital or their own homes.

Lucille, black and in her thirties, runs the multiracial Rialto Neighbourhood Council from a 1950s walk-up estate a few yards from the burnt-out Rialto. She is even more definite. 'No, we weren't frightened, because we knew just what people were going for.' Her neighbours (both white) agree. There was the shop where someone's brother, over from Africa, went to change a fiver and came out with a pound note and a shoebox of sweets, the shop where an old women went in for a light and was charged a penny for a 'lucy' (a match).

The Chinese chippy was left untouched ('Mrs Ling is all right'). But people hadn't forgotten that when the Rialto was a dance hall it was barred to blacks. Eventually they only allowed black women. Anglo-Saxon womanhood was protected from seduction by black men.

Now, with the Racquets and the Rialto gone, it's just the police. 'They won't be satisfied until every kid round here has got a record,' one of the women says. 'We're supposed to have a community policeman round here, but you can be sure he wasn't to be seen on Friday or Saturday. There's no end to it. There'll be more trouble, believe me. The CID will be round to every flat looking for the looted stuff. And when they don't find it, the whole thing will go up again.'

Feeling about the police doesn't just run high on the streets. Ewan Gillespie, who runs the youth club in Beaconsfield Street – which is the most popular black club in the area – says of them: 'The police treat all youngsters round here as criminals, as less than people. There's no respect any more.'

Behind the clubroom's steel doors, the black kids, furiously playing pool, snooker and table tennis, say they've nearly all had trouble with the police, are on the dole or the 'schemes'. But Gillespie doesn't think that unemployment ('though a very big problem') caused the riots. 'If the copper who pulled that lad off his bike last Friday night had even known his name, it might never have happened. But they don't apply that standard of policing round here.'

The political parties, he says, are happy to talk about the environment (1,400 new dwellings in the past ten years, mostly low-rise and many built to defensible-space rules). 'But what about the police? There's rarely a word about that. What can you do to change it?'

This Friday afternoon, at its special meeting a week after the riots began, the city council gets its chance. For a rare moment the people from the tents outside are prepared to note what those in the citadel have to say, and the gallery is full of black faces.

The black community leader, Wally Brown, pleads for the police to be made more accountable. The Tory leader thinks the police and fireman should be given a civic reception. Labour and Liberal leaders squabble about the Militant Tendency. Toxteth is promised, as usual, 'that full account of its hopes and needs will be taken'.

The fourth-worlders go home to streets where the police walk in fives and unemployment nears 50 per cent. The irony of the town hall busts of blackamoors and elephants and the council motto – GOD HAS GIVEN US THIS LEISURE – is not wasted on them.

16 July 1981

10
The joys of joyriding

Howard Parker

Up to 200 cars are taken and driven away from Liverpool's city centre each week. Although joyriding accounts for only a small proportion of this number, it is still regarded with concern. This is because joyriding escapades involve extensive damage and often the total destruction of the vehicle taken, as well as damage to other property and possible injury to pedestrians. For these reasons, the joyriders are called particularly unfriendly names such as 'mindless' and 'a danger to society'. These labels lead to rhetorical questions like, 'How do we stop it – lock up the ringleaders for a long time?' (That was one senior police officer's potential solution.)

Joyriding in Liverpool is largely an early adolescent activity and is distinct from the more common adult 'borrowing' of cars to get from one place to another. The joyrider is not mainly concerned with saving a taxi fare or carrying stolen goods. He is looking for excitement, competition, status and adrenalin-pumping stimulation. This, in short, means *action* – the taking of risks which can otherwise be avoided. The vehicle is taken without permission, to be driven for the action offered by the whole process of getting an illegal self-driven car ride.

While young joyriding teams are growing up throughout the city, I shall just be writing about one inner neighbourhood which has the most extensive and sophisticated adolescent joyriders in the city. My information is based on conversations with locals, taped interviews and direct observation.

Ths neighbourhood has become increasingly recognised by officialdom as more than just another inner-city problem area. Vandalism, delinquency, tenant unrest, rent refusal, landings of empty flats – all indicate a community tension in an area of high unemployment, butt-end jobs and minimal facilities. Juvenile delinquency is partly a symptom of this malaise. When the early adolescent is not at school, he is likely to be hanging around the neighbourhood. Nearly all the joyriders I spoke to said they were rarely at home and always 'out', since the flat was 'dead boring' and 'full of whining kids'. The youngster pushed into the street by such family pressure has to create his own excitement and he is likely at some time or another to be delinquent. 'That night we took that dumper truck, remember, honest to God we had a laugh. We were only standing there when Tony says, "Come on, let's take that dumper round the block." Only it steered dead funny and we were crashing it and everything. In the end there was a whole load of us on it . . . and I only came out for some ciggies.'

It is difficult to say exactly why joyriding has become an important activity in this neighbourhood specifically. What can be said of delinquent styles here is that while they are partly transmitted by various sources, such as older adolescents, they are also transformed by each new generation. Joyriding is one such recent transformation. Misdemeanour involving theft from, and taking and driving away, vehicles accounts for 33 per cent of offences recorded in the Liverpool area. Joyriding is one branch of a larger and more complex shift of delinquent styles involving the car.

The rise of the car to its now immense status is important for understanding joyriding. The potential joyrider soons tunes in to street-corner talk about the status of the car. Talk about the 'whizz merchants', 'going on the cars', 'screwing cars' and 'robbing cars' has its impact on the young pretender.

The car symbolises material success. The few locals who own cars (3 per cent, according to an independent survey) are seen as 'doing OK', or having 'got it made' because they 'drive a smart danny'. Even the probation officer who 'thinks he's Stirling Moss' is viewed with admiration. A car's desirability also creates the opposite reaction, in that envy is easily turned to resentment and aggression towards, for instance, the 'jewboy', the 'poser', the 'toffee nose' and the 'business classes' who sport expensive and powerful cars.

All these street-corner attitudes affect the youngsters, eager to be 'big' and 'hard'. These youngsters consider these views, along with press and television's portrayal of the car and its connection with manliness; add some personal touches; and conclude that the car is desirable, the car matters.

Joyriding in this part of Liverpool developed from several roughly simultaneous sources about four years ago. The most significant innovators were a group of then 13-year-olds, who sometimes helped in the nearby car auction rooms. Here they learnt about the car and took tentative drives around the forecourt. With a knowledge of key codes, and a few keys of their own, the next stage was to go around the city, trying to open car doors. Sometimes things would be taken from the car; other times the engine might be turned on and revved up before everybody would run away. 'It was bound to happen sooner or later. In the end, Moggy found a car with the key in the ignition and he drove it up to the block. That was the start of it and after that it just spread.'

Early joyriding was limited exclusively to Minis, which were easy to get into, start and drive – especially if you were a rather small 14-year-old. Minis were infinitely more potent than the traditional ride on the stolen bike or moped. From these beginnings, with no more than half a dozen mid-adolescents being spasmodically involved, joyriding has escalated into a craze – especially during the summer months when excitement is most needed to fill the time.

The situation is now rather complex, with age differentials having widened from the 13 to 15 into the 10- to 16-year-old bracket. 'It was just a few of us, Micky's lot and our lot, but all the kids want to do the cars now. They want to show off, like show the older blokes that they're just as hard. You can't blame them, like. We was like that over robbing when we were their age.' This growth means joyriding escapades can now be simultaneous and independent of each other, and indeed actually competitive, as well as interdependent and shared.

This increased knowledge, sophistication and competition has led to major changes in the nature of joyriding. Considerable escalation has occurred with, for instance, the members of the auction room network. As their contest with the police has intensified, they have taken their own precautions. Since two members of the group were arrested during a joyride because, in their terms, 'we'd no chance, the motor wasn't worth a carrot', these senior joyriders have become more selective about the vehicles they acquire. Higher-status cars have become desirable, and Cortinas and any GT models are being sought. The added power of these cars, the boys feel, is necessary to compete with the police Morris Marinas. Indeed, very recently, a Marina itself was acquired and driven around the area. They seem to feel that if the police drive Marinas around town 'like fuckin' lunatics', why shouldn't we?

This senior joyriding group claims to have partly initiated 'the chase', examples of which have increased annually. Since this group and other contemporaries have ventured outside the neighbourhood on their pleasure trips, their chances of being spotted by the police have multiplied. Such an encounter may lead to 'the chase'. This is a still rare but much talked-about confrontation, whereby the joyriders return at top speed, pursued by the police, into the privacy of their neighbourhood. Its familiar complexity will usually let them abandon the car and get away successfully. Thus, older and more sophisticated joyriders can then bathe in the glory of standing around with their mates when several police cars come screaming up five minutes too late. 'We just stood there like all innocent and asked the busy the time. He just gets on the radio and says – car found abandoned and all that – all the kids was laughing 'cos they knew we'd done it, but the busies never caught on. We had a really good laugh.'

The escalation of joyriding and the increased number of vehicles 'abandoned' in this neighbourhood has led to a different kind of use of the car. This has, in turn, led to joyriding being viewed as conventional vandalism by officialdom. As the American sociologist, Philip Zimbardo, reported in his experiment with an eventually vandalised car, certain cues reveal that a vehicle is abandoned before the 'steady parade of vandals' begin their business. Youth in the neighbourhood tend not to vandalise a stolen car while it is mobile. It is only when the potential joyriding use of the vehicle is exhausted (for example, when it runs out of petrol) that the vehicle is abandoned or re-abandoned for other purposes.

The metamorphosis for the unfortunate vehicle tends to be a set pattern. The example of a newish 8 cwt van is typical. The van was first illegally taken from outside the neighbourhood by a couple of fairly local adults to move a 'load of stolen gear' (clothes) from A to B. It was then deliberately left in one of the tenement courtyards, where it stayed for a couple of days. In this case, the cues that the van was already stolen, and thus fair game for local kids, came through a series of channels. The van was not known, it was parked in the wrong place to be a local's, and it was unlocked. Questions were asked and soon the word got round it was 'robbed'.

Next day the van reappeared, at the other end of the neighbourhood (where cars were usually abandoned), with a dented wing and seven more miles on the clock. Other youngsters tried to re-start the car but without success. Its joyriding use was over. At this point the van became a different type of object and interest to different members of the neighbourhood. Early in the parade came the 'scrap merchants'. They were the local adults, who were keen to remove any part of the car of value – the battery, wheels and unscrewable accessories being the most profitable.

The van was now regarded as expendable. It no longer interested the older adolescents or 'scrappies'. The 'little men', the joyriders of tomorrow, now take over the vehicle and continue their apprenticeship. One sits in the driver's seat, while his mates push to try and move the van. Not so easy as the other week, when that Mini went rolling off and smashing into the railings. Once completely immobile, the 'little men' (9- to 12-year-olds), will, over a day or two, vandalise the vehicle. They will smash up all the glass, rip out the seats to make sledges, jump on the roof and so on. In between these smash-ups, really little children will explore this new toy and play their own inventive games till the older boys return and chase them away. The van must now suffer the latest aspect of its new fate – which means cremation. The wrecked car is nearly always set fire to, repeatedly if necessary, and empty aerosol cans are sometimes thrown on the blaze for good measure. The blaze is inviting, the possibility of an explosion exciting. The car is almost totally consumed and its carcase left to rust.

Joyriding is a craze and, because it matters to the lads concerned, it is not something police attention will easily eliminate.

There is some evidence that police intervention has increased the habit. Any effective action would have to come from the immediate community and here there are many problems. The joyriders quite deliberately 'abandon' cars away from their own blocks, so they can be sure their parents won't see them. Since dilapidated highrise flats prevent not just parental supervision, but community solidarity, it is unlikely that strangers will intervene either. However, residents who are concerned about the neighbourhood as a whole will take action.

The police are regularly informed when a stolen vehicle *first* appears on the scene. 'They come and look at it, sometimes they lock it up and then they bugger off and the kids just come back and carry on smashing it up.' This apparent reluctance of the police to intervene and remove the car, which otherwise quickly becomes a write-off, is a source of bitter complaint among the residents. However, because liaison with the police is at a minimum, many don't realise that the law does not allow the police to remove a vehicle until it has been reported missing, and that is often too late.

In general, then, the 'vandal' label does not apply to the joyrider. Indeed, the joyrider himself rarely smashes up. And the 'smasher-uppers' don't see their behaviour as deviant either. As far as they are concerned, the car is abandoned, has no owner, and is fair game since its destruction does not cut across neighbourhood taboos. For the youngsters, smashing up is merely play. The 'scrappie', too, is just being 'smart' by taking things which are 'lying around for the taking'. The stolen car brings something *for* the neighbourhood in various ways, and as those involved are protected by the community's 'say nothing' stance, they feel their action is condoned.

While joyriding is a delinquent action, it is motivated by respectable and conventional desires. There is too much about the downtown joyrider and his style to allow him to be classed as mindless or psychopathic. The desirability of having a car key, of parking 'your' car in a semi-private area for future use, smacks of conventionality. Is the 14-year-old – dressed in a trilby and raincoat he found in the back of his newly acquired car, who drives down the main street of his neighbourhood using his traffic indicators – really unresponsive to social standards? Are mid-adolescents who drive two cars around a playground in a tight circle for an hour, mindless vandals? Or are they acting out something important, which they would otherwise never have a chance to do? Are they not entering into the character contests of the racing driver, and acting out what their mates regard as important? The youngster in this neighbourhood who appears at the wheel of a furniture lorry and receives such compliments as 'the mad fucker' – how else does he make it?

Joyriding is undoubtedly dangerous. Someone, sooner or later, probably will get killed; and the smashing up of other people's property is indeed something society could do without. But the downtown adolescent's moral character and rationality should not be judged just in terms of the consequences of his delinquent actions. And while we should be talking about the utility of schooling, butt-end jobs, housing and so on, should not the very need for breaking out itself be appreciated and accommodated?

3 January 1974

11
The Duke Street story

Norman Dennis

Duke Street, Millfield, is a row of terraced bungalows in Sunderland, County Durham. These single-storey dwellings are to be found in their thousands in the town. Locally they are called 'cottages' (as distinct from 'houses', dwellings with two or more storeys).

Views about Duke Street vary. Mrs Douglass, for example, does not want to leave her cottage. She is 91. A farm girl, she was brought to Sunderland with her parents when she was ten, and came to live in Duke Street as a bride of 25. She does not see her cottage in any way as being a slum, or unfit for human habitation, or not reasonably suitable for occupation by her and her daughter, Mary. Nor does she feel isolated or exceptional in this, as her view is shared by her neighbours and nearly everyone with whom she normally comes into contact. To her, the eccentric view is that there is anything substantial about her cottage to criticise.

Charlie Jenkins is 67. He was born two doors away from where Mrs Douglass now lives. He is a retired bookmaker, and lives down the street with his family, including his son, Ian. Ian is the proprietor of a nightclub in Sunderland; clearly he could live virtually wherever he wishes. He choses to live in Duke Street with his father and mother. The Jenkinses' cottage is a scene of luxury, with a pine-panelled ceiling in the living room and every comfort and convenience that can be squeezed into their small home.

Mrs Robson has lived in the street all her married life. (One of her daughters is now married and has moved to a block of council flats which she heartily detests. As a result, the daughter spends most of her daytime at Duke Street, at her mother's house, which she loves.) When Mrs Robson moved into the cottage it was in poor condition, but her husband (a 48 year old crane driver) has improved it out of all recognition. As the family has grown and the need for more space has arisen, he has built extra bedroom space for the children with his own hands.

Captain Gray is another resident. He is an ex-army officer who lives a bachelor's life in his cottage, without the housewifely neatness of decoration and furnishings found elsewhere in the street. His living room is a place for his typewriter, his papers and antiques (some valuable, some not), and in the hearth a pint pot of tea. He feels a free man.

Mrs Hodgson is a gentle, self-effacing pensioner whose husband and house are the centre of her life. Her cottage is immaculate yet homely. Next door to the Hodgsons are the Atkinsons. Jack Atkinson is a 48-year-old labourer, unable to work because of sickness. The Steinbergs are another family in the street. They, too, have improved their cottage, and find it difficult to understand how anyone can reasonably hold a view different from their own – that it is a pleasant home, and that the balance of advantages for themselves by no means lies with residence in a council house.

The council, however, feel differently. It wants to pull down the north side of Duke Street. Why?

The slum clearance proposals are a straightforward case of a power struggle in several ways. First, only a small number of families are involved: 19, plus a joiner whose workshop is in a converted cottage. Second, the pattern of opinion in Duke Street is clear, strong, solid and unproblematical from the residents' point of view. Third, the history of the slum clearance process is uncomplicated, as compared with other disputed slum clearance areas in the same part of Sunderland. Fourth, it reveals the contrast (without complexities arising from other matters such as road proposals) between the formal model of slum clearance procedure and actual events.

Such relative simplicity is unusual among the decisions that I have been studying, both as political scientist and as town councillor, in Sunderland. Most decisions have the advantage (for those taking the decisions) of what Richard H. Rovere, in his study of Senator Joe McCarthy, calls 'the multiple untruth', which few people have the stamina or interest to unravel. In their tangled history, and ever-changing tracks of responsibility, as the file moves from office to office and from promoted officer to new appointee, decisions also have the advantage provided by obscurity and volatility. The citizen does not know with whom he is dealing or what their authority is. At a very much more serious level, this is the state of affairs discussed by both Hannah Arendt and Alan Bullock as basic to totalitarian domination.

The Duke Street story begins with the still-valid Sunderland development plan, which was approved by the minister in 1952. In that plan, Duke Street was programmed for re-development by 1972. In 1968 a survey was carried out of all pre-1914 properties in the town, the cottages of Duke Street among them. Then, on Monday 12 July 1971, the chief officers concerned with slum clearance met. The medical officer of health said that it was plain that since 1968 ten areas, including the north side of Duke Street, had deteriorated to such an extent that they ought to be included in the slum clearance programme.

One aspect of the Duke Street story is the scientific accuracy of the reports on the properties from qualified public health inspectors, other council staff, newspaper reporters, ward councillors, neighbours and the Duke Streeters themselves, whether based on observation or not. The *truth* of the reports, and their relationship to the law, are not questions that can be satisfactorily dealt with here. Not even *perceptions* of reality, which would require knowledge of whether or not various people believed what they themselves were saying, can be dealt with here. This article will be concerned with *presentations* of reality, within the particular context of slum clearance, using a small case in an unimportant corner of a not very well-known town. The question is, in relation to Duke Street, on whose presentation of reality were decisions based – ie, became 'the facts' for all practical purposes – and by what means did that presentation of reality prevail?

The proposal to demolish Duke Street came to councillors for the first time in preparation for the committee meeting of September 1971. The Duke Street councillor (as I shall call myself) objected. First, he was already involved at that time with the difficulties of rehousing families in his ward from a nearby clearance area. An expanded and accelerated programme would mean even less choice and/or an even longer wait under clearance-area conditions of vandalism, theft and arson. Second, the findings of the survey of 1968 were questionable, and no real evidence had been produced to show deterioration since 1968. Third, the existing staff of the local authority was unable to cope with the current programme. They could not cope with an even larger programme, except at the expense of the families affected by it. Members were advised by officers, however, that these resources of manpower would be forthcoming; the housing programme was revised (the supply of dwellings was increased by one hundred *fewer* than the increased number to be demolished) and, in December 1971, the new clearance programme was approved by the council.

On 6 November 1972, the programme was again revised. The realities since September 1971 were that the local authority was unable, with its resources, to accelerate the programme as planned. On the contrary, the programme was being fulfilled even more slowly than before 1971. But *on paper* the programme was to be still further expanded and fulfilled even more quickly in the future. A new strategy was approved by the housing committee, at the same meeting at which it approved the further acceleration and expansion of the slum clearance programme. The social problem of 'retaining communities' and of 'helping old persons' was to be tackled. Individuals in slum clearance areas were to be kept 'fully informed of the effect of slum clearance on them personally'. And in January 1973 the official civic newspaper, *In Touch*, announced 'a bright future for older houses'. There was to be an end to 'public misery' and to 'widespread property demolition'. This was the corporation's 'new thinking' and 'an historic turning point'. The same story was being told in national journals. The May 1973 edition of the *Municipal Review*, for example, carried a report on Sunderland's 'planning for involvement', in which (it was said) the emphasis was to be laid on the community, rather than on the official.

What was the actual experience of Duke Streeters? When they had been put into the clearance programme in September 1971, the fact was not even reported in the town's evening newspaper. (Rehousing of Duke Streeters was to be completed in January

1975.) Nor was the revision of November 1972 conveyed to Duke Streeters, whose rehousing was now to be completed by the end of May 1974. Individuals, on inquiring at the Civic Centre about rehousing, received vague and ambiguous replies. As late as 10 July 1973, less than nine months before rehousing was programmed to commence, an inquirer could be sent a reply which stated that it was 'anticpated' that her north-side Duke Street cottage would be 'demolished' 'within the next two years.' The usual rider was added that the information was believed to be 'accurate' but was given without any legal responsibility for supplying it. The first information volunteered by the corporation was the announcement in the edition of *In Touch* of January 1973. Here Duke Street was simply listed as one of the 21 areas included in the slum clearance programme for 1971–75, with an invitation to residents in the 21 areas to contact the health department for more information.

On 11 June 1973, the housing committee, *without either being given or asking for any evidence*, approved the medical officer's recommendation that the north side of Duke Street should be declared a clearance area because all the dwellings were unfit for human habitation, and the demolition of all the buildings was the most satisfactory method of dealing with the problem. The Duke Street councillor, who was on the committee, protested at the lack of information supplied to him, to the committee and to Duke Streeters. He would inform the Duke Streeters of the housing committee's recommendation and he reserved his position until he had learned their reactions.

When he and his fellow-councillor for the Duke Street area saw the families who lived in the street, a clear pattern of social evidence was immediately apparent. In the middle of the north side of the street was a block of seven dwellings, the defects of which the occupants eagerly displayed. Towards the western end of the terrace was an unbroken block of five cottages, the advantages and merits of which the occupants displayed as eagerly. When they discovered that clearance was almost upon them the message at each one of the five was, in effect, 'over our dead bodies'. At the extreme western end of the street was a cottage in poor condition, where the Ross family (long-standing residents in the street) wanted to remain if, but only if, they had financial help in improving the cottage – financial help beyond what was legally possible. So rehousing was not unwelcome here. At the eastern end of the street the situation was more complex. There were seven cottages at the east. Two were in poor condition, from which the Lau and Urban families wanted to be rehoused. They would need to be expensively rehabilitated or, more expensively still, demolished and new cottages put in their place. The other four families were attached to their homes (two of which were probably the best in the street); and the joiner was very attached to his workshop. They were indignant and bellicose. For them this was 'the first they'd really heard of it'.

At the meeting of the Labour group of councillors which decides which way they will cast their votes at the next meeting of the council (where Labour is in a majority), the two Duke Street councillors proposed that only the central block of seven should now be declared a clearance area. The three families who wished to be rehoused by the council should be rehoused, and the vacated cottages either rehabilitated or demolished and replaced. The remaining nine families should be allowed 15-year grants for their cottages if they wanted them. They were not successful. But the Labour group agreed to vote in the council to send the clearance recommendation back to the housing committee for re-consideration.

Everything now depended upon the decision which would be taken at the next meeting of the housing committee on 9 July. The Duke Streeters sent a petition to the committee. The vice-chairman of the committee, who would be taking the chair, visited the cottages and talked to the families. As a result he came out strongly in support of the 'small' clearance area proposals. Then, on Saturday morning, 7 July, two days before the council meeting, members of the housing committee received for the first time (there was no covering letter saying what it was or who had sent it) the official evidence for the clearance for the whole of the north side of Duke Street (the evidence on which, in theory, they had 'based' their original decision of 11 June). It condemned the whole north side. When the sheet describing his cottage was shown to Ian Jenkins, he seized a pen and wrote 'Rubbish!' and other comments of disagreement over the sheet. Obviously, whatever defects could be 'proved' to exist by anybody else, the views and wishes of the Duke Streeters had not been a factor in the council's deliberations.

On Monday 9 July, the Labour members of the housing committee met in normal caucus. The chairman for the evening recommended that the housing committee (ie, the caucused vote of the Labour majority) should declare only the central seven cottages a clearance area, investigate the best way of dealing with the three dispersed poor cottages, and make the other nine eligible for grants. To all appearances, the vote was so caucused. To all appearances, therefore, and according to all precedents, these would be the housing committee's recommendations and the council would accept them. The chairman, the Duke Street councillor and some other Labour councillors supported the proposals relating to the 'small' clearance area. But the rest of the speakers, officers and members of both parties, addressing themselves largely to the medical officer's evidence received the previous Saturday, argued that with properties so grossly and irredeemably defective, it was not possible to exclude the nine cottages from the clearance area.

The debate turned on this kind of question: was the fact that a water closet opened directly into a food preparation room (as it did in the Jenkinses's cottage, a shocking and insupportable state of affairs, referred to by several speakers) *in itself* sufficient to make a property unfit for human habitation? The medical officer replied that it was in itself sufficient, *and that this was laid down in section 4 of the Housing Act, 1957.* 'That's funny,' said a Labour councillor. 'I've just been on the annual inspection of the council houses, and the council's modernised houses at Marley Potts have toilets straight into the kitchen.' No rejoinder. (In fact, this item is mentioned in a ministry circular – MHLG 68/69 – which gives guidance on section 4 as amended. The inclusion of this item as a 'bad arrangement' is quoted in the circular as an opinion of an advisory subcommittee.)

The 'small' clearance area proposals were defeated. The housing committee was to re-submit its recommendation to the council that the whole of the north side of the street should be declared a clearance area.

The *Sunderland Echo* reported the decision of the housing committee under the headline, 'Little palaces of Millfield to go after all.' The editor was immediately sent a letter signed by eight of the nine families, saying that it was by no means settled that their homes would be pulled down. 'This is going to be the hardest slum clearance the council has ever taken on, because it's the stupidest.' A reporter was sent to find out what was going on.

Mrs Robson told the *Echo*, 'I'm just not leaving. It's as simple as that. I've lived here all my married life. We've done all sorts to our home. How dare they say it's slums! The Duke Street nine will win.' 'We have spent all our time trying to make the home as nice as possible,' said her husband. 'There's still more I'd like to do. It's not right to call it a slum house. It's just not true.' Other Duke Streeters, when they were interviewed by Radio Newcastle and subsequently by Tyne-Tees Television, made similar statements. More letters were written to the *Echo*. Mrs Douglass wrote an open letter to the chief executive officer which was widely reported, announcing that she was looking forward to the council's decision, looking forward if necessary to the public inquiry and, if necessary after that, to the council's attempts to evict her: 'Fighting this lunacy will keep me entertained for a few years yet.'

Meanwhile, attempts were made to obtain written answers to various crucial questions from the technical officers. In particular, *which* items, singly or in combination, listed on the medical officer's sheets, were defects which were such as to make the cottage not reasonably suitable for occupation in that condition (or dangerous or injurious to health)? The results of these attempts were far from satisfactory to the Duke Street councillors. A list of questions was tabled for the chairman of the housing committee which, under standing orders, he would be required to answer publicly at the council meeting. The questions were designed to confront the chairman with the facts which proved that suggestions that Duke Streeters would be re-housed in the locality (and therefore had no reasonable objection to being moved) were mistaken or bogus.

When the Labour group of councillors met to caucus the vote of the full council, the chairman of the housing committee appeared with an amendment. The cottages would not be cleared, the amendment ran, until new houses for rent were provided in the Millfield district for Duke Streeters. Specifically new houses for rent would be available (i) within twelve months, (ii) on the nearby Potts Street site. That this was an improvisation of the previous few hours, and that no particular arrangement had been made (or perhaps even thought about) up to that time, is proved by the fact that 24 hours later Sunderland's Labour MPs were

pleading in the House of Commons for a ministerial recon-
sideration of the decision which had made the Potts Street site
available for Duke Streeters. The Labour group agreed to vote in
council for the clearance of Duke Street and for the re-housing
amendment. At the council meeting no vote was needed. The
proposal and the amendment received all-party support – but not
the support of the Duke Street councillors.

Following the council's decision, the Duke Street nine
announced, as a body, that they still 'emphatically rejected' the
assertion that their homes were slums. Though they were
pleased that, 'if the worst came to the worst, they would at least
have the opportunity to stay in Millfield', this was not 'in any
way' a sign that they preferred to move.

But local re-housing was guaranteed. One cheer from the nine.
Perhaps two from the Hodgsons. Three cheers from those of the
other ten families who wanted to be cleared anyway, and who
wanted to live in Millfield. The fight of the nine had won that
much. But the council had decided that they must be com-
pulsorily cleared and re-housed against their wishes. The judgment of the chief officers, contained in their memorandum of
their meeting of 12 July 1971, two years almost to the day before
the 'evidence' was seen by the 'authoritative decision-takers',
the councillors, was vindicated. The political processes and decisions
which ordinarily would have assured the exclusion of the nine
from the clearance area – especially the Labour Party caucus
decision of 9 July – had been defeated.

*   *   *

Duke Street is an example of the kind of work being undertaken
by several political sociologists in the north east, on the basis of
four principles.

The first is that politics is about power. The second is that
politics is about what actually does happen, no less than about
what people say happens or believe has happened. Conse-
quently, this approach depends less upon reports and recon-
structions than on the direct observation of decision-taking. Our
main technique, therefore, is participant observation. Our main
arena is municipal politics.

The third principle is that modern societies create facades to
protect every nook and cranny of organisational life. So one of our

operating principles is that they are penetrated, ripped aside, or shattered, by the activities of the researcher himself. In Brechtian terms, everyday life is lifted out of the realm of the self-evident by means of an 'estrangement effect'. In some of the best known examples of this method, the estrangement effect is created negatively, by *violating* the apparent conventions. But it can be created just as well, in some situations, by faithfully *abiding by* the apparent conventions. Both the positive and negative versions of the 'estrangement effect' aim at the same thing – namely, discovering what sort of behaviour is actually approved and allowed, and which behaviour is condemned in practice: in this case, discovering how a decision was made, and what happened when different groups attempted to exert influence.

The fourth principle is that, above a certain level of abstraction, the fabricators of illusions and the falsifiers of the record come more and more into their own. To know who is powerful, therefore, it is necessary to keep close to the details which the generalised reports will eventually purport to describe and from which they will be claimed to have been derived.

The great drawback of this technique and of this field of inquiry (you may have felt this yourself on reading this account) is the inability to generalise from any particular detailed study. But by all means let us be shown different results, perhaps obtained by other methods. This account has sketched, in very broad outline, how the Duke Street clearance decision was really taken. How are decisions really taken in your town?

4 October 1973

12
Portrait of a lady

Jeremy Seabrook

Miss Milner was 82 when she died. Her late-Victorian villa, with its tessellated garden path and oak-leaf carving in the keystones above the bay windows, was as immaculate as it had been every day for more than 50 years. The sash window was open a little, as it always was, in even the coldest weather. The white Scottish terrier sat on a chair in the bay, lightly frosting the glass with little evaporating clouds of breath.

Miss Milner was born in 1892 into the family of an architect. She was the youngest of seven children. The attic of her house was a shrine to her father's work, full of neatly displayed water colours, designs and plans, meticulously detailed, predominantly in pale yellows, ochres and browns. Many of his buildings dominated the town until quite recently: a monumental church on a hill-top, with a spire that pierced the sky; a row of neo-Jacobean mansions built for boot and shoe manufacturers in the reddest brick I have ever seen.

Until she died, Miss Milner walked the half mile into town every day, although the sedate thoroughfare had become a main road. Many of the houses had been turned into offices and the protective evergreens had grown gnarled and spare. Miss Milner still stopped and spoke to everybody, whether she knew them or not, asking them with the gentle, though authoritative, insistence of her caste to give an account of themselves, their family circumstances, their health; offering advice on child-rearing and domestic economy. She was never rebuffed by the objects of her critical attention; rather, she was regarded with indulgent detachment.

She was brought up to a constant accompaniment of how well or poorly-connected people were; how far from, or close to, low origins. Breeding was an overriding preoccupation; not so much in relation to her own family, but rather to the absence of it in others, which of course banished them from the possibility of acquaintanceship. This made most people 'unsuitable', 'not gentlemen', or even 'impossible'. Despite the long-won gentility of their condition, the family was acutely conscious of the danger of any contaminatory contact with those beneath them. An exciting but menacing population clamoured beyond the wrought-iron gate of Miss Milner's sequestered childhood. It was the women who were the principal custodians of social propriety. It was felt to be a fitting avocation for females, and because the women specialised, they were deferred to in this, if in few other areas of life. In this way, elaborate ramifications of hierarchic precedences and superiorities were devised by quite ordinary women, who were otherwise the wives of solicitors, doctors and farmers. They were often philistine and uninformed; sometimes illiberal and uncharitable. But at the same time they were puncti-lious in their observation of correct behaviour. They spoke in undifferentiated and authoritative tones on all subjects, and did not distinguish between social issues, moral judgment or per-sonal caprice.

Miss Milner's childhood was disciplined and ordered; she was taught frugality and self-denial, and learned to efface herself beneath the austere, obliterating influences of her upbringing. On Sundays the children sat with their mother in the nursery while she read *Sabbath Gems*, and told them stories about indi-viduals who were the embodiment of abstract virtues: the con-sumptive washerwoman who represented Patience, the orphan who represented Resignation, the blind fiddler who represented Hope. Left-overs from the family table were given to a family called Smith – bread that was no longer fresh, puddings that had been less than successful in preparation or cooking. Miss Milner visited the Smiths with her brother. They carried the bits in a wicker basket; in consequence of which, the recipients of their charity were known as the 'Bits-Smiths'. Miss Milner later felt ashamed of her thoughtless absorption of the insulting attitudes which were felt proper to her condition. Her mother once took her to see the daughter of the Smith family, a girl of 15, who was dying of consumption. The visit was intended to arouse a sense of social duty, combined with a salutary awareness of her own mortality: a real-life lesson. The mother lit a solitary candle from a spark of fire, and then took them into a bedroom which contained nothing but a bed in which the girl lay. On the same winter afternoon, Miss Milner was taken to see a dead baby in a dwelling nearby, a child of one year that had died of whooping cough.

Miss Milner's family was considered to be liberal, if not latitudinarian, in its beliefs and attitudes. Miss Milner attended a dame-school in the centre of the town; an establishment that offered embroidery and the pianoforte. This school was run by two women, both of whom dressed in mid-Victorian black, with white lace at the throat. At one time they suggested that school should be divided, girls from the professional classes being segregated, appropriately, in an upstairs room; the daughters of trade being left to the lower storey. Miss Milner's father threatened to remove his daughter from the school if any such move were carried out. It certainly wasn't that he was unaware of the abyss of unknowable people beneath them; and he knew that his daughter met some of them at school. Once she had caught fleas from the daughter of a haberdasher. Miss Milner could not be certain that the fleas had infested the tradesman's child; but it was commonly agreed that fleas were somehow more proper to the bodies of those in such doubtful occupations, despite Miss Milner's assertion that that particular girl was probably one of the cleanest children in the class. Her mother was deeply ashamed of this occurrence, enjoined her to the strictest secrecy, and spent an hour every evening for a week going through her hair with a fine comb.

As a child, Miss Milner saw no money, apart from a penny on Saturdays, which was spent on sweets or a toy from the penny bazaar. Children knew nothing of the provenance of money. But the fact that they never knew hardship meant that they were brought up to expect certain standards; many people of Miss Milner's age group lived to see their decline, but they were then helpless and splenetic at a world that robbed them of obsequious tradespeople, proper service and a supply of replaceable maids.

The family ate cake only on Sundays. On other days of the week, tea consisted of bread and butter. Lunch was the children's main meal of the day: poached fish, milk puddings, stewed fruit, roast meat only occasionally, with potatoes every day. Eating was, if anything, a self-punishing process; sparing of sugar and salt, cooking was bland and tasteless. Nobody would have committed the sin of gluttony. It was nipped in the taste-buds, as Miss Milner wryly said.

Because life was austere and frugal, moments of ceremonial stood out with greater definition – like May Day, when the poor children called, and were admitted into the garden, with clothes baskets containing a doll inside a hoop, entwined with daisies and bluebells. Miss Milner's mother's birthday fell on Midsummer Day. Their father hired a waggonette for the day, and they went into the woods at Yardley Chase; they collected wild flowers, mallow and herb-robert, which were crushed between newspaper under a pile of books.

All the domestic arrangements were characterised by order and frugality.

'Mother was always busy, showing indifferent maids how to do things the most efficient and economical way. In fact, the amount of time spent in instruction could very well have removed all need for the employment of domestics. I remember her using rice water to starch table linen, removing iron mould on sheets with salts of lemon, cleaning cruet bottles, using mutton fat in a tin lid to save money on candles. It was all polishing and scouring; wiping away.

'But of course we accepted everything we were told. Their morality was so much an expression of our parents' concern for us. There was a very subtle blend of love and control . . . I suppose people would find it hard to understand today. I remember one day going to a birthday party with one of these tradesmen's girls. We'd been given some money to buy a box of chocolates as a present. She suggested that we should buy the box and chocolates separately, because of course that was cheaper, and we'd then have money left over for some chocolates for ourselves. I can't describe with what misery I ate those sweets. My mother never found out, but I often wish she had. It pursued me for many years afterwards, in fact, until I was quite grown up. I remember looking at her and thinking, "My mother doesn't know that I've been deceitful, she thinks I'm still the same as I was before I was dishonest."

'I'm troubled now when I think about it of the way in which

servants were treated. They were a quite different kind of human being from oneself, you understand. We had a maid with us from 1898 until 1910. She slept in an attic – not that that was a bad thing, because my sister and I slept in the other one. This girl had two half-days off a week; but on those half-days she had to prepare tea for the family, cut all the bread and butter before she went out, and then wash up when she got home. There was a woman who came in to do the family wash twice a week. Everything for nine people, except the sheets.

'Occasionally I went out to tea with my mother. We were made to feel that this was a really adult privilege. I was very young, perhaps eight or nine. I was expected to sit absolutely still, and follow the conversation, and agree with something quite trivial from time to time. There was one man who used to boast that he was the only gentleman in Northampton because he didn't work. As we walked home, my mother said, "How could you tell he wasn't a real gentleman?" It was almost a catechism. Of course I didn't know the answer, but apparently he would never have felt the need to assert such a thing if it were really true.

'We never went to the seaside for our holidays. I did go once, when I was about eight, but only because the others were at boarding school by the sea. I went with my mother and brother, and we stayed in lodgings. I shall never forget, because in the morning at breakfast the woman asked, "Do you want tea or coffee, madam?" I'd never been asked what I wanted before. Children were just not consulted.'

Outside, two boys about 13, going home from school, start fighting. Miss Milner, frail, over 80, hurries down the garden path. 'What do you think you're doing?' Incredulous, 'You don't want to *hurt* each other? We should none of us hurt each other, however angry we may feel.'

*   *   *

Miss Milner's house has been turned into offices; a filing cabinet stands in the bay; the black and white tiles are obscured by the muddy imprint of fashionable shoes. Along the windowsill, a row of paper cups. Inside, a young woman in a pink cardigan sits at a typewriter.

18 April 1974

13
Those who do the butt-end jobs

David White

'Which of us is to do the hard and dirty work for the rest – and for what pay? Who is to do the pleasant and clean work, and for what pay?'

John Ruskin here distinguished the real alternatives of work: hard and dirty; pleasant and clean. The distinction is important, for it lies deep in our conceptions of work for the poor and work for the better-off. 'Better' jobs are advertised as 'clean, light work in pleasant conditions'. By implication, the worst jobs, the jobs for the poor, are dirty, heavy work in unpleasant conditions. Jobs involved with dirt and its removal. Enid Mumford cleans a bingo hall in south London. Her job involves picking up, by hand, the torn tickets, ice cream cartons and cigarette ends left by patrons. Her husband empties the cess-pits of Green Belt householders for the local authority. 'He's wasted away through the work,' she says. 'His legs are no thicker than my broom handle. And he throws up every meal.'

A 'better' job distances its holder from this dirt. And the distancing enables workers to distinguish their work from that of others. 'We clean up for the nurses,' hospital ancillary workers point out. 'We do their dirty work.' In hotels, the dishwasher and kitchen porter are only technically supervised by the manager. In practice, the chef, the head of the kitchen, is their boss. And their work is defined because it is placed in relation to his; they wash up the plates he has filled, and dispose of the remains of the food he has cooked. Again, they do *his* dirty work.

The status of a poor person's work is reflected in the pay it commands. In 1970, a survey of 126 national negotiating groups by Incomes Data Services showed that 117 of these groups had basic rates of pay for men which were below the TUC's target level of a £16.50 minimum basic weekly rate. Some, notably those whose minima are fixed by the Wages Councils, were well below. The minimum for the lowest grade of worker in industrial and staff canteens was found to be £8.80.

Why so low? Chiefly because there is so little pressure to raise low wages. Reports by the National Board for Prices and Incomes have noted the small fragmented union memberships in the cleaning trade, and among hospital cleaners, porters and general helps. Perhaps more important, employers outside London do not have to compete to fill these jobs. Nowhere are they competing for skills. A survey of hospital ancillary workers showed that, not surprisingly, only 5 per cent had stayed on at school beyond 16.

All that the unskilled, barely educated worker can offer an employer is his time – lots of it. The farm worker earns an average weekly wage £10 below the average industrial wage, for ten hours' more work than the average industrial worker. The hardness of Ruskin's 'hard and dirty work' can be found in the way in which a job controls a worker's time rather than the other way round. The poor suffer from this more than other people do. Overtime, shift work and night work curtail people's 'rights' to a full home or family life. A waiter at a central London hotel, whose wife is a receptionist at the same hotel, explains: 'We neither of us get off work until eleven at night, so we only use our television to watch the late-night movie. And we have to rush back to catch that.'

In 1964, it was estimated that there were nearly 70,000 women, mostly unskilled, working a 'twilight shift' in industry – that is, a short shift following immediately on the normal working day. And today, probably around 2,700 cleaners (1,800 women and 900 men) work full-time night shifts. The 'poor worker', therefore, lacks the choices of the better-off – what to work at, when to work, and where to work. Whether he works in toy manufacturing (1970 minimum £5.80 below the TUC £16.50 target) or in cotton spinning (1970 minimum £5.68 below the TUC target) will depend merely whether or not he lives in Devon or Lancashire. And whether he works at all will depend on whether or not he lives in an area of high unemployment. Even the *prospect* of unemployment will further limit his choices.

Liverpool ties with Sunderland in having the largest percentage (7.9) of unemployed of any local authority area in England. Over 48,000 – of which nearly 37,000 are men – are out of work. Liverpool must also have one of the largest percentages of derelicts, the shuffling poor who cadge small change outside the four-star Adelphi hotel in Lime Street. The street seems used to the contrasts: on one side, the businessmen stride out of the new Trust House Forte hotel on their way to the Philharmonic: on the other, two ex-seamen are thrown out of Yates's Wine Lodge.

The highest proportion of poor people still live in this central area, an area roughly within a two-and-a-half mile radius of the Pier Head. In spite of council efforts to woo them to the new bleak estates on the outskirts, they cling to the decaying courts of Liverpool 8, 3 and 5. Within these areas, there are pockets of real poverty; the notorious Bronte neighbourhood, and the Soho Street/St Anne's Street district. Adshel, a company which erects bus shelters paid for by the advertisements it displays on them, has said bluntly that these areas are unsuitable for such shelters. The money isn't there. 'Nobody saves, unless it's for one glorious night a week at the pub,' a social worker says: 'but they're not encouraged to save. Go and count the number of fish and chip shops in Everton, and then count the number of banks.'

The respective sitings of the employment exchange and the social security office seem equally pessimistic – the first in Renshaw Street (a fair walk off), and the second very locally. Certainly, among the families in the tenements, earnings supplement social security benefits, rather than the other way round. Out of 5 families, for example, in one block – large families, some as large as 13 – only 3 people have any sort of employment. Two of these are the mothers of families. Both women have cleaning jobs, one part-time and the other full-time. The third is a van driver, living on his own, earning between £25 and £30 a week, and faintly surprised that his neighbours cannot find work.

What work is there for the poor of the central area? More important, what work will they take? The aspirations of two 15-year-olds give some clue. Geraldine is ambitious and slightly ashamed of her tenement home. Ashamed enough not to want to bring friends back. Recently she made up a telephone number to disguise the fact that her home hadn't got a phone. When she leaves school in a year's time, she wants to work for the Tate & Lyle sugar refinery in Love Lane.

Her brother, Jimmy, 'lives for each minute and no further', his mother says. He won't think about a job until he has to. He's good with his hands, and has a talent for electrical repairs. But he can hardly read. '"Oh, Mam," he says to me, "I can always get a job on the fruits."' The 'fruits' is Liverpool's new open-plan fruit market, a bus ride away on the Prescot Road. The old market in Cazneau Street used to be just up the road from St Anne's Street, but Liverpool 3 loyalties have followed it eastwards. Central-area poor will travel as far as the Kirkby, on the north-eastern out-skirts, for work. But, curiously, they will not 'cross the waters' to find work in Birkenhead or Wallasey.

The 'fruits' is an acceptable job for the central-area poor, because it is a 'man's job'. The distinction between men's and women's work is far more rigidly adhered to in Liverpool than in London. Catering and hotel jobs are thought degrading, women's work; and few men admit to considering them. Even in London, men pushed into catering by necessity can be thorough-ly ashamed of the job. An ex-employee of a central London Lyons teashop remembers: 'We had this man who'd been a military policeman washing the dishes, and he was always saying that his job was only temporary and not the sort of work he normally did. But he badly needed that job because his wife was pregnant. I got "promoted" from the kitchen to table-cleaning and told him about it. He was really jealous, but covered up by saying he was only temporary. I went back there about 15 months after I left and he was still there – but he'd been "promoted", too.'

A man's job in Liverpool is a docker's job, with a docker's pay of around £50 a week. But the dockers are a closed shop. Only men whose fathers are dockers are admitted. Then there's Ford and Vauxhall at Ellesmere Port. Vauxhall employs over 11,000 workers, and pays good money – if you can get in and can stand the working conditions. Inevitably, therefore, a man's job boils down to outdoor work – labourer, road sweeper, market porter; or grubby indoor jobs – carpet cleaning, warehouse work or the slaughterhouse.

The slaughterhouse – the Stanley Abattoir – stands back from the Prescot Road at Old Swan, a mile to the west of Ken Dodd's

Knotty Ash. When it was built in the 1930s, it was reputedly the best-equipped abattoir in the world. Today, in spite of the arrival of the new 'fruits' across the road, it still commands attention. Not least because of its two massive chimneys, which bequeath to the area an overpowering smell of boiling offal. Even in the Cattlemarket, the slaughterman's pub, the smell lingers, carried in on overalls and thigh-length waders.

Thursday is pay day; and inside the public bar, the cutters, meat porters and slaughtermen are settling debts. These are the 'front end' of the meat trade, the skilled, better-paid end. Slaughtermen, for example, can take home over £40 a week. Their position in the workforce hierarchy is even defined by the location of their work – towards the cleaner, pleasanter, front end of the abattoir. The 'back end' workers help dispose of what's left, what the slaughterman rejects. They cart off the offal, boil it down for glue and soap. Being at the back end, they rarely frequent the Cattlemarket.

'Sure, I know I stink,' says Mike McKenna candidly. 'It's a dirty job. But you get used to the smell after a bit. I've got so as I don't notice it. All my wife asks is that I have a bath when I come home.' McKenna, a 21-year-old 'back end' worker, has worked at the abattoir for about 18 months. 'It's not a job I'd choose if I had a choice,' he says, 'but there wasn't much else, and this is an easy job to get into. And the pay's all right, better than what I was getting at the Post Office.' On average, he earns £21 a week. This includes overtime worked on Saturdays and Sundays. His wife doesn't work. 'There's a kid on the way, so I won't let her.' Even so, he says he manages three nights out with her a week.

He has some misgivings about his job. 'I didn't want to be an apprentice slaughterman, because the pay was so low. I wish to Christ I had been apprenticed now.' Besides their earnings, the 'front end' men get the perks of cuts of meat. And theirs is a trade, with chances of promotion. The best McKenna can expect is eventual promotion to foreman. But he doesn't bother much about prospects. He merely assumes he will be working in the same job in about five or ten years' time. He hopes shortly to move from his £3.50 a week council flat to a council house in Skelmersdale. 'I shall still come in to work here, though,' he says. 'I'll have to get a bike.' Skelmersdale is about 20 miles from the abattoir.

A quarter of a mile down the Prescot Road, another 'back end' man is at work. James Hesketh, a 28-year-old road sweeper employed by Liverpool corporation, is grappling with an eddy of tattered newspapers. Hesketh, like McKenna, left school at 15. Unlike McKenna, he 'went for a trade'. But he soon tired of it, and drifted through a variety of unskilled jobs. For the last two years, he has been unemployed. 'You don't apply for this kind of job,' he says. 'You hear about it. I took a mate's place.' The money's surprisingly good – £22 a week with a guaranteed £6 weekly bonus and opportunities for overtime. 'It's like the fruits,' he says. 'You got to be around when someone leaves.'

In both these admittedly dirty jobs, both workers have been able to work reasonable and regular hours: McKenna from 8 a.m. to 5 p.m., and Hesketh from 7.30 to 4.30 p.m. For McKenna, overtime is obligatory; for Hesketh, with his bonus, it is not. But the hard and dirty, 'somebody's-got-to-do-them' jobs also include those which curtail time. Jobs which turn a working day upsidedown.

'Them fellows on the buildings get £40 for a 38-hour week. I do twice those hours, for less than that.' The nightwatchman who watches the entrance to a large new office development near Liverpool's dockside has worked at the same job for 48 years. 'When I started, it was the only job that someone crippled like me could get,' he says. 'Now there's young, healthy lads that want to do it. It's the money they're after.' The money has improved over 48 years. When the watchman began work, he was paid 8s 4d for a 15-hour night shift. Today he is paid 31p an hour for a slightly shorter shift. But the job hasn't changed. It is still a lonely, tedious and sometimes dangerous job. Inside the building site, there are Securicor patrols, with radios and guard dogs. Outside, 'young lads kick over my lamp just to get me out of the hut,' he says. 'Then they set on me. And it's no use calling the police. Nowadays it's the police who need protecting.'

At 10 p.m. each night, a trickle of men and women pass the watchman's hut, bound for the Pier Head, for buses home or the ferry across to Wallasey. They have just come off the night shift at Bibby's, the vegetable and animal oil millers. Bibby's draws much of its labour fource from the poor of the central area of the city. It ranks lower than Tate & Lyle in the poor-jobs hierarchy, but not much lower. It introduced family allowances to employees in

1919, 27 years before the national scheme, and became a pioneer of the five-day working week. Yet, for all that, Bibby's jobs for the unskilled remain unalterably unpleasant; animal fats again bequeath their pungent smell to workplace and workforce alike.

But Bibby's is not exclusively a man's job. The firm, like others, aims to recruit married women. The combination of man and wife, both unskilled, both working awkward, late or shift hours produces those conditions that label jobs as 'jobs for the poor'.

A young couple living in one of the Three Ugly Sisters – the nicknames given to three tower blocks in the Soho Street area of Liverpool 3 – have struggled desperately to avoid those conditions. 'My wife has to do cleaning in a shop, because – well, not because we're poor but because we could not move out of the house in the evenings if she didn't,' says the husband. 'As it is, I don't see her until gone nine in the evening.'

He works as a hoist operator in a carpet wholesalers in Jamaica Street. He earns little over £20 a week, and pays just under £5 for the rent of his flat. His job is his first; and he says that if he chucked it, he would never get another one. 'Not without shift working, anyway. As it is, I do Sunday work. Sunday's the day people do a lot of shopping now, so we stay open. But I told them I got to have Saturday afternoon off – to watch the football.' His wife earns just under £5 a week.

The idea that married women go out to work for pin money or company got a sharp tap on the head from a report of the National Board for Prices and Incomes on contract cleaners' pay. A survey of a sample of cleaners showed that, while 78 per cent said they worked because they needed money, only 14 per cent said they needed it for themselves. And the board recognised the social consequences of this need: 'It is clearly not a desirable state of affairs that wives with husbands employed full time during the day should look after their homes and children in the day and attempt to carry on a full-time night job as well.'

It may not be desirable. But is it not inevitable? Who else, but women with large households and small incomes, would work these hours at these jobs? Women who have no skills, but still some of their time to sell.

It is possible to define the kind of work that devolves so inevitably upon the poor. It is work that makes use of their time, and little else. And it is work that brings them into close contact with dirt, with the butt-ends of other people's work. Often too close for much comfort.

8 February 1973

14
Making ends meet

Paul Harrison

Poverty breeds proverbs: man is what he eats; buy cheap and buy twice; buy cheap meat and you smell what you have saved; and so on. But the actual content of poor people's lives is still fairly uncharted territory in the second half of the twentieth century. You can find all the figures you need in the Family Expenditure Survey and the National Food Survey – but they convey nothing of the actual experience of being poor, and all the stratagems, frustrations and humiliations that involves. What do low-income families eat – and what would they like to eat? How do they spend their money – and how do they make it spin out? I spoke to four Gateshead families in detail about this.

Gateshead, just across the River Tyne from Newcastle, is one of those genuinely homogeneous working class communities like the south Wales valley towns or the East End of London, where there is no middle class to speak of. Unemployment is high: 9 per cent of males on Tyneside were unemployed in January, as against a national figure of 4.1 per cent. Not a few councillors even have been on and off the dole in recent years. The generations don't live far from each other and extend a helping hand, lending money from week to week, doing the shopping, giving old clothes. But, as often as not, the helping hand can only just afford to help itself.

It was not obvious at first sight that the families I spoke to were poor. With one exception, their homes were neat and tidy. Like most of the ordinary poor, their struggle was all the harder in fighting off the appearance of poverty. Florence Archer's home, in St Cuthbert's council housing estate, for example. The Archer home showed no outward sign of poverty: not much furniture, a newish three-piece suite, an electric fire with a decorative wooden surround; sparse but very clean.

Florence, who is 34, lives with her four children. She is seeking separation from her husband, who is in hospital undergoing treatment for alcoholism. The total weekly income of the family is £18.45. This consists of: £12.15, share of her husband's sickness benefit; £3.80, supplementary benefit; and a contribution of £2.50 from her eldest daughter Karen, a 15-year-old machinist. Total weekly expenditure between £18 and £19: rent £3.02 (Florence is also paying off £20 arrears incurred while her husband was still with them, at 30p a week), electricity £1.20 a week, clothing club 50p, hire purchase for suite and fireplace 85p, fares to school £1, food £11–£12.

The family can save nothing at all from week to week, and there is nothing to spend on luxuries. 'I have to think very hard every time I want a tin of furniture polish,' Florence told me. And the spending schedule is geared very closely to the exact days on which benefits are paid: Saturday the share of her husband's sick pay, Monday the supplementary benefit, Thursday or Friday Karen's housekeeping. Any hitch in the timing can be disastrous. The week before my visit, the sickness benefit Giro didn't turn up. 'I was down to the office and in the queue at 9.30 when they open, to find out what had happened. They finally sorted it out. But I was frantic. You can't make seven days' money go into ten.'

The splitting up of the income means that buying in bulk – even just enough to last the whole week – is impossible. Florence tried it once, but found she had no money left to cope with an emergency. Hair shampoo she buys in four individual sachets a week, because she can't afford a bottle. The family manage to eat some kind of meat most days – usually mince, chicken or pie meat. Their meal that evening was bacon, eggs and beans. 'Sometimes they come home very hungry. If they've been on the last sitting at school dinners, there's often not enough to go round.'

Clothing is a major difficulty. Florence pays 50p a week to the 'ticket man' from the Provident. Every 22 weeks she gets a cheque for £10, so she is paying a shilling in the pound extra. The cheque can only be spent at certain shops (the Provident is much better for choice than most other clubs), so shopping around and buying from market stalls is out. 'I'd rather have £10 cash in my pocket any day. If I'm really beat for clothes. I've got to ask the social security. They might give you £9 for two coats, or £4 for two pairs of shoes. So you've got to buy cheaper things, and it's more expensive in the long run because they don't last.' Sometimes the social security people refer her to the WRVS, who give out second-hand clothes to people who have a letter of recommendation from a social work agency. But Florence would rather get clothes from friends. She unpicks sweaters and makes new ones with the wool, or rips up men's trousers and salvages good material to make pants for her son, George.

Last September the children had no shoes for school, but the supplementary benefits officer assessed them to be 39p above the income limit for free ones. The three schoolchildren stayed off school for a fortnight until the commission decided in their favour. 'They make you fight for it, it's humiliating,' says Florence.

How does the family cope with emergencies or special occasions? Over Christmas, Florence relied on her working daughter to buy presents for the other children, and borrowed £6 from her mother for extra food. When decorations are needed, the Provident cheque is used; so the children go without new clothes for another 22 weeks. The children get free holidays with the social services department once or twice a year. Florence stays at home. A few extra pounds come along every couple of months when the TV slotmeter is emptied. It costs 5p for an hour's viewing, but they get back everything paid over 50p a week.

The family was, in fact, far worse off than it is now while the husband was with them, even though he was working much of the time. 'I didn't know in advance what I had coming in. If he wasn't drinking, it could be £20 or £25. If he was, it could go as low as £6. I couldn't work things out at all. If he knew he'd given me extra one week, he'd be liable to take it back another. And he broke stuff – china, glass. Once he wrecked a sideboard. Sometimes we missed the rent for four weeks running.' When her husband went into hospital in November, the council asked her to agree to pay off his rent arrears – then £20 – before they would sign the tenancy over.

It is quite possible, therefore, for a man to be getting a decent

wage and to be fairly well-off himself, while the rest of his family
is in extreme poverty. Another example of this was the McCormick family who also live in St Cuthbert's. Barbara McCormick is
a tiny wisp of a woman, with asthma and TB, aged 43. She has
five children, aged between two and nine. One of them has a
heart condition. Her husband, Bill, is a labourer whose wages
fluctuate; but when he is working, they average £40. He pays her
'wages' of £20 a week, and she gets family allowance of £3.90.
Because of the husband's large wage, the family does not qualify
for any rebates, allowances, family income supplement, free
school dinners or anything else. Rent is now nearly £6, and
Barbara is paying off £1 a week of the £20 arrears accumulated in
the course of the builders' strike last summer.

Out of the housekeeping, Barbara has to pay all outgoings,
including her husband's food. Bill eats well: steak or two chops
for dinner, bacon and eggs for breakfast, sandwiches and cake for
lunch at work. The rest of the family is practically starving.

'We're vetarians (sic),' says Barbara. 'We don't eat any meat. If
we could have toad in the hole every night, they'd all have it; but
we can't afford it. In general, I give them what they ask for – at
breakfast, it might be crisps. The children go to their granny's
near school for lunch. They usually have soup. They don't get
much for tea – an apple, or sweets and biscuits. I don't eat much at
all myself – a cup of tea and a cigarette.' Barbara relies heavily on
the social services department for help. She gets most of the
family's clothes from the WRVS. 'I can't afford jumble sales.' The
children's Christmas presents were second-hand toys from the
social services department.

There are, of course, elements of sheer bad management in
Barbara's budget. After their skimped tea, the children often get
hungry in the evening, and clamour for fish and chips. Barbara
goes shopping once a day or more; but she buys almost everything at the supermarket on the estate, where prices are not
cheap, rather than walk the 15 minutes into the town centre. The
house was very dirty inside; the children were shabbily dressed,
with blotches of dirt on their faces; the walls were covered in
filthy fingermarks. By any external financial criteria – and these
are the ones that government agencies apply – the family are not
'poor'. But, in fact, Barbara and her five children have less each,
after the rent is paid, than Florence Archer – £2.59, as opposed to

£3.08. And this is taking no account of the fact that Bill gets the lion's share.

I met Mary and Clarence Atkinson at an old people's lunch club, in a prefab canteen in the Saltmeadows area of Gateshead, where cold mists and wind from the nearby river add to the expense of heating. All the old people there looked poor, with threadbare clothes, torn or patched, made to last longer than their lifespan. For a shilling, they could get a nourishing hot meal twice a week. That day they were having meat pie (surprisingly little fat and gristle), cabbage and dollops of mash, with rice pudding for afters. The table conversation was about the cost of living, and the cold weather.

The Atkinsons – Clarence is 68, Mary 71 – did not look to be among the poorest. Appearances were deceptive. Their pensions are a little higher than basic. Clarence's is £7.10, and Mary has her own of £5.94 because she had opted to pay stamps on her own account. But they were not claiming supplementary benefit. Until November, Mary had a job cleaning at £6 a week; but then she cut her leg open falling off a bus and had to give it up. They then became entitled to a rent rebate of £1.49, but this still left them £4.50 a week worse off than before. This, plus a rent rise of £2 since May of last year, has left them considerably poorer than they were twelve months ago. Mary told me, 'We had to cut out new clothes for summer, and we were going to buy a new carpet – this one's terrible, we've had it for ages. But that was all knocked on the head. Before, we were trying to put away £1 a week; now we can't save anything. We've got £4 in the bank; that's all our savings.'

They cash Mary's pension on a Monday, Clarence's on Thursdays, to make the money stretch. It costs them 16p a week in fares to collect, because there are no local post offices. They cover the larger bills by saving week by week towards them – stamps to cover their electric bill, about £3 a quarter; and stamps to pay for their television licence, which at £7 a year is a hefty sum to pay out at one go. The gas bill is £2.75 a fortnight; and they get a rebate every six months if they consume less than this.

The Atkinsons spend nothing at all on luxuries. Neither has ever had a holiday, even when they were working. Last year, they had a free day trip with the social services department. 'We went to a zoo, it was a really good run-round. They paid for your cup of tea and we had a knife and fork dinner.' But even essentials they go short on. Mary: 'Meat, we'd eat it every day if we could get it, but we can't afford it.' They eat fish and chips, spare rib when they can afford it. Mostly, they make soup with bones.

They are even worse-off for clothes. Mary has two frocks with which she rings the changes. Clarence has only the trousers he stands up in. 'What will you do when they wear out?' asked Mary. 'Blacken your legs? Or you can put on a pair of my bloomers and pretend you're a runner.' If they had any extra money, they would spend it on clothes. 'A pair of shoes and some good underclothes so I could go out decent,' says Mary. Despite their poverty, the Atkinsons have never been in arrears with the rent, except once during an abortive rent strike last October.

George and Sarah Renwick, on the other hand, often defer payment of the rent when they get the electric bill. 'You've got to keep the light on, haven't you?' says Sarah. The couple, aged 64 and 60, live in the Teams, one of the classic slums, with very bad housing conditions and a high rate of delinquency and other social problems.

For the past three years, the couple have lived on George's sickness benefit, at present £11, plus supplementary benefit of £1 which covers their rent of £1.07. What they save on rent, they more than make up for on fuel and light, because they stay in most of the time. Their large living room, where the clothes hang on an overhead rack to dry, is heated by a coal fire which is kept in all the time. It takes three bags a week and costs £2.70. Three quarters of the heat goes up the chimney. They cook on a gas stove, paid for by the dearest way of all – shillings in the slot. Sarah says it can take up to 25p a day if she is cooking a lot. Their fuel bill is thus about £4 or £5 per week, nearly 40 per cent of their income. George draws his benefit on a Friday. But it only lasts till the following Wednesday, when every week Sarah borrows £1 or £1.50 from one of their daughters. This is faithfully paid back again on the Friday. 'We just manage,' says Sarah, 'and we're grateful.'

The Renwicks skimp on food even more than the Atkinsons. Sarah has kidney trouble, George an ulcer – both are supposed to eat plenty of greens, fish, lean meat. But like the other poor people I spoke to, they cannot afford their diet. Most of the time they live off soup. If they have meat, it might be half a pound of sausages for tea, or bacon bought by the quarter or even two ounces. Sarah: 'I'm ashamed to ask for it in such small quantities. We have lentil or split pea soup – if you get some good soup down you it's not so bad. But I really miss my meat. Even a year ago, we always had a meat dinner, liver or chops. Now maybe we fry a few chips. The other night I put two Oxos in with an onion and a few taties. It was very nice and tasty, though. But I'd really love to go in a hotel some time and have a nice sitdown meal.' 'I reckon half the Teams is starving these days,' said George.

Like the Atkinsons, the Renwicks have only the clothes they stand up in. Sarah has one change of dress. George gets a new pair of slippers every year from his daughter. Sarah gets clothes from jumble sales – even her underclothes. They pay £1 a week to the ticket man, but when they get the cheque they often spend it on other things than clothes – paint and wallpaper, for example. They don't go out because they have no clothes to go out in. They have no savings at all. 'We had a shilling or two a couple of years back, then they all went,' said George. 'That's the way it is when you've been on the sick for a long time.'

No one outside the family has bothered to explain to the Renwicks what extra benefits they might be entitled to. They both need new glasses. Sarah's are patched with glue, George's too weak. But, through a strange logic, they feel they ought not to ask for anything else from the national health just yet, because they both had new false teeth last year. George: 'We had our teeth money last year. That's enough for now. We don't want to impose.'

The Renwicks' massive fuel bill is only one example of a general problem: the poor pay more, not less, than the better-off. They need to keep a little in hand for emergencies, and their money comes in dribs and drabs on different days of the week. So they are forced to buy in small quantities, from day to day. They have no cars to get to discount supermarkets. For larger bills, they pay little by little, saving with electricity stamps or the clothing club. But they get no interest on their savings, and indeed pay the club an extra 5 per cent to cover the cost of the weekly door-to-door collection. Furniture they get on hire purchase at high rates of interest. They often pay for power at the very highest tariffs, and the Supplementary Benefits Commission will not pay for conversion to cheaper methods of heating.

To cope with all this, the poor have evolved their own distinct financial way of life. 'The poor man's banking system,' it is called by Virginia Bottomley and Richard Drabble of the Child Poverty Action Group, who have just completed a survey of family poverty in London. They point out that large weekly payments such as rent or HP play an important role as sources of emergency finance that can be broken into – but only at the risk of being evicted or having the power cut off. The CPAG survey found a consistent excess of expenditure over income – as high as 13 per cent in the case of the unemployed. They also found a massive fluctuation in family income over short periods; as much as £10 per week up or down. This was due to changing fortunes, redundancy, sickness, withdrawal of overtime, and so on. It meant that, like Florence Archer before her separation, housewives were not budgeting on predictable incomes. The survey also found that the proportion of family income going on the unavoidable items of housing, food and fuel was much higher than that found by the government Family Expenditure Survey.

It is clear that the basic experience of life for poor people is almost unimaginable for those who are not subject to the same constraints. Their diets are different. They eat far more of the things that dentists and dieticians say are bad for you. This is not through ignorance. Most of them know what they should be eating, but can afford the right things less and less. Their pleasures are few. They go out on day trips maybe once a year, to the cinema or theatre never. They take no holidays. Practically all of them have televisions, and for the old it is their only pleasure (except when the time comes to pay the licence).

None of those I spoke to were very bitter about any of this. They had come to terms with it as a way of life. They struggled on with the always-losing battle of making ends meet, often, at the cost of their pride, forced to accept charity, cast-offs, second-best. Perhaps it is because their situation is so hard to understand and so rarely talked about openly that we fail to realise that hand-outs – even if they were all taken up – at present allow people only the most meagre of existences.

15 February 1973

15
A tale of two sisters

Jeremy Seabrook

Phyllis and Gloria are sisters, brought up in the Jamaican country-side. Phyllis is now 40, Gloria five years younger. Phyllis left Jamaica 20 years ago for London, where she settled, and married a man from Trinidad. Gloria left Jamaica twelve years ago, and went to live in New York with her husband, a Guyanese in the United States army.

Phyllis left two older daughters in Jamaica, who are now grown up. She and her husband have four children, and live in an old 1930s LCC estate in south London. Six years ago, her husband became incapacitated with heart disease, and the family lives on invalidity benefit.

Gloria and her husband have three children, the youngest of whom is less than a year old. Two years ago, she sent for her oldest boy, now nearly 13, and he went to live with them in the north Bronx.

In many respects, the fortunes of the two sisters are com-plementary: Gloria represents success in a harsher society, and Phyllis represents relative failure in a milder one. They haven't seen each other for 20 years, but their relationship with each other and with their country of origin remains complex and subtle.

Gloria and her family live in a huge New York apartment block on Unionport Road, built by the Helmsley Corporation in the 1950s, which the company is trying to sell off as 'condominium' apartments. Gloria doesn't want to buy. You never know who your neighbours are going to be, and she prefers to save up for a house. She pays rent of about £150 a month. The flats are well maintained and substantially built; and although there is no liveried doorkeeper as there would be in more expensive flats, there is an intercom so that everybody who rings the bell has to account for himself before the door is opened. There is a good shopping area nearby, with a branch of Macy's.

It is about six miles from Manhattan, where Gloria works in a big office block on 'maintenance', from four in the afternoon until 10.30. She passes through the south Bronx and Harlem, areas of great nineteenth century blocks with Italianate architecture, some of them blackened and gutted by fire – whether by tenants firing their own apartments in the hope of getting better accommodation, or by landlords wanting to claim the insurance money, is an argument that seems to preoccupy many better-off New Yorkers.

Phyllis and her husband live in a south London estate that is rundown and neglected. Blocked rubbish chutes overflow onto the pitted asphalt, and the staircases are littered with ordure and waste paper. Phyllis is proud and fastidious, and her flat is well-kept inside. Even so, rust has corroded the window frames, and condensation has rotted many of the carpets. There is no room for a table in her flat, and her children have never sat down there to a communal meal in their lives.

Gloria's apartment is spacious and well furnished. In the living room there are two sofas, and an expensive music centre, a colour television in an ornamental cabinet, and wall-to-wall carpeting. There is a dining table, which seats six people comfortably. Even so, her three boys have to sleep in one room, which contains, as well as three beds, their bicycles and toys and considerable accumulation of possessions; and in this respect, they are little better-off than Phyllis's family, whose three girls have to share a slightly smaller room.

The dereliction of the south Bronx – which is only a half a mile away from where Gloria lives – acts not only as a spur to getting on materially, but also as a constant warning and example to people who don't make it. You get a strong impression that an at least equal part of the rewards-and-incentives argument is its other side – the visible and threatening presence of failure; and it is this that gives New York so much of its energy and sense of excitement.

Of the people in the south Bronx, the illegal migrants, the

misery, crime and despair, all those destroyed by drugs and alcohol, Gloria says: 'They have a better life than I do. They come from all over the place to New York just to get on welfare. They get more than I do by working, they get food stamps, everything they want. I get nothing given to me. They lie in bed all morning, then go out enjoying themselves all night, dancing at discos.'

She makes no connection between her theory of why people are on welfare and the fate of her own sister, partly perhaps because she assumes things are different in England. She knows that her sister is not culpable; but to believe that the people of the south Bronx lived there for any other reason than merited punishment would be too painful.

Everything supports Gloria's sense of success: she and her husband have just become American citizens, and this reinforces the feeling of achievement. She is now in a position to sponsor other aspiring migrants, which brings with it real power – shall she sponsor Phyllis's two daughters (who, she feels, should never have been left in Jamaica), or Phyllis herself, or maybe even one of Phyllis's children in England?

Gloria is horrified by what she hears of the poverty in England, and she sends her sister a jar of coffee as the most useful present she can think of. 'Why doesn't she get a job?' Gloria asks. 'At home she was always such a worker. She was always much happier working on the cultivation than I was.' But there are few jobs Phyllis could do in her part of south London. If she were to commute into the city to do office cleaning, like Gloria, travelling costs would bite more significantly into the much lower wage she would get.

Gloria is more hedonistic than her sister. She likes to enjoy herself, goes to shows on Broadway, to discos and restaurants. Phyllis likes dancing, but she would never go into the West End, and has never been to the theatre. But perhaps the most painful difference in the lives of the two sisters is that Gloria doesn't feel that she is cut off from her roots in the way that Phyllis does. On the contrary: from New York, Jamaica is only three hours away, and Gloria goes back every two years to see her parents, Phyllis's daughters, her aunts and uncles.

Gloria says, 'I love to go to Jamaica. There is the sun and the sea, but life can be hard. It's terrible there at the moment, they can't get enough to eat, they have to stand in line for everything. I love the sun and I love the sea, but you can't live on sand and fresh air. You've got to help yourself, not wait for fate to do it for you. You wait for ever that way. God isn't going to help you – God helps them who help themselves. I love to visit Jamaica, but not to live there. The opportunities for my children are here.'

Gloria's youngest child is the only girl in the family. When she was born, Gloria stayed at home for six months before going back to work. With the previous child, Carey, she resumed her job after only two months. 'I think that's maybe why he is a bit aggressive at the moment. This will be my last child. I've got a nice little family, but no more. That's it now.'

Phyllis has never been back to Jamaica since she left in 1959. Partly because of this, and partly because life has somehow failed to live up to her expectations, Jamaica has taken on something of the aspect of a lost paradise. She hasn't her sister's matter-of-fact attitude, which comes from closer, more realistic contact.

Tears come to Phyllis's eyes as she talks of the piece of land where she worked as a young woman. 'My father had the land where the house is. He had cane, banana, plaintain, coffee and breadfruit. When I was going to school, you could have guavas or June-plum. You have golden-apple and mangoes, all different sort of mangoes. You just burst the fruit and suck the juice out.'

One of her ways of communicating with people at home is by 'dream-seeing' them. 'When my grandfather died, I knew. I dreamt-see him in the night. By the way I dreamt-see him, he tell me, "Look how long I gone," and he is going. So I say, "Where you going?" He said, "I have to go somewhere." I see him sitting under the plantain tree, and I see him just pull his hat over his face. . . . The way I see him sit, he look so sad and I knew that he gone.'

Her life is a more leisurely and melancholy one than that of her sister, who has no time for such introspection. Phyllis consults the stars and hopes that fate will bring her a lot of money, the chance to go home, to visit America, to get out of the flat in south-east London. Gloria says she doesn't understand why Phyllis stays there, tied to a sick man, when she isn't getting younger and life is passing her by.

Phyllis still talks of the spirits and ghosts of her rural Jamaican childhood. As a girl, she would get up early in the morning to help cut cane, and she remembers there were 'spirits everywhere;

but they don't worry me. . . . You see like a figure coming down;
you don't know if it a man or a woman, and when they get in front
of you they just disappear. . . . I turn round once to look at one,
and I see him spring up tall, tall; and when I tell me father he tell
me I shouldn't do that. It could turn my head if I looked at *them*, it
could turn me head behind me so that it could never come back in
front.' Gloria has had such memories ironed out by the vitality
and immediacy of her life in America. She has time only for what
is tangible and credible.

Although the sisters were close as children – Phyllis always
used to look after Gloria – their experience of migration has
reversed their roles. Gloria is now protective and slightly conde-
scending towards her sister. She is a far more friendly and
spontaneous person, while Phyllis is reserved, self-conscious,
more insecure. In part this is a temperamental difference, but it is
obviously far easier to be a migrant in the Bronx than it is in south
London. Ironically, Phyllis sees the migration as more irrevers-
ible than Gloria, although she feels less secure in England than
her sister does in New York.

In many important aspects their lives are similar. 'In this
country you have to give the children everything they want. You
have to give them money whenever they go out, even when they
go to school,' Phyllis says. 'You didn't want sweets all the time in
Jamaica. You have a June-plum. You reach and take the fruit from
the tree, and that's it. And if you got plenty, and your friends
poorer than you, you just hand it out.'

The children, both in New York and in London, are still
optimistic. Gloria's oldest boy talks with great enthusiasm about
his wish to become a famous baseball player; one of Gloria's girls
wants to be a fashion designer; her boy wants an apprenticeship.

In some ways, it is difficult not to feel that the lives of the
children have been in some ways impoverished. They have
surrendered all contact with a sense of Jamaica as home. They
don't even have Phyllis's profound and sorrowful attachment to
its landscape. The children have forfeited everything for a promise, which is unlikely to be realised, the promise of a lot of money.
In this way, they have abandoned all the resources that people
develop to cope with poverty, in anticipation of getting rich. Both
families have believed promises which were made by no one, but
which are implicit in the whole experience of migration.

Both sisters said they had felt lonely at times since they left Jamaica. Both had found that, removed from traditional supports and disciplines, they had been tempted to leave their husbands, despite the knowledge that there was no possibility that any other relative would look after the children, as would happen in Jamaica.

Phyllis found herself a boy friend, but she hesitated too long before leaving her ailing husband; and the truth was that she found she was more attached to him, and certainly to her children, than she had realised. When Gloria and her husband grew dissatisfied, each returned for a time to their separate families in Jamaica and Guyana. There, they found the will to carry on together; not in a sentimental way, but by getting a glimpse of what might happen if they split up – going home would represent a failure even more complete than sinking into the slums of the south Bronx.

The two sisters illuminate in a dramatic way the intractable relationship between success and failure. Gloria exemplifies the energising influence of the need to succeed when the alternative is so disagreeable, Phyllis the more passive acceptance of that alternative when it is not so bleak. At a deeper level, both sisters symbolise the eternal sadness and hope of migrations; the promise of a better life which, however fully it may be realised, always involves forfeits and losses that can never be calculated.

11 September 1980

16
'If a miner tells you he likes it, he's lying'

Tom Forester

Just north of a line between Barnsley and Doncaster in south Yorkshire, the belching steelworks and filthy coking plants of the Don and Dearne valleys give way to a flatter, more rural landscape, where the Pennines dip down toward the Humberside basin. A saucer-like shallow valley carries the Inter-City railway line from London to Leeds and, from the OS map, we are told that the area has been well and truly carved up with ancient, dismantled ones.

Trees rustle on the hilltops and plumes of smoke rise from the rows of NCB and council houses in the linked mining settlements of South Elmsall, Moorthorpe and South Kirkby.

Half a mile underground, on G20 face of South Kirkby colliery, the early shift are struggling with the final hydraulic prop on the advanced technology face. The 100-metre face hasn't moved for a month now, held up by an oblique fault line across the ten-foot seam which is causing repeated roof falls. Sure enough, as we crawl through a dust storm in the tailgate entrance, the roof caves in on cue, opening up an eerie cavern 80 foot high.

The faceworkers retreat, their faces and near-naked bodies coal-black and glistening with sweat in the 80-degree heat. Now it will be more digging out and manoeuvring with hydraulic rams before another ounce of coal is cut (and G20 can move 1,800 tonnes in a shift when it's working). We retreat from the heat, dust, muck and water before claustrophobia sets in. Riding the narrow conveyor belts for the two miles or so through narrow tunnels back to the pit bottom, the smell of virgin coal and the

145

soluble oil used in hydraulics clings to our overalls. Our throats are dry with the dust. I worry about pneumoconiosis.

Recently, the National Coal Board announced a £19 million loss for last year, the first loss in five years. With coal production down by over a million tonnes to 119.9 million, and a financial squeeze caused by massive expenditure on a huge investment programme that has yet to produce results, 1978–9 was not a good year in the pits.

Despite the new incentive bonus scheme, which the Labour government used to buy off the miners in 1978, overall pit productivity rose by only 2.2 per cent. Power station stocks reached their lowest level since the winter of 1974. An NUM claim for a 65 per cent wage rise is to be lodged shortly.

South Kirkby colliery is a typical British colliery. It will be 100 years old next year. It has three deep shafts, five faces and an annual production of 750,000 tonnes. It is also the pit where Jimmy Saville worked for four years before he got rich and famous. They still talk in South Kirkby about that 'astute young fellow' who got out. Many of Jimmy's contemporaries have been invalided or else are dead with the dust by now.

New investment and proven reserves ensure that South Kirkby colliery itself could have a long life ahead of it. However, in recent years, like many NCB pits, South Kirkby has run into trouble. Declining seam thicknesses, geological problems and a shortage of labour, especially skilled men, have brought total production down from one million tonnes in 1975. Last year South Kirkby made a loss of £3 million on a turnover of £18 million.

Colliery manager Roy Beeforth resembles Arthur Scargill, and was a childhood friend of his in Worsbrough Dale, Barnsley. He worked his way up from the face through the study of mining engineering. He is one of a new breed of ex-worker managers who replaced the chinless-wonder sons of coal-owners, and the ex-army officers put in after nationalisation in the immediate postwar era. Roy is naturally not happy about the pit's productivity at present, but adds that it is not due to the failure of the pay incentive scheme: 'You have to ask yourself what would have happened without the scheme. It has boosted attendance. People think twice now about not coming in because they lose the shift bonus.'

Even so, although official NCB figures for the Yorkshire area show a creditable drop in average daily absenteeism (from 20 to 16 per cent), Kirkby's geological difficulties are reducing productivity – and thus all but eliminating the shift bonuses. About 30 per cent of South Kirkby pitmen work a four-day week and a hard core of 5 per cent work just three days.

'I don't think there will be a bust-up this winter,' says Beeforth. 'In '72 and '74 the country asked for it. The miners had a very good grievance. They had dropped to about 17th in the pay league.' 'You can only go so far,' says the production manager, Chris Hindley. 'The wages of the miner have got to stay up top, yes. People need motivating. But at the end of the day we have got to show the public that we are getting the coal out. In another seven years I expect there will be another change in the wages system when the effects of this one wear off.'

Outside the manager's office, in the pit yard, the men are coming off the early shift. In batches they march into the pithead baths, faces blackened, some hobbling, others plodding wearily and looking much older and far less brawny than the standard image of miners. Dust masks are left for cleaning in the room next to the chromium-equipped hospital block, a constant reminder of the brutality of a miner's life and the closeness of death.

Next stop up top is the canteen, where pies with mounds of chips and mushy peas are the order of the day, along with mugs of tea. There's 'coal talk' aplenty but most want to get away to the coaches and the bright blue and yellow NCB minibuses that take them home to towns and villages perhaps ten miles away. A car park of battered Cortinas provides more personal transport for those that can afford it. Others head for the racks stacked with mopeds.

South Kirkby is what they call a 'cosmopolitan' pit. Nowadays, 80 per cent of the miners come in from around, mostly from Hemsworth, Wakefield and Barnsley. Yet 20 years ago nearly every South Kirkby miner was from South Kirkby. The local NUM president, 38-year-old Frank Clarke, says: 'The system of controlled labour means that you're just a number now. You're sent where they want you to go and you have no say in it. What we have seen is the break-up of the village pit system.'

'One of the peculiarities of mining,' a local NUM branch delegate, George Buckley, says, 'is that the mine has always dominated the community. All the men worked down the pit.

But here we've got an unemployment rate of 13½ per cent in South Kirkby and the pit is 250 men short. The youngsters won't go down the pit these days. The NCB are recruiting like mad, but they're fighting to stand still. All the men come here for is the money. That's why, when the money's wrong, you've got trouble.'

What is the money? A youngster of 16 will earn £7.40 gross for a 7¼ hour shift. This rises to £42 per week gross for a 17-year-old and £50 at 18, when they are first allowed underground. The basic for an adult faceworker is £84, but the bonus on top can vary enormously. Frank Clarke's pay slip for the previous six-day week revealed the following: gross £114; net, after deductions, £64. But the deductions include £4.85 rent on an NCB cottage and loan repayments of £3.41. True take-home, therefore, with which to keep a wife and three children – £72 (for six days).

But Frank works on 'headings' (new tunnels). Another NUM branch delegate, Charlie Covell, has the misfortune to work in G18 seam. Here, the face is 2 foot 6 inches high and runs for 300 yards. He spends 5½ hours a day on his knees or belly in two inches of mucky water. Again, for six shifts, Charlie's pay slip reveals a true net weekly pay of £78.

Not surprisingly, there is a high rate of absenteeism on such faces: 'You've got blokes off all the time with cartilage problems, slipped discs, cracked knees, damaged fingers and all kinds of strains. You're like swimming in muck trying to lift 12-inch steel props. And you try having a shit lying on your side in two inches of water. No, blokes don't last long at the face. You're no good unless you're on top form.'

Frank and Charlie's bonuses for that week were pretty average for South Kirkby, but the anomalies among workers in different sections of the same pit are extraordinary, an indication of the inherent divisiveness of the incentive scheme. Of four headings at South Kirkby, the shift bonuses in the same week were £3.04, £15.63, £9.10 and nothing. Thus the lucky ones in a good week might cream off £160 gross, while colleagues in the tunnel next door could be down on the basic £84. The variations from pit to pit are just as bad, and greatly increase tension between miners.

The blokes on the surface earn less – 40 per cent less than underground workers. Their bonuses, if any, are also 40 per cent less. 'A five-day week man on the surface simply cannot live. He has to work weekends,' says the NUM surface representative, Roy Onions, who in his spare time is an accomplished painter. 'Many, if not most, of the surface men have had to come up through no fault of their own. They have either been injured, sent up by the doctor or rejected for facework.'

Typical is Billy French, aged 31. He started at 16, worked underground for two years, then smashed two fingers. One is now permanently bent, the other permanently straight. How do you feel? 'I feel old,' he says.

Margaret Jones, aged 23 and mother of two, is a South Kirkby housewife. Her husband Stuart had to come out of the pit because of blackouts. They came on after a workmate had a bad accident. Now he is on the surface in the coal-washing plant, an unattractive job at the best of times. It pays £57 gross for a 40-hour week. Only by working five night shifts, plus all day Saturday and Sunday, can he gross enough (£99) to take home £73. Margaret's dad was crushed in a pit accident, her granddad died from pneumoconiosis, and her husband's father is an invalid with dust on his chest.

They haven't had a holiday for years, but this year they were offered a cheap week in a caravan near Skegness. Apart from that, they have only ever been to Blackpool once and a rugby final in London. Happy? 'Yes, we're happy. I've got my bingo and Stuart goes down the British Legion.'

'This is the only industry where you start at the bottom of the wage scale and finish at the bottom,' says Kevin Delaney, a skilled engineer who is having to work (because of the skill shortage) seven 12-hour shifts a week. He takes home good money in this, his prime, but worries about the future. No big spend-up for their holidays this year: a modest two weeks in Weymouth, an indication of the conservatism of miners and their marked reluctance to venture abroad. As one retired miner, Charles Hayward, put it: 'There's nowt to go abroad for. There's nowhere better than this country.'

In fact, Charles and wife Lilian have only ever been to Bridlington. They have never been to London, let alone pottered around the Cotswolds or taken a peep up private drives in the Stockbroker Belt. So they've not seen much of the country they are so proud of. Charlie, one of 16 children, spent 49 years in the pits from the age of 14 to retirement at 63. For that he got a £500 golden

handshake and a cheap-looking Certificate for Long and Meri-
torious Service (to the industry and 'the country').

Starting as he did in 1928, Charlie well remembers the days of
the pick and shovel, pit ponies, and the tin bath in front of the
fire. 'It's a lot easier and safer is mine work today. The money's
better, but they tek it off them in tax and other ways.' Yet Charlie
has no romantic illusions about the past: 'To tell 'e the truth, I
didn't like it. But there were nowt else but the pit. If a miner tells
you he likes it, he's telling lies.' Charlie now has emphysema, a
respiratory disease that many miners get which doesn't qualify
for compensation. Between wheezes he looks up at the certificate
on the wall: 'I don't think it were worth it, mi'sen.'

Just down the road from Charlie's, Moorthorpe cemetery offers
its own judgment. There, the blackened tilting gravestones on
miners' graves, a remarkable number explaining that their occupants had been 'accidentally killed' at local collieries, testify that
mining isn't worth it.

As you go on through the Coronation Street backstreets of the
three towns, South Elmsall-Moorthorpe-South Kirkby reveals
itself to be a poor area: judging by the way folk down south talk
about £300 a week miners, you would expect to see the roads
choked with BMWs and Jaguars. In fact, there are very few new
cars. South Elmsall market is dominated by stalls selling sweets,
biscuits, net curtains and cheap plastic toys – hardly signs of great
affluence. Tatty corner shops sell cheapo goods at discount
prices. It's the kind of area where only the pub and the ladies'
hairdresser make money.

But even in the pubs and clubs, things aren't exactly booming.
At Mill Lane social club, they've found a tendency for people to
come out later in the evening, with the inflation in beer prices.
And the lengthy bingo sessions in the miners' welfare centre
make for a cheaper evening out. Yet the legendary generosity of
the miners shows no signs of dying out: in South Kirkby each
miner gives away a quarter of his 12-ton annual coal allowance to
retired miners and their widows. The mayor of South Kirkby,
Horace Clark, explains that the Labour-dominated council now
provides 'one shilling' TV licences for old folk, intercoms in all old
people's homes and a comprehensive meals-on-wheels service.
'You have to remember that 40 per cent of our retired are
geriatric.'

*   *   *

Of the past, Frank Clarke remembers most of all the walks in the
nearby countryside. 'People just don't walk to the woods now. I
suppose telly and bingo has put a stop to that. But basically we
haven't changed much. We're a mining community united
through coal and united through our suffering. Here you go into
a club or pub and you can tell everyone is a miner. The little
blue-black scars are the mark of a miner. Once a miner, always a
miner, they say. We don't change.'

A few miles down the road from South Kirkby, at Great
Houghton, there is one of those postwar roadside police houses
of the kind that provide law and order in rural areas. It stands
empty, its garden overgrown. It was declared surplus to needs.
The miners, through their conservatism, and their tight-knit
communities, evidently police themselves.

20 September 1979

17
At the doctor's

David Selbourne

'Is it an emergency? What's wrong, love?' 'What name is it, love?' 'What's he done, love?'

The phones don't stop ringing. It is 8.30 a.m. Behind them, the medical records – 17,000 of them – stand on metal racks. It is all women's voices, white coats, Dr Scholl's wooden sandals, broad vowels and the first brew-up of the morning.

This is Hyde, in Tameside, on the Lancashire-Cheshire border, land of Lowry, made – and unmade – by cotton. If the Pennines can be said to have foothills, then we are in them. When the light came up, it was not so much rosy-fingered, as the colour of liver sausage. Round here, the word 'love' sometimes seems the only beacon in the darkness. I am in the Clarendon House group practice, as the morning rush hour of the halt, the lame and the anxious begins to press in on its seven doctors.

A fat chap with a moustache, hair down his shoulders, and with a beery paunch hanging over his trousers, appears at the reception window. 'What time do you want, love?' 'I'm not bothered.' 'Your address, please, love.' He gives it. 'Half-past eight on Friday morning. Will that do, love?' 'Ta.' A man on crutches, in blue denim and with tattooed fingers, limps down the yellow linoleum. 'They're at the window,' Dr David Livingstone, the head of the practice, said to me later, speaking of the six ladies at the counter: 'They see a lot.'

This is a dismal neck of the woods, if ever there was one, with 3,000 jobless in the town, chronically low wages – 10 per cent below the national average in textiles, 20 per cent in clothing and footwear – and with the staple industries declining. 'There is a pervading atmosphere of physical neglect throughout Tameside,' says an official profile of the area; and 'no obvious growth sector in the local economy has been discovered'.

The prospect, it says, is 'disturbing'. But here in the large waiting room, clean as a clinic and shining with polish, faces seem impassive. 'Be a patient patient,' it says on the wall. They are.

Browsing through the *North Cheshire Herald and Hyde Reporter*, I see that Stalybridge Celtic have been 'humiliated', four-nil, by Prescot Cables. 'It was pathetic fare,' writes their man at the match, 'with nary a semblance of challenge, spirit or resistance. For this current Celtic side, defeat simply does not hurt enough.' Perhaps that explains it.

'Tebbit takes on the unions,' screams the *Sun*. No one bats an eyelid. Drs Beenstock, Bennett, Farrar, Livingstone and McGillivray await them. The colour supplements, *Cosmopolitan* and *Woman* stand in neat piles on the table. It is all running like clockwork.

Hyde is not quite the place I remember from my own wartime childhood in the area. In those days, it was – or seems to be in memory – all bruise-coloured brick, looming crowded mills, and rookeries of crouching terraces and dark ginnels; a place of smoking chimneys, sooty privet and blackened churches.

My father was a doctor in neighbouring Dukinfield; and through him, I still see it as a world of asthma, bandylegs and bronchitis. In our waiting room in wartime – dingy and coal-lit and smelling of the sourness of defeat and poor bodies – the patients used to sit in a muffled fug of coughing and spitting, reading *Picture Post, Blighty* and *Reveille* till the pages fell apart in grey, dog-eared tatters. Today's anti-rickets posters are in Urdu.

In a starched white coat – 'in them days' – my father spent his life on these towns' bodies, which always seemed to be sick and tired. It was as if everybody was bowed down, bent double, by labour. In the wind, before the Clean Air Act, the whorls of smut and smoke would swirl and billow in the down draughts, roof pots rattling.

Now slum clearance has smashed through the terraces, which used to follow each other up hill and down dale, leaving more vacancies and worse dereliction than the bombs of war could. They say 4 per cent of the land in the area is derelict. From here, a bird's eye view would make it 40.

Under this morning's waiting-room neon, and in such polished conditions, the wounds of unemployment and the new depression seem bloodless and centrally-heated. But this single-storey utility style of Welfare Britain is also the new working-class wasteland: of communities laid waste by clearance, planners and already clapped-out postwar public building.

They built the new Jerusalems round here – and everywhere – with warped hardboard and breeze blocks. It is the wattle-and-daub of the twentieth century, a new desert for an old dunghill. It is made of show houses and flyovers and motorway-blue road signs at one end of the spectrum, and the fear and unease of trying to make ends meet at the other, as the tide of local unemployment rises.

'They're not coming in such large numbers for "a week on the sick" with a bad back, like they used to,' says Dr Stephen Farrar, one of the partners. 'The chap who has a few weeks off every year I don't see so often. They're frightened', he says, 'of losing their jobs. They fear that firms will look at the sick-list and say, "Who's first?"'

He has recently seen a personnel manager with 'anxiety-type symptoms'. This man has been handling the firm's sackings. 'It is making him ill,' says Farrar, 'or, rather, he felt it was making him ill. He doesn't like doing it. It isn't very nice for him having to tell people they're out.'

'There is also a continual rumour about ICI,' Farrar adds. (With Walls and Senior Service, they are major local employers.) 'Members of the workforce are jittery there,' he says. 'But most patients don't talk about it. You have to extract it from them.'

The well-wrapped waiting-room silence is not what it seems; anxieties are deep-coursing. 'It is a class thing,' he says. 'People of my class think that if they're unemployed, they deserve it. But working-class people are very worried.'

In the waiting room there is a blur of medical posters: 'Anna Ford says, "I would like to help someone live after my death"'. Her lips are pouting, her lipstick glossy. 'Get a donor card from your doctor.' Her eyes seem to be beckoning and winking. But the come-hither falls flat on these customers, silently waiting for the buzzer and a recipe for their own survival, not someone else's.

Dr Norman Beenstock's position is different. (Or, as Dr Farrar wrily and accurately puts it, 'Medical attitudes to the problem of unemployment depend upon your political views, as well as your clinical judgement.') He says: 'The economic climate is having an effect on people's health. There's more anxiety expressed in hypochondriacal illness, seeking help for minor day-to-day complaints, and depression. But the poorer are still smoking as much as ever, with their colour TVs on from 9 a.m. onwards.'

Out in the town, Lowry's stick-figures have long ago vanished. The tripe shops sell televisions, and Ladbroke's rubs shoulders with the Dacca Oriental Delicatessen. The dull uniform of wartime hardship, the threadbare, patched and grey clothing of northern labour have gone for a Burton. (And so has Burton's.)

There are no more knotted kerchiefs and balaclavas, waistcoats without jackets, or shirts without collars; no more clogs and Bisto-kid faces, no more thin black pumps for children with bony knees and running noses. The view to the Pennines is as clean as a whistle, the grey-green hills delicately snaked and squared with black stone walls.

Yet the community is up against it, in a depression both medical and economic; the townscape less soiled, but as sallow and downcast as ever. Half the factories in use were built before 1914, and the population is growing older also. Dr Beenstock is worried as well as angry about the run-down in resources, though his argument is a complex one.

On the one hand, he has a real fear of a 'breakdown on the clinical front', when 'patients will actually die because of the run-down. Sooner or later something will hit the headlines and people will say, "How disgusting. It shouldn't happen"'.

On the other, 'People who have had services expect them' he says. 'As far as the public is concerned, the welfare state is an open-ended system. They make their demands as of right. And since the doctor, for many people, is their main contact with the welfare system, it is the doctor who gets the bashing for its defects. If it doesn't tally with their expectations, we get their phlegm.' 'Phlegm?' 'Yes, phlegm.' It is a good bronchitic metaphor, drawn from practice.

Behind the reception counter, opinion is similar, but more

strident. 'People are wanting more and more, expecting more, not less. They expect it as part of their rights. And the people who are greedy, and won't help themselves, are the first to start moaning.' She is a kind person, who calls everyone 'love'. 'The working class know what they can get to the last detail.' (Dr Farrar disagrees completely: 'The services are there, but the working class don't know it.') 'They ask for such silly things,' she says, holding out her fingers, 'Like, "I want my plaster changed."'

She is positively cross, getting quite flushed with it. 'They take it all for granted. People are so arrogant, there's just no contentment.' You wouldn't have guessed it. In the waiting room are only muted and cautious whispers. Their suffering is in silence, criticism of them raucous.

'Then,' she says, warming to it, 'there's the blackmail. On the phone they say, "I'll get the doctor out," if you can't get them an appointment when they want it.' (What, these lambs – or sheep – wrapped in their fleeces?) Her kinder, northern self says, 'Some of these patients are a bit cheeky.' 'Quite a number do it,' agrees Dr Livingstone, unruffled. 'They'll call you out for a toothache.'

My father used to describe it as a 'wandering fart', in the old days, when doctors did open battle with their patients. Livingstone himself is laconic, mild-mannered. 'I don't think it's any different from what it used to be. You get the minority who'll always complain. They're unbalanced, paranoid or something of the sort,' he says shrugging, dismissive.

But as the health service comes under pressure, the whole underlying argument about the nature and purposes of welfare is becoming intenser and more urgent. Beenstock says of the welfare state that 'As an ideal, no one could fault it. But in practice, in an acquisitive society, you can't have people demanding things as of right in an open-ended system.' It is a view from the trenches of an infantryman under attack from swarms of patients, and tired of defending himself with prescriptions and potions.

Farrar's priorities seem different. (He has been in practice 8 years, Beenstock more than 20.) 'The fact that the welfare services are getting worse, and publicity for them diminished, is very short-sighted,' he says. 'The health of society, as opposed to its sickness, is the major problem.' But the health service is 'not a sacred cow. Mine is a practical assessment. It is simply the best way I can see of working.'

He is a socialist, but thinks that 'to legislate private practice out of existence' would be 'totalitarian'. Instead, he'd like to see the health service 'so good that no one wanted to be a private patient'. He adds that the 'true red-hot red dismisses the principle of self-help. But a balanced view has to include it.' 'The first social service,' Livingstone says briefly, 'is your friends.' I expect that these three voices, between them, constitute the voice of the medical profession.

I go out with Livingstone on his visits. A Glaswegian, he started in practice in the area in 1937, went to war, and on VE Day was in Bari. He ended up as a captain anaesthetist in the British hospital in Quetta. The sun is shining, a clean breeze blowing. We are in Newton. It was stale here once, death-grey; ashen, in recollection. There are chrysanthemums in the windows, yellow, white, red-brown, tawny. Most of the sooty privet of wartime has vanished.

His patient – 'a young girl', he calls her – is 40, and has lung cancer. I wait in the car. There are small stained-glass swallows in the leaded windows, dark-blue, bottle-green, wine-red and yellow-orange. They fly with leaden wings in their jig-saws of coloured glass. These are northern mosaics.

He comes back after only a few minutes. 'She is dying of it, poor girl,' he says. 'She is very thin, poor thing.' He starts up the engine. The front gardens, low-walled in red brick, are neat and tidy. 'She weeps, she's not very happy about it. She has to work out a philosophy, and wonder why we're here at all,' he says quietly.

Hers is a depression beyond reach of unemployment, or any prescription. In this street, there is a sudden beauty. It is in the eye of the beholder, thankful for small mercies in the face of terminal disorder. 'To appreciate this kind of thing,' he says, gesturing towards the Pennines, and reading the moment, 'you have to be well.'

Back in the market square, with its stalls and striped red-and-green awnings, the Pakistani stall-holders are putting away their bric-a-brac. There is an acrid smell in the air; the 'Kingston stink', the locals call it.

Once it was the bitter aroma of bodies worked to the bone and picked clean by hardship, the fagged-out fragrance of old clothes and worn-down pavements. Now it is the stench of the local bone-factory, boiling up the carcases. Round here, you always seem to be sunk in one miasma or another, even when the sun is shining.

3 December 1981

18
Dole-queue rock

Peter Marsh

Ever since rock and roll was declared a 'communicable disease' by an eminent psychiatrist, we have grown used to witnessing the meteoric rise to fame of 'bad men'. The classic giants of the 1960s pop world – such as Elvis Presley, the Rolling Stones, The Who, even the Beatles in the early days – all seemed threatening and corrupting. But then Elvis cut his hair and joined the army, The Who stopped smashing up their hotels, and the Stones became part of the establishment. Their predecessors like Bill Hayley, Chuck Berry, Jerry Lee Lewis and Little Richard, along with the late Buddy Holly and Eddie Cochran, merged into rock history to become the alleged inspiration for any rock and roll player who could finger three chords and keep a steady beat. Against this background, lesser bands in the rhythm and blues and rock and roll revival moulds have come and gone – some achieving brief notoriety before being totally forgotten.

The pattern of events in this ephemeral world is predictable. The bad men become millionaires and their fans grow into marriage and steady jobs. The millionaires sit back in retirement and watch new 'demons' of the pop scene emerge – to be hated by the same kind of people who once despised them, and loved by a new generation of equally adoring young fans. All this makes it rather difficult to understand the collective insanity which has characterised the reaction to the latest pop phenomenon – punk rock. For those who have been living on a different planet for the last six months, this is a chance to catch up on the story of how society has managed to turn a handful of young amateur pub-

159

rock bands into a new *cause célèbre*. More important is to look behind the image and make sense of what punks are actually saying.

Punk music has been around in this country for some time. It was inspired by American groups, such as the New York Dolls, and by the man who has been called the Godfather of punk rock, Lou Reed. In this country, Dr Feelgood, one of the most competent bands to emerge from the pub-rock circuit, is credited as the major pioneer in Britain. But in the last year, a new wave of punk rock bands have emerged, which have taken on both the musical style and the general air of nihilism of the New York groups.

Expressing their contempt for anything and everything that was around them, the Sex Pistols had become firmly established in London by the summer of 1976. Two other groups, the Damned and the Clash, joined them as front runners in a movement which has since gained considerable impetus. Together they spawned groups like Siouxsie and the Banshees, the Buzzcocks and Vibrators. The average age of members of these bands was about 19. Following them came the real schoolboy punk groups, such as Subway Sect, Eater and Jam. These have recently had trouble in convincing the police that they are over 14 and old enough to be allowed on licensed premises.

Until about six months ago, very few people outside of the rock world had even heard of these bands. They played almost exclusively in small London venues like the Hope and Anchor, the 100 Club and a few other pubs. But bands like the Suburban Studs in Birmingham and the Buzzcocks in Manchester were beginning to spread punk music to the provinces. Things began to happen. The music press began to pay them some attention and both *New Musical Express* and *Melody Maker* started to carry reports of the Sex Pistols' London gigs. A few other papers also commented on the strange style of dress that some teenagers were adopting. Ripping up perfectly sound denim jackets and then holding them together again with hundreds of safety pins was novel. So, too, was the wearing of ear-rings with razor blades dangling from them. And then the real spark came. Someone at the 100 Club threw a glass which shattered and a girl was blinded in one eye. Overnight, punk rock became dangerous and a subject for vilification.

During this time, the Damned had secured a recording contract with Stiff records and the Sex Pistols were snapped up by the entrepreneurial Nick Mobbs of EMI. On the basis of the advance from the EMI contract, Malcolm McClaren, manager of the Pistols and owner of a sex boutique, financed a first British tour by punk bands. This included the Vibrators, Talking Heads and a New York band called the Ramones as well as the Pistols. But as the Pistols' image of violence and obscenity began to spread, the support bands pulled out and the punk rock scene started to splinter. To save the planned tour, the Damned, the Clash and the Heartbreakers rallied to the Pistols' side.

Then came Bill Grundy, whose interview with the Sex Pistols on Thames Television created the biggest furore since the yippies invaded the *Frost Show* in 1970. To add insult to injury, the Thames programme was screened live in the early evening to a very large child audience. 'The filth and the fury,' screamed the *Daily Mirror*, whilst the *Sun*, thinking that the Pistols' outrageous behaviour could be due only to drunkenness, asked: 'Were the Pistols loaded?' In true *Sun* style, the answer was provided: 'Punk group plied with booze.' The interview itself lasted just over one and a half minutes, short even by Thames standards, but in that time Grundy was able to talk himself into the headlines and a two week suspension from his job. For those who missed it, two extracts highlight the inanity of it all:

GRUNDY . . . They are the punk rockers – the new craze they tell me. They're heroes, not the nice clean Rolling Stones. You see they are as drunk as I am. They're clean by comparison. They are a group called Sex Pistols and I'm surrounded by all of them. . . .
GRUNDY . . . Go on, you've got another five seconds. Say something outrageous.
PISTOL You dirty bastard.
GRUNDY Go on, again . . .
PISTOL You dirty fucker.
GRUNDY What a clever boy.
PISTOL What a fucking rotter.

In the wake of this rubbish, something very close to a temporary nationwide hysteria set in at the prospect of the Sex Pistols spreading their influence around the country during their now much publicised tour. Predictably, promoters and theatre managers began to cancel some of their engagements. (The Sex Pistols' contract now no longer exists and radio stations are still refusing to put punk music on the air.) Even at this stage, however, little was said about what punk rock actually stood for. The Damned were doing a number called *White Riot* and the Pistols had just released their *pièce de résistance, Anarchy in the UK*. But there was little comment about the underlying political message that punk bands were trying to put across, beyond being out to promote violence, sex and destruction (in that order). Perhaps the fact that the Pistols' lead singer was called Johnny Rotten, and the Damned boasted a drummer by the name of Rat Scabies, was an obstacle to further inquiry.

With the Pistols' tour virtually written off, it was becoming increasingly difficult to see punk groups in action and to witness at first hand what all the fuss was about. In the south-west, however, folk get less excited about these things and Van Dyke Promotions were able to set up a venue in Plymouth for Clash, Heartbreakers and Pistols with little opposition from the city fathers. The Damned were absent from the billing. They had considered playing in Derby, even though the Pistols had been banned by the local council. Such treachery, it seems, is not to be tolerated and Damned were unceremoniously ditched from the rest of the tour.

The Woods Centre in Plymouth provides discos and live-group entertainment for Devon teenagers. Located rather incongruously above Montague Burton's in the main shopping centre, it seemed an unlikely place for such famous degenerates to be appearing. One couldn't imagine the Bay City Rollers coming here. But punk rock, it soon became clear, is very different from the neatly packaged pop products we have grown used to. Whatever else it may be, punk rock is *access* music. Despite the fact that the Pistols are headline material, there is no distance between them and people who regularly support them. You could even stand next to Johnny Rotten in the urinal.

A punk couple had been sitting, self-consciously and with great modesty, at a table on their own for hours before the groups were due to appear. The male half wore a long grey ex-WD overcoat for some time and it was not until he took it off that his tattered jacket, neatly kept in one piece by an appliqué of safety pins, was revealed to the world and to the German press photographer who also happened to be there. Both he and the girl with him wore tight drainpipe trousers – she with an imitation leopard-skin bikini top and he with a black satin shirt. Hair was cropped and brushed to a point at the front, but one wondered how they got those safety pins actually through their nostrils.

Other punks arrived during the evening, but most of the audience were noticeably unremarkable. There was a group of cynical rockers who, with weary expressions, said that they had seen it all before. It was a passing phase. Why had they come if they weren't interested in punk music? I asked naively. 'What else do you do in Plymouth?' one said, and at that moment Clash appeared.

It has to be said that if musical ability is a serious means of judging punk rock, then groups like Clash and the Sex Pistols are incompetents even in a field where gifted musicianship is an extreme rarity. No complex guitar riffs or elaborate harmonies here. Even the stage acts were clumsy and, at times, downright embarrassing. Joe Strummer, Clash's lead singer, managed to tie himself up with his own guitar lead at one point after trying to roll around the stage and play at the same time. Johnny Rotten of the Pistols, who appeared late in the evening, did a passable imitation of a ginger-haired gibbon as he swung menacingly from his microphone stand. But there was nothing here to compare with the strutting of Mick Jagger, the collective leapings of Captain Beefheart or even the skilful 'goose-necking' of Wilko Johnson in Dr Feelgood.

The idea that punk rock bands are a threat to society because their songs advocate violence and anarchy turned out to be quite absurd. The lyrics are unintelligible. Only when they played familiar oldies, like The Who's *Substitute*, did you get the experience of listening to a song rather than to a heavy noise. If this is the way in which revolution is to be preached, we are all going to need printed song sheets. As one local rocker remarked, through cupped hands placed against my ear, 'There's probably a message in there. The trouble is you can't hear the message for the music.'

It was, perhaps, because of the lack of any real communication that the punks, and the Sex Pistols in particular, got a rather unfriendly reception in Plymouth. 'A pile of crap', 'Wankers the lot of you,' yelled the cynics and a few glasses were hurled at the stage: It began to look more like a Spurs v. Arsenal match than a pop concert. Members of the other bands, and the few punks who had travelled down from London, tried to counteract the hostility by dancing in front of the stage, but to little effect. In no sense was Devon to be turned on to nihilism and revolt overnight.

So what, if anything, lies behind the image and the music that punk groups have generated?

Listening to the Pistols' recent, and only, record release, one can at least begin to decipher the words. *Anarchy in the UK* opens with this statement:

> I am an Anti-Christ,
> I am an anarchist.
> Don't know what I want
> But I know how to get it.
> I wanna destroy.

By contemporary standards, *Anarchy in the UK* is a good record. It is powerful rock and roll and the shortcomings of the Pistols as musicians don't come across at all. The lyrics, on the other hand, seem too simple to communicate anything other than total alienation and violent determination to hit back at an ill-defined enemy. The song is pounded out with aggression and force – it's the music that does the work, not the words. Contrast this with an extract from an almost Dylanesque song written by Mick Jones of Clash, called *Westway*:

> Now I'm in the subway
> Looking for the flat.
> This one leads to this block
> And this one leads to that.
> The wind howls through the empty blocks
> Looking for a home
> But I run through the empty stone
> Because I'm all alone.

In *Westway* we start, I think, to get close to the kind of social world which punk rock reflects. It captures something of the emptiness in kids' lives. Another Clash song, ironically called *Career Opportunities*, also begins to express some of the desperation of young people just out of school. In contrast to the rock and roll, which grew up in the 'You've never had it so good' 1950s, this is the music of the unemployed teenager. It's dole-queue rock, and the only way to really make sense of it is through some awareness of the kinds of lives which the kids who have become punks are leading.

Most of those involved in punk music have only just 'escaped' from the concrete comprehensive. Others are still waiting to do so. But, in fact, there is little to escape to. It is desperation and frustration, developing into a demand to be heard, that is reflected both in the songs themselves and the demoniacal manner in which they are performed. In the process, a new political rhetoric emerges which is quite unlike the more rational patterns of argument we are familiar with.

Punk rock demands a piece of the action. The song, *White Riot*, arises out of recent events in the Notting Hill area. If blacks can have an arena for fighting authority and the police, and if they can have reggae, then their white counterparts want similar opportunities and their own music:

> All the power is in the hands
> Of people rich enough to buy it,
> While we walk the streets
> Too chicken to even try it.
> And everybody does what they're told to
> And everybody eats supermarket soul-food.
> White riot, I wanna riot,
> White riot – a riot of my own.

The message is clear. It would be a mistake, however, to assume, as many have done, that the punk philosophy is fascist, or extreme right-wing in any simple sense. On the contrary, many punks are quite explicit about their opposition to organisations like the National Front and about their rejection of the emerging right-wing backlash. Admittedly, some punk bands have worn swastikas and iron crosses on stage, but groups such as the Clash and the Damned reflect a move away from convenient scapegoats and easy excuses.

While many young people in our society are only too content to sit back and allow blacks and social security scroungers to take responsibility for the current feelings of hopelessness, punks are trying to do something radically different. They may not actively like West Indians. They may even, ironically, complain about others who, like themselves, live off the state. But they attack much more. They attack everything – even themselves.

Punk bands only survive, however, because they are no different from the people who listen to them and take note of what they are saying. There must be thousands of kids in London alone who could play as well as the Sex Pistols or Clash, and that is really what it is all about. It is about people having access to their own music because the music is within reach of their own competence. As soon as a punk rock group starts to succeed, it will be dead; it will have moved outside of the milieu which gives reason to its very existence. You can't play dole-queue rock and eat well at the same time. And unless they develop genuine musical talent, they will have little opportunity to play anything else.

The only real future lies in their ability to make intelligible the message of despair which lurks, at times poetically, in the words behind the music – the words which are rarely heard and even less often given serious attention. But even this might be asking for the moon. Perhaps rock and roll and revolution will remain incompatible bed-fellows and the former will continue as a substitute for the latter. The Stones said it all ten years ago:

> But what can a poor boy do
> Except sing for a rock and roll band?
> In sleepy London town
> There's no place for a street-fighting man.

20 January 1977

19
Mad Mick Tracey and Kamikaze Les

Peter Woods

The banger racers assemble. Their battered machines are embla-zoned with identification numbers, names, colour coding, spon-sors, designs and lucky emblems. Mad Mick Tracy, Kamikaze Les, Dave the Rave, Hagger the Horrible . . . they are all there. By trade, they are ordinary people – builders, labourers, roof tilers, farm workers – but now they are transformed into banger drivers, a special kind of expert, lining up to pitch wits and machine against each other.

Most have spent all week preparing their cars – modifying them as stipulated by the regulations, strengthening the frame, resiting the petrol tank, removing glass, straightening the sus-pension, mending punctures, tuning engines, checking tappets, changing points. They are aiming for both the reliability and speed that will bring them a coveted position in at least one of the races.

Mr Starter leaps nimbly on to the bonnet of a car in the front rank, and jumps up and down, rotating both arms briskly. It is the signal for ignition. He beckons the cars slowly forward for the rolling start. The traditional 'popcorn' music comes on the loud-speaker system. The cars creep round the oval circuit in lines four abreast, 30 or more. The drivers rev furiously to warm up engines, waving to the spectators, flexing muscles, getting com-fortable.

The less experienced 'white top' drivers are at the front, the star 'red tops' at the back, yellows and blues in the middle. As they come into the pits bend, the adrenalin rises. Mr Starter on his

167

rostrum stands poised with the green flag held aloft. Then he waves the flag vigorously in all directions at once and, with a mighty roar, they're off!

The Mouthmobile goes into an early lead, but is spun by Super Gas on lap two. He, in turn, gets caught in a melee on the grandstand turn. Vern has steering trouble, and can only go back and forth across the track. With no chance of winning, he is going to make it as difficult as he can for others by lying in wait, then jumping out, cat and mouse, on the leader.

The Bin Yin and Iron Brian are having a private tussle, leaning on each other. But both have to stop at the grandstand melee. Here a dozen or so cars are tying themselves in knots, and are rammed for their pains by Vern, who now seems to be sitting in a pile of steaming scrap metal. But still it moves; and as Dave the Rave tries to accelerate through a sudden gap, Vern catches him with his back end, sending him into a spectacular somersault. Dave's car ends up on its roof, astride the kerb. Ambulance men and attendants rush from the centre green, and peer inside. An arm is raised to indicate the driver is safe. Dave emerges and scrambles clear.

Gorgeous George is going round with his bonnet lid open. Farmer Tarn is trailing part of a rear wing and trim, creating a spray of sparks. Hagger has a shredded tyre and is getting the black flag; but head down and eyes ahead, he doesn't seem to see it.

A brand-new Escort (as a banger, that is), beautifully painted and designed and without a scratch, has survived 14 laps; but it is spun by Kamikaze Les, and then rammed into the fence by Vern, from whence it rebounds, severely modified. The crowd cheer. They've been dying to see him get hit.

The Cockney Rebel comes up behind Yogi and gives him a little acceleration he doesn't need at the pits bend. Yogi's car wraps itself with an almighty clunk, amid a shower of rusty metal and escaping steam, around one of the fence stanchions.

Meanwhile, most of the star red tops have managed to evade the trouble, and have worked their way to the front. Toddy Bright is chasing Dave Inns, lap after lap. He is trying everything he knows, waiting for Dave to make a mistake. He takes different lines round the debris, the slower cars and the stranded cars on the bends, to get close enough to try a spin.

Mr Starter indicates five laps to go. Vern is after Dave; but Dave is too good for him, anticipating every move, knowing just when to accelerate, when to brake, which line to take, weaving the shortest route to the finish. Dave wins, Toddy second. The rest carry on scrambling for one of the first ten places before red flags declare the end of the race.

Puffing and steaming, scraping, bumping and rattling, the bangers assemble at the pits exit in order to carry out hasty repairs for the next race in ten minutes' time.

Ten minutes? But surely, several of these cars will never race again? Wheels pointing in all directions; steering mutilated; chassis distorted; engines grunting, squealing, hissing, leaking; cables trailing; tyres flat, in ribbons, or gone; some cars limping back, others being pushed, others lifted by one of three break-down lorries – they are surely wrecks now?

But no! In the pits there are scenes of controlled savagery. The drivers that have just bashed each other's cars out of shape, now bash their own into a new design. They free the wheels, straighten the chassis, square bonnets and boots, hack off excrescences. There's muck, filth, twisted metal, steam, heat, oil, and the ring of an orchestra of lump hammers knocking cars back into a state of trackworthiness. Here and there an axe, and even one chain saw, take shorter cuts.

Music wafts in from the loudspeakers. Spectators mingle with the drivers. There are programmes, hooters, favours. 'Clockwork Orange Rules, OK?' 'Scouse Power', 'Highway Florida Patrol', 'My Brain Hurts', 'Love', 'Sex', 'Sharon', 'Mother', 'Mafia GB', 'I choked Linda Lovelace'. There are bomber jackets, jeans, overalls that seem made of oil and dirt, summer dresses, dainty high-heeled sandals tripping through mud. Fathers and young sons.

Frank Wesby's car has been on fire and is out of commission. He spends the rest of the day looking forlorn. Some are all right. Time for fags, even perhaps a pork pie or hot dog, eased down by oil off the fingers and a pint.

There are snatches of conversation. 'You put yer foot down and there's nothing there.' 'If you see me flying into the bloody fence, you'll know it were the other one.' 'I put 'im on a barrel when 'e was lying second, 'e won't speak to me for a week.' 'Load of bloody bullshit 'e told you about 'avin' radials on the back.' 'I 'ave about half inch tread, the others none at all.' 'Greasy as hell on those corners after a race or two.' 'A nudge is all it takes on these corners.' 'If you let the back end drift out, you lose ground, don't you?' 'Get 'er well warm.'

Here and there, there are trickier matters to attend to. Why, for example, aren't Toddy's brakes working? The cognoscenti are consulted. 'Go and fetch Pete Archer, he'll know.' The car is on its side, propped up by an iron pole. Pete works with a hammer and spanner, and cleans the suspect part. 'Something else I've learnt,' says Toddy.

Two others are under a car, puzzling over its erratic steering. Stan comes to have a look. 'Yer shaft is bent, look, that's what it is!' A begrimed face emerges from beneath the car. 'So is *your* fuckin' shaft bent,' he says, 'an' it allus 'as been!' Laughs all round.

Air filters, distributor caps, spark plugs, carburettors, petrol feed pipes, cables and a hundred nuts and bolts receive attention. Wheels are changed, suspensions straightened, track rod ends replaced. Water is changed, petrol and oil topped up. In you jump, and off you go – engine revving, spitting up the dust, accelerating away with screaming tyres. Noise, dirt, excitement, adrenalin, danger, speed. A moment of calm in the ranks to collect one's thoughts and lay a strategy. Then the fence is stitched up and away we go again, men on wheels in suits of armour.

Banger racing is a way of life. Invariably you begin completely by chance, like Kevin, who happened to spot a banger outside Andy's house just after his own car had failed its MOT, and got into conversation with him. You become, in turn, interested, enthusiastic, excited, dedicated, and eventually addicted. The sport takes over your whole life. Toddy showed us his 30 or so write-offs on his allotment: 'They're my babies, they are. I can guarantee, when I've been on holiday, I shall come back straight up here before I've even reached the house, that's the truth. I live it: this is my life.'

Charles actually said he was addicted; he'd been packing up for years, but he couldn't, and it takes up all his spare time, including the winter: 'It's just never ended.' Brian has retired three times, but cannot resist coming back when someone finds him a car. Johnny says it's a disease. 'It gets in your blood and you just can't seem to shake it. All my free time, when I come home from work, is spent on the cars.'

Brian told us that as a schoolboy he always wanted to be a racing driver; but working six days a week, he never had the chance. Then, at 35, he discovered this sport and joined the Bedford Banger Club, 'picking the bits and pieces up from the rest of the team'. Colin told us how it had redeemed a bad diagnosis of him by a school careers adviser, who had told him not to become a mechanic.

Many have not, and would not, have learned these things anywhere else. 'All I've learned about mechanics,' says Brian, 'is what I've learned through banger racing, really.' Andy says, 'I used to race motor-cycles years ago in scrambles. But I hadn't really that much knowledge on cars. I knew how they worked, but I'd never worked on them before.'

What is remarkable is the unsystematic but thorough acquisition of knowledge. As Toddy says: 'These are not the sort of things you learn at school. This is something you pick up. I mean I couldn't have changed a gearbox here twelve years ago. I take it to bits now without thinking about it.'

There is considerable basic technology involved in the construction of the engine and the frame, wiring, suspension and aerodynamics of the car. There are the special 'wrinkles' in fitting cars up for banger racing – flaps on wheels, different engines, adapting gearbox housings, cutting handbrake cables, bolting on the front bumper.

Special skills are required during the race. 'You've got to know where to hit them, how hard and how to get out of it, otherwise you'll only land yourself in trouble.' There is much else besides: anticipation, fine judgment, good reflexes, lightness of touch, patience, controlled aggression, absolute command of your machine, knowledge of others and their machines, and of the track and its hazards. All in an atmosphere of fever-pitch excitement.

And there is always something new. As Andy says, 'Every race is different. You never get a race that's the same because the hazards are different.' As for commitment, Brian says, 'You tend to work ten times harder than you do in a normal day's work.' It is a test of physical as well as mental powers.

Though drivers are fiercely competitive on the track, cameraderie rules in the pits. They help each other, if extra strength, knowledge or tools are needed. It is a self-help and self-contained community. To a large extent, they generate their own special knowledge and tricks of the trade. They are masters of improvisation. If something needs doing, there is a way of doing it. No problem is insoluble. *Someone* will find an answer.

You learn through the community by various means. You 'beg, steal or borrow' (Charles), and 'pick people's brains, watch what other people do, trial and error, you learn as you go' (Toddy). Andy says: 'You find out the hard way. You do something you think is a good idea, and you find it's a disaster. The whole of the wiring will burn out, for example. Or you'll have to experiment to find the best place to route the petrol lines through. And also when you get the chance you look under somebody else's bonnet, and see what they've got!'

Colin recalls scrounging a steering box so he could take part in a final. Brian mentions a 'hundred and one silly little things you pick up like taping the plugs on'. In this way, experts are made.

So, too, apparently, are responsible citizens. As Andy put it: 'I drive for a living and I used to be an aggressive driver, but now I do banger racing. I've found I'm a very placid driver on the road. Because I know, if a car goes past me and cuts me up, I could roll that car over, and knowing that quietens you down a bit.'

The first national youth championship in banger racing was held at Wimbledon Stadium this March. It was arranged by the Ilderton Motor Project, a south-east London organisation which enables boys on probation to renovate old cars and race them at Wimbledon during ordinary race meetings. Another London organisation known as Itmek (Intermediate Treatment Mechanics), also uses banger racing to build confidence among local youth who have often been written off, like the cars, as losers. Lots of boys *and* girls, you suspect, would welcome such an opportunity.

As for the rest of us, there are other lessons to be learned. For example, do be careful the next time you are going down the centre lane of the motorway and there are two cars coming up fast behind on either side of you. They could be Mad Mick Tracy and Kamikaze Les, unimpressed by the supposed therapeutic quality of banger racing, or simply just forgetting where they are, bent on making a sandwich of you.

And if there's a battered, steaming wreck going back and forth across the road, it may be Vern. Put your foot down, say a prayer and watch for his back end.

4 June 1981

20
Ladies' dingdong night

Stuart Weir

Terri, the drag artist, introduces himself: 'The boys on this trip call me "Arsepro", for quick relief.' He is a heavy, middle-aged man. His body is encased in a red shiny gown, a fluffy blonde wig is clamped on his head. His florid features are made up with a calculated exaggeration, and he adopts an arch, matey way of talking, his fruity sibilance rubbed hoarse by a natural cockney rasp.

'Darlings, this is an evening of culture. At the end of each half comes the *pièce de résistance.*' He pauses. 'Cock. Our strippers are men of many parts, they come in all shapes and sizes. Had a stripper last night, he was like that. . . .' He holds up a thumb and finger, cocked together as close as points. 'I've had bigger gumboils.'

He chuckles in assumed complicity with the 50 or so young women, in their late teens and early twenties, who crowd into the upper-deck salon of the small Thames pleasure boat. They sit on long benches round the small salon's windows and in haphazard rows and circles of plastic stacking chairs. Most of them are drinking Balkan Prince white wine from slender glasses. 'A thought goes through my mind. We're all here enjoying ourselves, those miserable bastards are stuck at home for a change.'

The women, all in their party best, certainly do enjoy themselves. They join wholeheartedly in the sing-songs. They laugh long and loud at Terri's countless blue jokes, wholly uninhibited by his persistent swearing or by the jokes' bleak misanthropy.

How they laugh. The atmosphere is charged with an excited expectancy, stoked by the comic's constant reminders: they are here to see two men strip naked.

The boys on the trip call it a 'winkle trip', or 'ladies' dingdong night'. The girls are nearly all on office outings – there are, for example, a dozen from an office in Covent Garden, plus Nell, their tea lady, twelve more from hotels and restaurants in Surrey, six from a branch of William Hill's in south-east London. More than half of them have been before. As the *Enchanté* pushed out down the Thames from Tower Pier, I talk in the bar below to three young women and to Terry (as opposed to Terri) and Tom, the strippers.

Amanda, Jackie and Stephanie work together in a hairdresser's in St Albans. They saw an advertisement in the local newspaper. 'We wanted something different, not a pub crawl.' Terry is standing by the bar. Jackie looks him up and down, and decides she fancies him. 'I'm sitting in the front.'

Steph is married. 'I'm glad he's young.'

Amanda says: 'It's a bit frightening. We don't know what to expect.'

'What are they going to do?'

'Stick it in our drinks, tie ribbons round it?'

Jackie says: 'The lot.'

Steph says: 'I'm afraid I'm going to wet myself. See a pool on the floor, you'll know it was me.'

The bar doubles as the changing room. The three drag artists are already changing, opening cases, applying make-up. 'Can you get all these virgins upstairs now? We're very religious and shy.'

Terry is neatly dressed in jeans, blue shirt and red zippered jacket. He could be a professional footballer. He is dark, good-looking, with a dapper moustache, and as close as his shave. He refuses to be interviewed or photographed. 'I've turned down the *Daily Mirror*. I can't even tell you what my job is, or I'd be identified.' He smiles. 'My wife thinks I'm at a Tupperware party.' What's he paid? 'In notes.' Why does he do it? 'For notes.'

'Some of the girls know me. They come back. Oh yes, some of them even ask for me.' He turns to a pretty blonde girl in a decorous olive green dress and page-boy hair cut who is passing by. 'Leaving already?' She smiles.

'It's got other advantages as well,' he says. 'Still, if you came out with that in mind, you wouldn't score.'

Tom is burlier, balding and ebullient. He has a big fur-lined jacket over his white polo-neck sweater, a huge sparkling initial-led ring on one finger, and L-O-V-E and H-A-T-E tattooed across them all. He hasn't bothered to shave.

'There's about seven good male strippers. How did I get in? I was driving a drag act and a stripper never turned up. They asked me if I'd go on. I said no, but with a few Bacardis in me. . . .' He strips every night and doesn't work during the day. 'I'm quiet during the day. Jekyll and Hyde sort of thing. Though I'm starting a disco.'

His mate: 'When he's not signing on.'

Tom: 'Unquote.'

'I've toned down my act now. You should have seen me three years ago. I used to tie them up on stage, simulate sex, that sort of thing.' Indignantly he tells me: 'But I'm being done for perform-ing in an indecent manner. They had three plants in the show.'

Alec Coote, the organiser, is equally indignant. 'You don't know what's legal or not. It's ludicrous, this prosecution, a lot of bollocks.' He's been running 'winkle trips' for two or three years now. 'It gives them a chance to let their hair down. I think they really come to see the drag artists. Oh yes, they say, "It's smaller than my old man's" or "It's bigger." Usually, it's bigger.'

Shouts of laughter from the salon. 'I call him Knobby for short. Not for long.' More laughter. Outside, it is a bitterly cold and dark night. The Thames is black, but the waves pick up shifting silver reflections from lights strung in arcs along the starboard bank. Inside, it's warm and jolly. Empty brown bottles of Balkan Prince and ash-trays line the misting windows. Terri introduces the first stripper.

'Now, I want the girls with long nails at the back. Keep your mouths closed at the front, or you'll need false teeth. I want no touching or groping. He'll come among you, but don't worry, it wipes off. Girls, the one and only, the Rhinestone Cowboy!'

The young women cheer and giggle. Then, as the Rhinestone Cowboy fails to appear, begin a rousing chorus of 'Why are we waiting.' A girl shouts, 'What's the matter, has it dropped off?' The laughs turn to shrieks and screams as Tom, resplendent in an orange cowboy suit, bounds into the salon, grabs a girl's head, pulls it into his crotch, and holds it there as he vigorously thrusts his pelvis back and forwards in time to heavy rock music from two black speakers at the front.

The room is in tumult. The girls laugh in terrified exhilaration as Tom swaggers among them, a wicked grin on his face. And as he advances towards this or that girl and seizes her – perhaps to press her hand against his still-covered penis, to sit in her lap and embrace her, to try and push her hand over his broad black belt and down the front of his trousers – the laughter reaches peak after peak. The girls scream, and shriek, and squeal.

A girl at the front who has been screeching with laughter throughout turns to her friend, her hand over her eyes, presses her stomach and sides, grimaces, and then laughs still more. Her face is contorted as though she is sobbing.

The disco switches from Rod Stewart to *You Sexy Thing*. Tom pushes through the chairs to a blonde in black chiffon who collapses weakly behind a friend. He sits on her lap and pulls her hands as though she is masturbating him. He gets two women to take off his boots, puts his socks under the nose of a girl in a pink dress, unzips the sides of his trousers.

He drags a dark-haired woman in a blue Chinese print dress onto a chair in front, and ties her legs and hands together. By now he has stripped down to a kind of black leather romper suit. He is sweating heavily, and the hairs stick to his chest. He mimes the slinky dance of a woman stripper, gets everyone to clap, asks a girl who is swaying to the music to untie his costume. She can't look at him, and gestures weakly with her hands. Her friend, a cheerful toothy girl, makes her grab the thongs. She shuts her eyes and, shaking with nerves and laughter, pulls the thongs. Tom darts away and she turns and hugs her friend.

Tom looks about, like an overweight sprite. By now he's wearing only his cowboy hat, a handkerchief knotted round his neck, and black pants. Three women at the back sit upright and calm amid the pandemonium, and sip their wine from the slender glasses. They light up cigarettes, almost defensively, as Tom begins to prowl forward. The girl on the right leans across, her blow-dried hair falling in immaculate symmetry, and hisses in her friend's ear, 'If he comes anywhere near me, I'll tell him, "I'll stick this up your arse."' She jabs her cigarette fiercely upwards.

Tom retreats back to the girl he has tied and blindfolds her. He sits on her, pulls her hands round under his black pants, leaps up and stands behind her. He takes out a large banana and smiles mischievously at the women. They are nearly all abandoned to paroxysms of laughter. He rubs the banana against her neck, looks teasingly again at the audience, peels it, and pushes it into her mouth. Uproar.

The atmosphere is unimaginably intense. It's getting hard to breathe. Tom strips down to a silver G-string and pouch, and shoves his black pants down over a girl's head. He turns his back and plump white buttocks to the audience, there's a triumphant flourish, and now he's naked.

I've got the hippy, hippy shake . . . Tom presses a girl's hand to his penis. At first she's shocked, but as she pulls her hand away, she laughs.

. . . shake it to the left, shake it to the right. . . . He does. Then, as he leaves, he modestly covers his genitals with his hand. Throughout his act, his penis has remained limp; and, interestingly, while the boys on the trip believe that the women are closely interested in the *size* of the stripper's penis, I don't hear a single woman make any reference to the size of Tom's, or later Terry's, penis.

Tom comes back for a brief bow with pants on. A girl in a pink dress raises a full bottle of wine to her lips. They all clap, and cheer, and breathe again.

'He's quite a lad.'

'Yes, right down to his thing.'

'He's got guts.'

'I was killing myself laughing. I'm glad he didn't come my way.'

'You don't see much of it. I was expecting to see more. He kept his hand over it.'

I talk to the girl who untied his romper suit and her friend.

'I felt like dying,' she says. 'I nearly wet myself.'

'She couldn't undo it. I made her do it.'

'I nearly wet myself when he came over. I held my legs together real tight.'

'I couldn't look at him.'

'She said he smelt.'

'The girl he tied, she said that he was ever so gentle. He kept asking her if she was all right. It's all in fun.'

The girl he had sat on was with the Surrey hotel crowd. They'd sat in a boozy circle of chairs near the front. No, it wasn't sexually arousing: 'He's doing his job. There's nothing wrong, nothing disgusting. It was all joking.'

Her friends join in. 'It's nice to get out without the guys. It's all good, clean, innocent fun, nothing terrible. If a few more people let themselves go, there'd be less aggro. People *are* crude.'

'Most girls go out, have a few drinks, that's all. Why should the men get it all, and not the girls?'

The three girls who have held aloof are in the bar. All the women have been served their supper: chicken salad and a roll on a plate. 'We thought it would be a bit more sophisticated. Not so *blatant*. They treat you like you're a moron.'

'They think all we care is to see a naked man and we'll get all excited. I thought they'd dance, on a stage. No way did I think he'd go around sticking it in people's faces. What would people do if a man came up to you on a train and did that?'

'It was funny watching people being humiliated. If he'd come near me, I'd have run out. I'm not going to tell people I know, "Guess where I've been tonight?"'

'Are you going to write about *debased* womanhood? We're not prudes, you know, we know what it's about.'

'If he had got hold of me, I just couldn't have played along. I'd have been thinking all the time, *yehurk!*'

For the second half, I squeeze in at the front next to a small blonde girl. 'I'm married,' she says. 'I've seen it all before.' We've heard quite a few of the jokes before, too, and she begins casting warm glances at the ginger-haired drummer, who's now leaning back languidly on his stool. Then, finally, the drag artist introduces Terry. 'It's that big, if it had brains it would rule the world.'

Terry wears a red shirt and black trousers which shine. He begins like a disco dancer, ruffles a girl's hair, then climbs above her and wriggles his pelvis against her face. He gets the women to undo his shirt and take off his shoes, but a dark-haired girl goes limp when he indicates that she should undo his trousers. The blonde next to me does it instead, and pulls his trousers down. He pulls her head between his legs and rubs his crotch against her cheek.

Terry is more aggressive than Tom. He is a predator while, below his mischief, Tom really wanted to please. Terry struts, lithe, cool and vain, to the rock music and constantly leaps above the women. He's wearing only black pants now, and pulls them open in front of a girl's eyes. She looks away. Again, the blonde near me strips them off. Again, he leaps above the benches, his genitals encased in a silver pouch, and shakes them vigorously in time to a drum solo.

Down again, and the blonde strips him naked. He puts his hands over his penis and leaps agilely over the shoulders and heads of the audience. Finally, he stands erect on a bench, releases his penis and twirls it around like a baton. The girls clap and sway in time to the music.

He leaps down onto the vinyl tiles of the salon floor and stands, legs apart, swaying his penis before the blonde girl. She leans back, splays her arms and legs and mimes a dance in return. He leaps away again and, swivelling his hips, begins to twist and twirl his still limp penis remarkably fast. He even swings it back between his legs as he stands facing the audience. As the music pounds to an end, he turns, shakes hands with the blonde girl and insinuates his penis into her grasp. She shakes it.

The women cheer generously and cry, 'More, more, more.' But instead the drag artist returns and asks them to clear the chairs from the floor for a final 'good rip-off'. Six girls line up for a photograph, and push their right legs forward in unison. Then two kneel at the front, four shift to the back, and they raise their glasses high and smile for the flash. Terry comes back dressed and girls crowd round him. 'You were really good.' The disco begins and the girls dance energetically.

It's still not midnight when the boat docks again at Tower Pier. The girls go roistering off along the quay, arms round each other, singing at the tops of their voices. A woman tells her friends, 'I won't be coming back with you,' and goes off arm-in-arm with Terry. Men in cars and on motor-cycles are waiting for their wives and girl friends. The blonde climbs into her husband's mini. Tom and his mates are going to a club in Soho.

It's bloody cold, but it has been jolly good fun, hasn't it?

24 January 1980

21
The night people

Helen Chappell

At midnight in the Dunkin' Donuts cafe, on Ludgate Circus, the night shift is just about to begin. Bill Webb, night manager, checks out the storeroom at the back to see if anything is running short, and ties a striped apron around his middle-aged spread.

His eyes are red with lack of sleep, and his hands are already frosty with flour from the paper sacks stacked behind him. He is the only one serving behind the counter tonight. It's up to him to keep things organised. The blue plastic buckets, for instance, hold lemon curd; the huge tins, blackcurrant jam; the steel baths, chocolate sauce, strawberry icing and coloured vermicelli. Dough mix is one sack of flour to one block of yeast to one bucket of water.

He will work tonight until 6 a.m., but it's not unusual for him to work much longer. 'If there's a staff shortage,' he says, 'I've been known to work from midnight Saturday to 1.30 Monday morning. I don't mind. I'll work any hours.'

Back in the cafe, he wipes down the Formica-clad bar with a wet cloth, and fills up some doughnut display cases with nut/fresh cream and choc/coconut. There are two customers sitting on high stools at the bar. One is a gaunt elderly man in a brown Crimplene suit and a navy-blue anorak. One hand props up his thinning scalp, the other turns the pages of the *Standard*.

An empty stool away, a boy of about 20 in black leather gear drinks a cup of coffee. In front of him a crash helmet and motor-cycle gauntlets are tumbled on the counter. Bill gives him his change. Bill says he loves working nights. He prefers to be his own boss. He spent eleven years in the RAF, then eighteen months 'on security' – poking around deserted factories at night with no one to bother him or get on his nerves.

Newspaper delivery vans glide past the window, on their way to the railway stations. Bill tells Shahriar, the day waiter, to cash up before he goes. Shahriar is a 24-year-old Iranian – tall, slender with wavy black hair like a matinée idol. His eyes, when they abandon the defensive blankness of the servant, widen in a pastiche of the innocent abroad. 'I am here one year, four month,' he says. 'It is my first job in this country. I am very grateful for my governor to help me so much. I cannot go back to my country.'

Shahriar's family worked for the Shah. Doing what, exactly? He blushes. They were in the secret police. They used to have a very rich, very good life, but Khomeini drove them away. His father fled to America; the troubles have aged him. He lost everything in the revolution, but now he has 'a business' over there. Shahriar, his brother and two cousins, came to England. 'We hope the Shah's son will return soon to Iran and defeat Khomeini. If this happens, I will go back and fight.'

When he first arrived in London, he was found by a gang of Khomeini's men and beaten up. They broke his nose. So he moved house and took this job. He feels a lot safer now.

'It's a pity for them it's going to be a warm winter.' The elderly man has reached the end of his *Standard*. He's talking about the threat of a miners' strike. The boy in the black leather nods agreement. Don't they realise that if the money isn't there, it isn't there? The old man buys them both another coffee. Bill starts up the impressive brushed-steel Japanese cassette player that serenades the night shift. It looks out of place among the cardboard boxes and bottles of bleach behind the counter.

The two of them are regular customers; they come in every night. The old man cuts the grass and works as a caddy at the golf club in Coombe Hill, in Surrey. The boy is a newsvendor and distributor. He has worked nights for two years now, selling the *Daily Express* on Coventry Street from 1 to 5 a.m. He prefers night work. There's such a lot of pushing and hurrying during the day. No one has time for you. At night it is different. People are friendlier.

Bill's music centre is playing Spanish flamenco guitar. The

occasional clash of the cash register marks a steady trickle of take-away customers.

'Most of these golf experts', the old man, Eddie, says, 'are legalised con men. They wouldn't make golfers in a million years. Half of them don't know one end of a golf club from the other.' Although he lives down in Coombe Hill, Eddie spends most of his nights up in town, nearly always in this cafe. He makes sure he gets a seat near the electric fire in winter. His job on the golf course is seasonal; so, in the off season, he takes another job on security. As an ex-porter, ex-RAF man, there's no problem.

Even in the Air Force, he worked nights. 'We used to work from 4.30 p.m. to 8.30 a.m. the next morning on the radar. They used to call us "the moles".'

Outside the plate-glass window, taxi-cabs swim into the light. The drivers swoop in for a quick take-away or linger over a cup of tea. Bright, cold neon light brings out the grey tones in their faces. 'It's the only time this city comes to life,' says Eddie. 'Most people don't know London at all.'

Bill produces a copy of the *Sun*. 'You can't win tonight, Eddie,' he says. 'It's my turn, I've got nine cards going at the same time.' Eddie studies the Superbingo pages thoughtfully. 'What would you do if you won?' he asks. 'Go out to Australia,' says the newsvendor, whose name is Phil, 'have a fresh start.' He yawns. 'Nobody sleeps well who works nights. It upsets everybody.'

'The body is at its lowest point at 3 a.m.,' Eddie says. 'When the body is at its lowest point it's on the floor,' says Bill.

'Well, it could be six feet under.'

'I'll let you know when I get there.'

They laugh. Phil pulls on his balaclava helmet and gauntlets. 'I'm off now,' he says. 'See you again at five.'

A pair of policemen walk past the window. Eddie looks critical. 'They used to have to be six foot once. But it's been downgraded now.' Bill says they get quite a lot of police in during the night. For the best reasons, of course. 'I have a very good relationship with the police. If we get any trouble, they're here like a shot. A couple of years ago, this place used to be pretty rough at night. Notorious. Loads of tarts and drunks. But now (touch wood), we've got much better clients – though the odd drunk still comes in for a peaceful cup of tea.'

Eddie perks up: 'What happened to that bloke who used to sit in here all night crying?' he asks. 'He was a weirdo. Kitchen porter, I think. Then there was that old boy who used to write cheques for his bill on envelopes and bits of paper tissue.' The door swings open, letting in a blast of cold air. It's 1.30 a.m.

A fat, middle-aged man in a sharp leather jacket joins the group. He wears a fine polo-neck jumper under the jacket, festooned with gold chains and medallions. His greying hair is swept back like a rock star, his moustache is a tabby mix of orange and black. The others greet him like a long-lost brother. 'You're speaking to the only American cab-driver in London,' he announces. 'I may look like a pimp, but I'm not.' This is Jon – a fully paid-up member of this unofficial night hawks' club.

Jon is in a jubilant mood. He's just had that cab-driver's dream – a party of provincial businessmen, up for a conference and out on the razzle. 'There were *five* of them,' beams Jon, brandishing a £50 note. '"Can I recommend a club?" they ask me. Jesus. Just when I was wondering how I was going to make up my money until 3 a.m. when the discos turn out.'

Jon, like other all-night cabbies, gets a substantial kick-back from nightclubs for any new patrons he sends their way. 'I took them to the Cabaret in New Bond Street,' he says. 'It's a burlesque place – striptease every 20 minutes, topless waitresses, and all that.' He orders a coffee and a strawberry doughnut, and lights up a cigarette.

'Mind you,' he says, 'the Cabaret's a respectable joint. The girls aren't pros or anything. I got £9 a head for that lot. Shouldn't have taken all five of them in the cab, but what the hell.'

Jon seems particularly interested in prostitutes. At King's Cross at 2 a.m., he says, you can watch them hopping from car to car. They get constantly harassed by the police, but the canny ones pretend to be waiting at the bus stop. Which can be hard for any respectable women trying to catch a bus. 'They're terrible-looking birds,' says Jon, wrinkling his nose. 'And the later it gets the cheaper *they* get.'

He came over from New York in 1971, when he married 'an English lass'. He speaks in an odd mixture of transatlantic and stage cockney. His wife is a shadowy figure established in splendid surburban isolation in Chingford. For all his stories, Jon is anxious to remain anonymous, to escape her wrath.

'I picked up a girl in the Fulham Road last month,' he says. 'She was pissed out of her mind. Her boyfriend gives me ten quid to take her home to Dagenham. When we got there, I asked for the address. Nothing. She was really gone. I tried everything to wake her up, even slapped her face. Suddenly she comes to and grabs me round the neck. She was so stoned she thought I was her boyfriend. So she points out the house, I follow her in, and end up in bed with her.'

Jon is obviously pleased with the effect his tale has had on the others. They all agree that drunken women are *the worst*. 'I hate to hear a woman swear,' says Jon. 'I don't know why. It just doesn't seem right.'

Empty buses pass the window, diesel engines panting. An old man in an oily mac comes in and takes a stool. He tries to move it but realises it's screwed to the floor. He unfolds a copy of the *Star* and starts the crossword. Jon stubs out his fag-end and pauses for breath.

Yes, women do the craziest things. There was this old lady he picked up outside Harrods, who *played with herself* all the way home. 'I mean – she was really *old*. She lived at this really flashy address in Kensington, too. I couldn't believe it.' Eddie is looking down into his coffee cup, deeply embarrassed. 'But it's the pros who really kill me,' Jon continues, regardless. 'I picked this one up once who was going to service an Arab. She says you never say a price to an Arab. If he is satisfied, he could hand over up to £500. "I'll only be 20 minutes, love, so wait for me," she says. And she was.'

The door opens again to admit a post office worker, an oil-streaked printer, and Phil again in his crash helmet. 'You're early,' says Bill. 'Had a row with my boss, didn't I?' explains Phil. 'Stupid old bugger tried to blow me up for being late. Said I could sod off.' Underneath the bravado, Phil looks worried. The others ignore him, as if they sense his vulnerability.

A couple of girls come in and sit at a table by the door. They order cream doughnuts and Cokes. They are in their early twenties, dressed in rabbit furs and vertiginous stilettos. The older one, Karen, says she is married, and Julie is her friend. They seem anxious not to give the wrong impression. Karen comes from Middlesbrough, Julie from Leeds. They both live now in Bethnal Green, but they met each other at Gulliver's nightclub in Park Lane.

They love London nightlife. 'In the daytime everyone is always in a rush,' Julie says. 'They push you around, they're so ignorant.'

Karen says emphatically that she is a housewife and Julie is on the dole. They don't think London is a very friendly place, not like up north. They've made a few friends here, but mostly other northerners.

'It's getting like New York in London now,' Karen complains. 'The other night we saw this old tramp being mugged. These yobs just knocked him down. There was a terrible crack when he hit his head. Everyone was just standing around, watching. We thought, "Surely someone will call the police?" but no one did.' Julie bites into her doughnut. 'Did you see *The Generation Game*?' she asks.

A young black roadsweeper walks past the window and looks in at the girls. It is 3 a.m. He reminds Karen of a story. 'We were in this Indian restaurant the other night, when this young Rasta comes in. He orders this huge meal and puts the lot away. Then, when he gets the bill, he says he hasn't got any money. Didn't bat an eyelid. "Sorry," he says to the manager, "can I wash up, mop the floors? Do you want my jacket?"' 'Bloody nerve,' says Julie.

By the ice-cream machine, a pair of teenage lovers are having a silent row. She stares relentlessly down at her tea cup, while he holds her hand and tries to coax her to speak. She just keeps shaking her head and mopping at the stray tears with a Kleenex.

'Evening, William,' shouts a young man with a beard and an army surplus greatcoat. 'Here comes the Marble Arch contingent,' says Bill. The young man is followed in by three others – a skinny middle-aged man with long, greasy hair, a small elf-like figure in a donkey jacket, and a white-haired man in a white coat with *Daily Express* printed on the chest. They fill up a window table with tea cups and ashtrays.

Pete, the young bearded one, has been an all-night newsvendor for three years. 'Before that,' he says, 'I did everything. Picked grapes in France; worked in a hostel for young offenders; in a factory; was in the Coldstream Guards for five years; in the Royal Corps of Transport for seven. I heard about this job from a bloke in the dole queue.' He speaks with a soft, middle-class accent which contrasts oddly with his street-wise appearance. He wears thick grimy boots and hiking socks, and has a couple of teeth missing.

He says he is self-educated. He reads a lot of books. He has a theory about people who work at night. 'They're returning to the womb,' he explains, rolling a cigarette in a tin on his lap. 'I believe a lot of day people, who hate their jobs, are frustrated night people. There ought to be a test to determine whether you're nocturnal or diurnal.' He starts to fill in *The Times* crossword.

Next to him, Harry sips his tea behind a curtain of lank hair. He must be in his middle forties. 'I'm a wanderer,' he says, 'a night owl. I was trained as an engineer, then went into the Catering Corps. I was even a baker at one time – delivering door to door. I can tell you one thing: if I was married, I wouldn't let a baker or a milkman call on my wife. The things I've seen! Whoof!'

Bill consults his digital watch-calculator and announces it is now 4 a.m. A Bee Gees tape has been playing; he changes it, and Greek bazouki music fills the cafe. He serves a solitary girl and the cash register bleeps into life. She looks around the tables, catches the curious or hostile gazes and hurries out. For several minutes a tramp has been standing outside the window, staring in. He stands quite immobile. His face and narrow eyes are focused on a pair of hands inside, mechanically kneading and rolling out dough. In the kitchen, Imran has arrived to make up the dough-nuts for the day shift.

Imran is in his late twenties – very thin, with deep-set eyes and nut-brown skin. He comes from Morocco. For the last two years he has been working the late night/early morning kitchen shift, from 4 a.m. to 10 a.m. He doesn't like night work. It doesn't pay any more money and it's hard to sleep during the day: his children make a lot of noise. His cheap plastic sandals and cotton trousers are dusty with flour. He badly wants to get a day job, perhaps as a lorry driver, the job which he had back home.

His hands toss, pummel and flatten the light grey dough like automatons. He stamps out the shapes with a battery of tin cutters, and covers blackened baking trays with the results. 'The pay is not good,' he says grimly. 'I get £75 a week for six days. The rent alone is £26. I have two children, my wife cannot work. I ask for £5 raise one year ago. It is not much. But *he* [gesturing in the direction of the bar] will not give it to me.'

The kitchen is heating up now that all the ovens are alight. On the hotplate, a huge vat of cooking oil simmers. The air feels warm and greasy. Imran narrows his eyes. 'When I complain,' he mutters, 'that fat one [meaning Bill], he hit me.' He points to a couple of purple marks on his cheekbones. He lifts up his T-shirt to show deep scratch marks down his back. 'But what can you do? Maybe I go back to Morocco in a year or two. But it is so difficult to save money.'

Bill admits they had a bit of trouble in the kitchen last night. He fingers the sticking plaster on his eyebrow, and smoothes back his Brylcreemed hair sheepishly. Phil bobs in again, reconciled now with his boss. 'I don't think he really meant to sack me. He just got the wind up.' He passes the door on his motorbike and beeps the horn. Bill and Eddie wave. A siren wails as a fire engine goes past.

Eddie is on his fourth cup of coffee. He looks maudlin. He wasn't always on his own, he says. He married a German girl in the RAF, but after a couple of years she died. Leukemia – nothing they could do about it. That was fifteen years ago. 'If she'd lived,' he says, 'I'd probably have stayed in the RAF. But at the time I couldn't think straight. Couldn't settle down to anything.' He opens his cigarette packet, but it is empty.

'I tried to find consolation in the bottle,' he says portentously. 'I was drinking like a fish. Finally I said to myself, "I'll have to stop this or I'll soon be dead." It was only self-pity. Everyone has bad luck.'

'It's almost five o'clock,' Bill says. 'My favourite saying in a minute.' He goes up to the till. 'Time, please!' he yells.

A young policewoman walks past the window and comes inside. She orders a couple of jam doughnuts. 'Don't put them in a box, love,' she tells Bill. 'I'll eat them now. Bit cold out there this morning. Cheers. See you later.' The cafe empties, the door is locked, and the CLOSED sign put up for an hour or so while the doughnuts are baking for the day shift. Part of the furniture, Eddie has still not budged from his seat. No one expects him to leave.

Bill and Eddie appraise the result of the Miss World contest and fulminate over the latest spy scandal. They start to reminisce about the war, the RAF, street parties, the okey-kokey, Tommy Handley, the Ark Royal. Out in the street, the sky has lightened to an intense blue.

A brisk wind is blowing off the river. Cleaning ladies hurry past on their way home, coats blowing open to show nylon overalls. Postmen and postwomen are walking to work in twos and threes. There are a scattering of lights in the surrounding office blocks.

'It's funny,' says Eddie, another night older. 'Half an hour makes all the difference. One minute the world is dead, then all of a sudden – boom! – the streets are full of people, the lights go on, and there's a bloke on the radio telling you the Blackwall tunnel's blocked again. . . .'

17 December 1981

22
Red light district

Paul Harrison

Maria has a baby doll look that might appeal to the older man: with hair cropped short, big eyes, rouged cheeks and a turned-up nose, she can't be more than 18. On an upright chair in the bay of a terraced house in Newtown, Southampton, she slouches, legs up on the sill, chain smoking, staring vacantly. The lace curtains are drawn only over the front of the bay, so clients coming from either side can see her: when one arrives, she gets up, stubs her cigarette, and pulls the curtains to show she's engaged. Outside on the street, Sikh children too young for school play tag, a fat Hindu grandmother swathed in saris waddles to the shops, and a West Indian bus conductor on the late shift buries his head in the bonnet of a rusting Ford Zephyr. Maria is one of 30 or 40 prostitutes who operate in a densely populated residential area. As long as they're careful not to make any encouraging or suggestive gestures from the windows they all sit in (under a red light at night), they're completely immune to police action.

The Wolfenden report, back in the late 1950s, made recommendations aimed at dealing with 'the presence, and the visible and obvious presence, of prostitutes in considerable numbers in the public streets of some parts of London and of a few provincial towns'. The Street Offences Act, 1959, was brought in to make it illegal 'for a common prostitute to loiter or solicit in a street or public place for the purpose of prostitution'. To make sure innocent women were not arrested, the police had to issue a formal caution to a woman on two separate occasions before they could prosecute her for soliciting. According to the recent report of the Working Party on Street Offences, the act 'has demonstrably had considerable success in its aim of clearing prostitutes from the streets'.

Certainly, convictions for loitering plummeted after 1959, from 19,663 in 1958 to 2,828 in 1960 and 3,466 in 1972. But it now seems that the 'nuisance' didn't go away, but simply popped its head up elsewhere. To take one city as an example, the middle-class shoppers in Manchester were spared the sight of whores in leopard-skin coats and stiletto heels leaning against the windows in Lewis's arcade (as I remember seeing them as a schoolboy). Instead, the girls went to Moss Side and Whalley Range, where the police weren't so thick on the ground, and working-class and immigrant inhabitants were less vocal in protest.

The girls have found ways around the system: most of them simply walk the streets till they've had two cautions, then move on to another area or another city and work under a different name. And now it's not so much the girls who create the nuisance as their clients. Most of the large industrial towns in Britain have their own red light area, usually in an inner city district already suffering from multiple deprivation and with high concentrations of immigrants: places like Chapeltown in Leeds, Balsall Heath and Handsworth in Birmingham, St Paul's in Bristol, or Newtown.

Every city has its dark side: a world of unfulfilled fantasies or frustrated natural urges. It shows itself in the seedy cases tried by Southampton magistrates in recent weeks: a 28-year-old ice cream salesman gave a lift to a 12-year-old boy and indecently assaulted him; a 17-year-old boy was committed to crown court charged with having sexual intercourse with a girl of 13; a Royal Navy sailor from Rochdale was found guilty of breaking into a house with intent to rape the housewife.

Alongside these cases are the few where the police nail the prostitutes or their pimps. Doreen Hobbs, aged 27, was fined £20 for soliciting from the window of her house in Newtown. When challenged, she said she needed the money to buy clothes and shoes for her three children. Patricia Cutujar claimed, with unconscious irony, that she took up prostitution to buy a house 'away from the vice area'. Her husband, Emmanuel, banked nearly £3,000 in unexplained earnings in a three-month period (one indication of the money the women can make). He said he got it by 'selling finches to pet shops'.

Newtown is typical of many inner city areas that have seen better days. It's cut off by two main roads and the railway line, and blessed with gas works, coal dump and shunting yard. There is a very high rate of home ownership here, but more than half the houses are lacking in at least one amenity, and overcrowding is as much as ten times above the Southampton city average. This is the principal immigrant area of Southampton. In some streets, two thirds of the residents are of New Commonwealth origin. Unemployment is high, as is the proportion of young children. Residents have the usual complaints against the council: bad lighting, poor repair of roads, lack of play facilities, and planning blight. The bottom half of the area has had the threat of a new four-lane highway hanging over it for fifteen years.

Now most people hope the area will soon be declared a 'general improvement area', and they're acting as if they are determined to make the place as habitable as they can: new roofs, new windows, porches going up everywhere, with bright, fresh paintwork. It is no exaggeration to say that the chief bane of their lives is now the prostitutes. The women used to be concentrated in two streets that were demolished to make way for a round-about. Then they scattered themselves in houses, mostly along Derby Road and the side streets that lead off it. They sit in their windows, filing their nails, reading the paper, doing crossword puzzles, staring aggressively at male passers-by; at night with one eye on the TV and one eye on the street. Their ages run from around 16 to around 40, their looks from attractive to plain or downright repulsive.

Take one row of three, each next door to the other: a fat Spanish woman of around 25 in hot pants, and a sleeveless blouse, with heavy make-up failing to hide an acne-scarred face; a bulky black woman, with green eyeshade, mini-skirt and brown curly wig, about 29, who threatened to 'kick my ass in' for prying; and a woman of 20 whose customers were obviously undeterred by her studied self-neglect: NHS specs, curlers and headscarf, and not a trace of make-up.

Toni, one of the few women who would talk to a non-customer, started on prostitution six years ago, when she was 17. She claims a West Indian put her up to it: 'He bought me a box of rubbers and a box of tissues and put me on the street. I couldn't do it at first. Every time a car stopped I'd walk past it. I used to say they didn't offer me enough money. Then he stood in a doorway and watched to make sure.' When she got fed up with him beating her, she turned him in for living off immoral earnings. He spent five months in jail on remand, but got off at the trial because there wasn't enough evidence. He had covered himself by having a job as well. Now Toni is a 'part-timer', married to a painter and decorator, with a baby, and very fat and matronly. She says she only does it two or three times a week with regulars, at £5 a time, and she intends to give it up altogether as soon as her son is old enough to have an idea of what she's up to. But some of the women earn £20 a night and £100 at weekends. Toni is exceptional as the women go, in that she's local and gets on very well with her neighbours.

Rosina, a friendly northern woman of 27, has more trouble. She's only been in Newtown a year – she came after reading a story in the *News of the World* about the area. Her living room is about as cosy as a railway waiting room, with a threadbare fawn carpet, two plastic kitchen chairs and a sofa with one cushion missing. 'The neighbours here give you a lot of trouble,' she told me. 'They're against you whatever you do. They give you bad looks and abuse you. Half of them are uneducated twits.' Rosina, who calls herself a 'business girl', sees herself as performing a service. 'If we weren't here a lot of other girls would get into trouble. If a man's not got an outlet, he'll lose his head.'

Both Toni and Rosina say their customers are anything from bank managers or solicitors down to lorry drivers or labourers from the bed-and-breakfast places on nearby St Mary's Road. From about noon on, the clients in cars drive up one street and down the next, circling and doubling back on their tracks, peering into windows and staring back at every nubile woman. At night there are no women at all on the dimly lit streets: they're afraid of being taken for prostitutes. The trade generates heavy traffic: for example, a couple of Rolls driven by Italian-shirted men in their thirties, a dark-red Jaguar XJ12 driven by a balding 50-year-old in a smart suit, a moped ridden by a bearded chap with a crash helmet and a Dayglo anorak.

But extra traffic isn't the only thing that other residents have to put up with. They find *they* can't sit in their windows, or have red lights or curtains. And whether they do or not, they get people knocking at the wrong door, asking where they can find a girl. They have the noise of car doors slamming till late into the night, and frequent arguments between the women and their customers or their pimps. One Sikh family I spoke to live right next door to an attractive white prostitute. The bad-tempered dog she keeps for protection goes for the children every time they go into the back yard, and has torn a new turban off the line. Because they complain about this, relations with the girl are appalling. 'She curses us every time she sees us,' the daughter of the house told me. The Asians are particularly offended by the trade because of their more straight-laced morals. Amarjit Sohal, a 42-year-old crane driver, told me: 'I don't like my children to see that thing. Sometimes when I come home from the late shift they are still shouting in the street. If the government don't stop this bad thing, in my opinion I will sell this house and buy somewhere else.'

Prostitution has added to racial tensions in the area. The Asians and the whites get along surprisingly well: but both are less at ease with the West Indians, who are more free and easy, and tend to have noisy all-night parties and shebeens. Most of the residents are convinced that the women are being run by West Indian pimps.

The residents have tried, or at least thought of trying, every conceivable method of dealing with the nuisance created by the prostitutes' presence. The most original was proposed by some of the Pakistanis: the women would soon go away, they suggested, if two of them were dragged out of their houses down to the middle of Derby Road and had their throats slit in public, *pour encourager les autres*. They have been dissuaded from this course. Most residents have at one time or another called in the police, and had them staked out in their sitting rooms doing surveillance, watching for the slightest nod that could be called soliciting.

Last year, three community groups were started in the area on the prompting of the city social services department. One of them, the Newtown Community and Improvement Group, was built around the fight against the prostitutes, largely through the efforts of its first secretary and chairman, Tony Larkin. Larkin, a short but dapper figure who burns with passionate conviction, returned last year after a long spell with the RAF in the Middle East, and had arranged that his Lebanese wife should follow on as soon as he had found a place. The estate agent took him by car to see his present house, in Hartington Road. He liked it, and was driven away again. Only when he moved in did he realise what kind of an area he had moved into, and was horror-stricken at the thought that his wife was due to arrive. He moved into battle fast, and, acting often as a one-man band, shot off letters to the Queen, the Prime Minister, Home Office minister Alex Lyon, Earl Mountbatten.

'Your majesty,' he wrote, 'if it is not possible for your loyal subjects to walk freely and unmolested through their own neighbourhoods after sundown, then the law of the realm in some respects needs a radical reappraisal.' The Queen declined his invitation to come and gape at the whores in their windows. To Alex Lyon, Larkin wrote that it was wrong to expect neighbourhoods like theirs to 'fester and rot in a cesspool of prostitution . . . blighting and crippling our personalities and outlooks from the cradle to the grave.' Larkin also wrote to the *News of the World*, who did a front-page piece on Britain's own red light district.

But underneath the rhetoric and the sensation, there were some interesting proposals. One was the old chestnut of legalising brothels. Another was that prostitutes should be licensed as traders, and controlled by local authority planning departments so as to direct them away from residential areas. The Home Office turned down both proposals flat.

And that is the stage they have now reached. A whole series of ideas has been thrown up, and thrown out one after the other: taking car numbers of customers (but where would you publish them, and would it be libel?). Sponsoring a special directory of women (but is it legal?), and putting pressure on the post office to get them phones. Giving out notices for all the ordinary houses to put in their windows to keep sex seekers away. One Newtown house already carries a notice: 'This bell is not a business bell so please referr you custom else where' (*sic*). Or picketing outside the whores' houses (but residents have just learned that you can only picket in trades disputes). Really they're very much at a loss as to what to do next, and no one else seems in any hurry to help them.

Not all the new red light districts are precisely like Newtown, of course. Take a south London example: Bedford Hill, in Balham. This road curves out of Balham towards Tooting Bec Common, through a very pleasant middle-class residential area, with rose gardens and privet hedges and prostitutes. Here, as in most other areas, the women walk the streets until they get picked up by a customer in his car. If anything, this way of operating works out far worse for other residents than the ingenious Southampton solution. Looking for prostitutes to interview, it was easy to see why. The problem is to find out which girls are the whores, and which are respectable. After all, lots of ordinary girls tart themselves up and look at you suggestively. I kerb-crawled behind one black girl who had done nothing worse than walk sexily, and only modesty stopped me from accosting another pair of girls in sexy mini-skirts – until I noticed they were in tennis gear. As I was circling round the streets, I noticed a dozen other cars doing the same, some of them braking suddenly in front of lines of heavy traffic while they shouted out to a pair of innocent females.

Local women tell you that they can't go to the shops without being accosted with some obscene suggestion. One man I spoke to said he once picked up his wife to give her a lift home, and was followed down all the side streets by two other cars. When he arrived home he asked them what they were doing. They asked him if they could have the next turn after he had finished with her. The lucky cars who do track down the genuine tarts – and there seem to be about six or eight girls operating at any one time – stop, haggle over a price, then drive off with them, or, sometimes, retire to the shadier bushes on the common.

I finally located two girls, who were wandering aimlessly up and down the same two streets staring at cars. Monica is 20, with straight hair brushed tightly down into a pony tail, wearing a black fur jacket, with extra-high heels and criss-cross straps around her ankles. Beverley is 22, in a loose-fitting flimsy dress and a mannish jacket. They're both attractive and open about their trade. They're from 'somewhere in the Black Country', and have been prostitutes for three years. Before that, Monica was a filing clerk and Beverley a computer operator. But they knew some girls who were prostitutes and making £100 a week and more. That plus the boredom of routine work determined them to start up, and now they're doing quite well.

Each of them has a car and they share an unfurnished flat,

which they're furnishing with the proceeds. They've not yet been cautioned once, perhaps because they move around a lot. They've worked in Norwich, Liverpool, Birmingham, and Southampton. In London they alternate between Finsbury Park, Hampstead Lane, Brixton, Soho and Park Lane. Sometimes they check in at four-star hotels and pick up clients in the bar. Their charges are way above the Southampton rates – £5 for a quick five minutes in the back of the car (or up an alley for a pedestrian); £25 to go to the man's place or their own; and £50 for all night. Both have had several dangerous experiences, being beaten up, strangled or locked in a room. Now they will not work apart; so for the basic price you can get a 'double act', too, if you want it. They work seven days a week, 'all the hours God sends'. But often that means just from nine till eleven in the evening. In a good week they can earn £300 or £400. The previous week, they said, had been a 'bad' one: they netted £40 each, tax free.

Newtown and Balham, in their different ways, show that the police have no hope of controlling the very disturbing nuisance to other residents caused by the presence of prostitutes. The gimmick the prostitutes have found in Southampton places them effectively beyond the law. In Balham they just don't stick around after two cautions.

The essential problem – and in a way it has been created by the Street Offences Act which banned soliciting – is one of recognition. Some men – soldiers, travellers, the ugly, the lonely or the perverted – will always need prostitutes, and some women will always want to be prostitutes as long as the rewards are adequate. The problem both groups have under the present law is how to find each other. At the moment both groups gravitate towards areas which, for one reason and another, have become notorious for it: then it's up to the clients to sort out the business girls from the decent ones by trial and error, and they do this by kerb-crawling. It's hard to think how else, in fact, they could do it, as long as the girls are not allowed to make it known that their wares are for sale. A law against kerb-crawling will either prove to be one of the most breached laws in existence, or criminalise a large section of the male population. It will not clear the red light areas or free decent girls from molestation. These things are unlikely to happen until prostitutes can be directed to operate in non-residential areas, and allowed to make signals to potential clients.

There are many ways in which these ends could be achieved: by legalising brothels; licensing prostitutes; tacit police agreement to ignore soliciting in certain designated areas; having badges or uniforms for prostitutes or for would-be clients. But none of these things can happen as long as politicians at national and local level are afraid of losing votes if they appear to be condoning prostitution.

In fact, they would be condoning it less than they are at present. They would be controlling it more closely, instead of allowing it to run rife on the doorsteps of some of the most underprivileged sections of the community. It's very curious that politicians are prepared to be liberal in the teeth of strong majority opinion on race or hanging, and not on this one. Perhaps, like most people, they don't really mind it going on, as long as they don't know about it. The residents of the red light districts have to pay heavily for this kind of moral hypocrisy.

10 July 1975

23
Whoring on the side

Sheila Yeger

'A little genteel whoring.' That's how Anna describes her work. She certainly didn't look like a member of the oldest profession when I met her the other day in the coffee bar of our local art gallery. She came in wearing an ordinary-looking tweed skirt, sensible shoes, an unspectacular woolly jumper with a scarf knotted round her neck, spectacles and no make-up. You'd have thought she was somebody's short-sighted secretary or the nice daughter of a Purley bank manager on her way to a point-to-point. Although the last time I'd seen her she'd been Mata Hari, complete with glossy black fingernails.

Anna, who has just turned 25, talks freely of being 'on the game', but you won't find her standing on any street corner in our large provincial town. As she said, 'I'd hate the thought of trying to pick somebody up; I just couldn't do it!' Instead, she works at home – 'home' being the comfortable flat crammed with books, records and paintings, where she lives with Oscar, her husband.

In fact, it was Oscar who gave her the idea in the first place. But then she is quick to point out that he *is* rather an exceptional man. A young writer, ambitious but still struggling, he is also something of a local celebrity. Egocentric, eccentric, likeable, flamboyant, he is seldom seen without Anna and his coterie of young friends and admirers – moths round a cultivated flame.

'Well, Oscar brought it up as a joke really. We'd read about *Contact* magazine somewhere and he said perhaps I should try it. Actually, I think he was a bit surprised when I decided there really wasn't any alternative and said I'd have a go. You see we

199

were in dire straits financially. I'd had various jobs since I'd left school – working as a clerk, for example. But we just couldn't stand being apart for all those hours every day. An hour or two and we'd miss each other. Working at home seemed the best idea.'

I asked her if she'd asked anyone else about how to go about it. 'No. I didn't know anyone else who did it and I still don't. I just bought one of those *Contact* magazines and studied the adverts. Then I wrote my own and sent it in. I got about two dozen replies straight off.'

I was interested in seeing the actual advert used, but she asked me not to quote it word for word – 'because I wouldn't want my clients to be hurt.' Actually, the advert describes her accurately enough: 'intelligent, attractive.' It lists her measurements, and adds, 'enjoys entertaining professional and business gentlemen.' She was anxious that I stress the word 'enjoys'. 'Of course I wouldn't do if it I didn't need the money – that's obvious – but I wouldn't want a client to think that's *all* I'm doing it for. You see it's important to them that they can feel that I get some enjoyment out of it.'

On receiving the replies, she writes back to each one giving more details about herself and making one or two things very clear, to avoid trouble later: 'I explain that my husband will be in the flat – that's in case they've got anything funny in mind. It tends to put them off. I tell them what I charge (£12 a session) which is for about two to three hours. I say I'm not interested in anything peculiar; if they want that, they'd have to go elsewhere. Actually I'm very wary of trying odd things with strangers; it's different with somebody you know and trust, when you've got to know their body and they know yours.'

I asked her how she had felt with her very first client. After all, it's not quite as simple as taking in envelopes to type. She looked into space for a minute: 'Well, I can't remember anything specific – except that I was very nervous.' 'Why?' 'Well, I was mostly afraid that I wouldn't be able to satisfy him. I wasn't afraid of getting beaten up or anything, because Oscar was in the next room, and I wasn't afraid that *I* wouldn't be satisfied – because I didn't expect to be – but I was worried that I wouldn't be good enough for him.'

Anna then described a typical encounter: 'I usually meet my

clients in the afternoon. I only work perhaps two or three afternoons a week, then I can use the mornings for cleaning up and things, and in the evenings we like to go out. I put on a pretty blouse, a skirt, stockings and suspenders. Men like suspenders. I still feel nervous when it's the first time with anybody – but I feel better when I realise that they're always more nervous than I am.

'At first we just talk. I usually make a cup of tea or coffee. They seem relieved that I'm not an old bag and that it's not all cold-blooded and businesslike. More often than not they're shy, not sure what to say or what to do. Most of them insist that they've never answered an ad before – that a friend suggested they do it for a joke. It's obvious that they feel there's something wrong with them if they have to pay for sex. No, of course I don't agree with that. I think they're just unfortunate. They're not at all sure what to expect and they're relieved that it all starts off low-key.

'The sex part, as far as I can see, is often less important to them than the talking and the tea. My regular customers – most of them are men over 40 – probably come as much for advice, sympathy, a chance to take "time out" for themselves, as for the actual sex. They're usually businessmen with lots of pressures and worries. Often they tell me that they have wonderful wives, nice children and a lovely home. It's just that their wives won't sleep with them any more. Sometimes they just accept it as a fact of life; or else they are puzzled and hurt and need help in understanding it. They don't want to threaten their marriages by getting involved with their secretary, or something messy like that, but they do need some sort of outlet and I can provide it. They don't want any kind of emotional involvement and neither do I. Once or twice it has happened that a client wanted to get too involved – started asking me out to dinner and all that – but I had to make it plain that I don't want that. Sometimes they accept it easily enough, but other times, if that was what they wanted, they just don't come back.'

I wondered if she herself ever felt more than professional interest in her visitors. She laughed. 'Well, I don't *like* it, if that's what you mean. I'd give it all up tomorrow and not miss it a bit. It doesn't mean a thing to me sexually – it's quite impersonal, in fact. But I must admit that I do like to make friends of my clients. In fact one or two I suppose I do count as proper friends: people who turn to me and to whom I'd turn if I needed their help. As far as sex is concerned, on the whole they're not physically attractive. Well, not to me, anyway. I'd say one in four of them is impotent in one way or another – either that or he has some sex problem like premature ejaculation.'

I asked her how she dealt with this. 'Well, I'm not an expert, but I have found that if you reassure a man that *you're* satisfied – fake an orgasm – then he can often improve his performance. And of course as he gets more confident, he gets better at it. Also I can sometimes give him advice about how to improve his sex life with his wife – how to turn her on and so on. I think I've saved quite a few marriages that way.'

I said I wondered how her work had affected her personally and what impact it had had on her relationship with her husband. 'Well, I grew up in an utterly straight working-class background. My father worked in a factory; still does. All my attitudes to sex of any sort were completely conventional in those days. I'm sure I'd never have dreamt that I'd end up doing something like this. I lost my virginity quite early – I was 13 – but it wasn't a bad experience or anything. Nothing traumatic. I went to a nice girls' school and did all the usual things. I met Oscar while I was still doing my A levels. Actually I was pregnant by somebody else at the time and he helped me through the abortion and everything. I thought he was marvellous – still do. We fell madly in love and got married a year later. It was really romantic. I'd never come across anyone like him. I'd always been attracted to reputations, especially that of a "rake" – I can't think of a good modern word for it – and he'd been out with most of the girls in my group. He didn't look quite so incredible in those days, but he still looked pretty amazing, bearing in mind the sort of place we were living. I used to think that I'd be the one to reform him: that was my only fantasy. Well, I've stopped fantasising about that because I've achieved it. I'm completely happy in my relationship with Oscar. Since I met him there've only been one or two blokes I've felt any attraction for at all, and then not enough to want to do anything about it.

'Of course, you want to know if my work threatens my marriage – everyone asks that. It might if I were married to a different kind of man. But Oscar is so sexually secure and so emotionally secure with me, that I really don't think that it's a threat at all. It was more of a threat when I went out to work and left him at home. It's a funny thing – our relationship: he's not faithful to me, actually; and in theory I'm not supposed to be faithful to him. But in practice it hasn't worked out like that. There just isn't anyone else I fancy! I don't even have sexy fantasies. I've got my marvellous man in real life. I don't need anything more. On a purely personal level I'd say this. I used to be a romantic, but now I'd call myself, would you believe, "a romantic cynic"? Life makes you into a cynic, but we – Oscar and I – have such a perfect romantic situation that I'd say, yes – definitely – I'm a romantic cynic.

'Moral scruples? That's another thing everyone always asks. Well, I don't have any at all. After all, you might as well sell your whole body for money as sell your mind or some other part, what difference does it make? Naturally I wouldn't really want my parents to know what I do, they'd be broken-hearted; but my brother – well, he knows, and he didn't seem all that shocked. He said he'd guessed, anyway. Otherwise I don't really care who knows what I do. I'm not a bit ashamed of it. I don't think or feel I'm doing anything wrong. If I were single, it wouldn't even be illegal; but I know that Oscar could be "done" for living off my immoral earnings, so I don't go shouting it around. On the whole, I feel I'm offering a social service. I see sex as just another physical act like cooking or eating a meal – something people have to do. I don't see it necessarily as an expression of love. No, it's really nothing to do with it.'

Lastly I asked her what she considered the most important things in life. She thought quite hard. 'Well, I don't want children. I don't like them at all. Of course, I might change my mind in five to ten years' time, but not now. Relating to people – though I don't find it easy – and especially to Oscar: that's the most important thing. And, yes, something else, I'd like to feel that I could add something to the world by being here.'

24 June 1976

24
The new vegetarians

Angela Carter

My neighbourhood wholefood shop – according to *Alternative England and Wales*, the best one outside London – is a genre masterpiece, a scrubbed pine and whitewashed gem of non-specific rusticity. There are baskets of splendid cabbages of many different kinds, of leeks, of kale, of ruddy-cheeked apples blotched and wenned as if on purpose so you can see at a glance no chemical spray has been near them. They're bakers as well: trays of solid, dark, hand-thrown-looking loaves, a slice of which, with nut butter, is a nourishing meal in itself; and all manner of cookies and flapjacks and goodies made with honey and dates and raisins, all the natural sweetenings – never a trace of the killer white sugar.

They don't stock sugar at all, in fact – not even that earthy, treaclish, fudge-coloured sugar that comes in chunks, which I'd have thought would have been All Right. But they started a few years ago as a regular macrobiotic food shop, which cut sugar right out. The first sign they were, in other ways, declining from their original rigour was when they started selling tomatoes, which, macrobiotically speaking, are nowhere. Poison.

They collect old paper bags and egg boxes and recycle them; there's a sign reminding one: 'It takes 17 trees to make one ton of paper – SAVE OUR TREES.' There's a back room, with bins, where you can weigh out your own beans and grains for a penny or two less than they cost if the staff has had to pack them themselves. There are moong beans; buckwheat; aduki beans; whole yellow millet; pot barley; lentils; black-eye beans; brown rice (Californian brown rice and Italian brown rice); red kidney beans; chick peas; haricot beans; and much else besides. Also nuts and dried fruit. And a roomful of jars of herbs. I am very glad of all these peasant comestibles. It is a pleasure to shop in such a place.

It's a positive aesthetic of unrefinement transformed into refinement. They don't, for example, wash their carrots. They may chip off a few of the bigger chunks of mud but those brick-coloured roots retain a substantial coating of the earth that bore them, a different order of foodstuff altogether from the scrubbed, supermarket carrot in its condom-like plastic sheath. Sometimes they come from a place which is called Paradise Farm. These are *real* carrots.

Wholefood makes you a whole person. The vendors themselves have a gnarled, hand-woven, organic look about them, in their smocks and collarless jumble-sale shirts and woolly caps. They come and go on a free-form democratic basis; it's a collective; it seems to work very well. Good vibes. There's been a cat, a marmalade cat with white paws, though I haven't seen him around lately. I asked them what they fed the cat on and they said: canned cat food. But canned cat food may be made from ecologically endangered whales. . . . They gentled me out of the shop, containing the possibility of aggro in a massive, vegetable calm.

The nice girl in the smock says she herself has nothing against people who eat meat though she personally doesn't like the taste and, furthermore, she didn't like what our society did to its animals, locking them up, pumping them full of hormones and so on. This is a favourite vegetarian ploy. I don't mind meat-eating in the least. If you want to poison your body with noxious substances, go right ahead, you have free choice; I don't want to preach to anybody. Diet has become a matter of morality. There's something of the air of a Nonconformist chapel about this shop.

I remember staying at a friend's where we'd reason to believe another guest was a vegetarian and my hostess wanted to roast a large joint of pork and so we asked, would that be all right? The perfidious vegetable eater said yes, fine; she wasn't in the least dogmatic and she'd join us in a slice or two of meat, probably, since it was planned as a special meal. When the roast was actually on the table, though, she rejected it and piled her plate with boiled potatoes. She said how good the potatoes were, really good. They always say that. 'It's really good', 'this is really nice', as if to restore 'really' from its neutral qualifying status to its original, non-debased sense, meaning 'authentically' or 'veritably'. Accept no substitutes. This is the real stuff. *Really* real.

Then, while the rest of us tucked into the pork in an embarrassed fashion, she remarked conversationally that she'd only become a vegetarian after a visit to an abattoir. She described the pools of blood, the gushing entrails, the mild, dazed eyes of the harmless beasts while the leg of pork lay there on its platter looking, every minute, more and more like dead pig. (That's another thing vegetarians like doing – chanting: 'Dead pig! Dead pig!' when they see a sausage.)

It wasn't the slaughterhouse reminiscences themselves that offended me. It was that she felt she'd got the moral right to try to ruin the meal for the rest of us, and, probably, she thought she was doing us a good turn. If she shoved in sufficient emotive detail, this Sunday dinner would prove a Damascus Road. When she got to the bit where the little newly dead lamb's hooves twitched uncontrollably, we'd push away our plates crying: 'Never again!' and eat brown rice ever after. What a display of moral superiority! It was delicious pork. I enjoyed it.

It seemed to me, furthermore, that she dwelt on these gory scenes with a good deal of masochistic self-indulgence: mightn't there be some degree of repressed violence in all this? And, anyway, according to the best counter-culture sources, vegetables are sentient, too. What pain the grain must feel to be stone-ground! Pythagoras wouldn't eat beans because he thought they might contain the spirits of his forefathers. Why should reincarnation abjure the kingdom of the plants? What is the ontological status of the carnivorous plant in the terms of the New Vegetarianism?

The New Vegetarianism – an alternative growth industry, a dietary sign system indicating spiritual awareness, expanded consciousness and ecological concern – has very little to do with the old vegetarianism, which was part of a lifestyle embracing socialism, pacifism and shorts, a simple asceticism expressing a healthy contempt for the pleasures of the flesh. Since Woodstock, you've got to *enjoy* your vegetarianism, dammit. 'Why live like vegetarians on food you give to parrots?' queried the man in song, before expressing his own preference for boiled beef and carrots. Because eating is a religious experience, that's why. 'Pure men like pure food which gives true health, balanced mentality, sustaining strength, life long enough to search – pure food which has delicate taste, soothes, nourishes and brings them joy – pure food that promotes the knowledge of God.'

This epigraph from the Bhagavad Gita adorns *Super Natural Cookery*, a typically camp title, written in the queasily flirtatious style which seems to afflict all Aquarian cookery books. 'Salads of fruit are not acid oranges, desiccated (and dead) coconut and dyed cherries, or an overcooked peach on a cardboard cottage cheese. Aren't you glad!' This is curiously flabby language in which to approach a sacramental food experience; a tone of sneering patronage, I call it. Some of the other manuals aspire to a hearty joyousness, often decorated with drawings of loopy-looking girls in smocks running through fields, which is really embarrassing. I mean *really*.

The New Vegetarianism claims that you can chew your way back to a lost harmony with nature: the way to the Kingdom of God lies directly down the gullet. 'Food was the core, the centre of the experience – in Boston, I found a large, loose-knit community of people from every conceivable background – whose common link with one another was primarily the whole, naturally-grown, unadulterated foods they chewed each day, food that was satisfying, delicious, healing. Food that was *alive*.'

This is a young man describing his first macrobiotic experience in a big, fat American magazine called *East West Journal* they sell in my health food store, along with the *I Ching*, various books about massage, *The Well Body Book*, and cook books.

Food that was *alive*. Curious choice of words. At least the Paschal lamb stayed dead. Now this young man's making himself a farm, committing himself to the 'mighty, healing land', embracing the mythology of a benign nature as if he'd never heard of the Lisbon Earthquake which shook Voltaire's belief in that benignity.

The ritual consumption of sufficient quantities of wholefood will restore man's lost harmony with nature. That's the theory, then. When did we lose that elusive harmony with nature, though?

It was, apparently, a shortage of the eggs, nestlings and fruit that formed its diet that sent the original ape down from the trees to forage in the undergrowth. He promptly almost exterminated a number of species of lizards and porcupines and other small mammals and reptiles, before he learned to kill larger animals by throwing rocks at them.

It's not surprising that the Aquarians and the New Age Seekers and the Natural Lifers turn against this unedifying scenario. *Seed*, the Forum of Natural Living, a homegrown publication, contains a brisk refutation of Darwin – claiming, among other things, that, since Darwin himself looked like an ape, he back-projected an analogy, rather than constructed a theory.

'Grain, the foundation of civilisation,' suggests the *East West Journal*. Hunter becomes herdsman, plant-gatherer becomes farmer when the ice fields retreat about 11,000 BC. At this point, then, we can identify a natural lifestyle superseding the unenlightened and unnatural past, about which the less said the better. This is the Golden Age, when, as the Harmony Foods ad on the back of *Seed* suggests, you could see the universe in a grain of wheat 'and heaven in a wholewheat loaf'.

The New Vegetarianism posits man as a microcosm. He has poisoned his own system with meat, white sugar, refined flour, chemical additives. He has poisoned his ecological system, which is an image of himself. The self-sufficient farming unit, beloved dream of most freaks – with its goat, its bean row and its beehive – is a model of an environment over which he will be able to exert maximum control. The macrobiotic diets are control systems in themselves. Dietary self-policing will keep the demons of psychic disorder away. Regenerated, man microcosm/macrocosm retains absolute control, of himself, of life.

After its busy day working in the fields, the communion of the elect gathers round the scrubbed pine table and consumes casseroles of chick peas and wheat grains, or lentil and sesame paste pasties, or mixed bean stews, ritually muttering: 'It's really good, it's really nice.'

Gibbon thought the primitive Christians, with similar rituals, were the straw that broke the camel's back.

4 March 1976

25
Village voices

Jeremy Seabrook

Market day in the little town still creates a vortex of excitement in the surrounding villages. It is the only time of the week when the buses are full; and the old women look round at the other passengers to see who's missing or who didn't catch the early bus that morning. The market stalls are erected round the triangular market place: ancient primitive structures, metal struts and dusty canvas, with a trestle stretched out to those who will buy. Much of the produce is unstandardised: apples misshapen and windfallen; plums unevenly ripened with leaves and stalks still clinging to them; the emerald folds of lettuce splashed with mud from yesterday's storm.

Small groups of women gather at the stalls, greet each other, dissolve and then meet again. They have time to talk: and even when they meet for a second or third time during the morning, they have thought of something new to tell each other. 'Have you seen the colour of Carol Porritt's hair this week?' 'She calls it vanilla.' 'Sounds like an ice cream.' The anecdotes are exchanged and run from group to group. 'How's that girl used to lodge with Mrs Forrest?' 'Worse, if anything. They say she has a taxi and sits all day outside where her chap works. Costs a fortune.' A local farmer had a cow that died of fog fever. 'Never heard of it. What's that then?' 'That bit of mist a-Tuesday morning. It got in the cow's lungs. It wasn't right on the Wednesday afternoon, they sent for the vet and he said: "I'm sorry, it's gone." Two hundred quid down the drain.'

When the women have finished shopping, they sit on one of

the memorial benches that flank the market place, made of
unpainted wood with a brown plaque saying in whose memory
the bench was presented. As she sits down, an old woman says,
'Oo that's better'; then, indicating the plaque, 'Been more use
since he's been gone than he ever was alive.' Some of the women
wait until late afternoon, because things that will perish are sold
off cheaply.

In the little row of cottages in the village, no visitor comes
unnoticed. 'That'll be the district nurse come to wash grandma.'
Whenever a car pulls up, people are impelled towards the window to see who it is. Sometimes the women just look at the clock,
bite off their darning thread and announce the name of the
visitor. 'It's next door's insurance man.' 'There goes Mrs Adams
home from work.' 'Amy hasn't looked in for a day or two, I expect
she's got one of her bilious turns.' A girl goes by on high platform
shoes. An old man standing in the doorway says, 'Who built the
scaffold for your shoes?' 'Cheeky old bugger.' During the day,
the women visit each other, walking in without knocking. Everything that is said by one visitor is repeated to the next one who
calls. Little by little, fresh items are added to a continuously
evolving narrative, which moves forward only very slowly. 'Mrs
Wilson seen old man Cowley sleeping in his van two nights last
week. Whether she'd locked him out, or he didn't want to go
home, I don't know.' 'Flo Billing's got a lovely new flat from the
council. She's got a cupboard so big she's got electric light in it.
She goes and sits in it sometimes.'

At the back of the High Street an old lady sits on the base of a
Windsor chair. 'If you'd a-come here when I were a girl, you'd
a-seen all the old women sitting at their doorsteps with their
cushions in front of them, making their lace.' Her bed has been
moved downstairs, so that she doesn't have to climb the narrow
corkscrew staircase which leads to a small upper storey.

'I shall be 86 a week a-Wednesday. I'm all right here. I can still
get about on the level. I've got eight grandchildren and twelve
great-grandchildren, so I'm never in want of visitors. It's only at
night that I get lonely.' Her next-door neighbour, who was over
90, died a few weeks earlier. 'She came into me every night for the
last seven years. Every night from seven while ten. Of course, it
were me as found her. Oo, I do miss her. It were a Sunday. She
stayed and watched the late film on the Saturday night and she

never done that as a rule. Then on the Sunday, she comes in three or four times for sommat or other. Then she said, "I'd better go and get meself a bit o' dinner." And I never see her alive again.'

We walk into the old back yard. The lilac bush is burnt on one side where the sofa and old furniture was destroyed after the old woman's death. The cottage is open, brown-painted door gaping, the window hanging broken from its hinges. Someone has been stripping the walls of paper; the bed, a metal rectangle with a mesh of tight springs, stands against a wall.

The past is not so easily obliterated in the countryside. Painted wooden signs on the outhouses at the back of the High Street announce obsolete economic functions: Farrier, Hay and Forage Dealer. Archaic notices authorise a pub to sell intoxicating liquor for the refreshment of persons attending the market on Monday and Thursday afternoons; commemorate the disastrous height of flood water in September 1796; declare that a Sunday school was erected by the curate of a parish at His Sole Expense in 1822. One evening I sheltered from the rain in an old man's stable: a dark and cobwebby place. Inside were some remains of farm implements: rusting wheels, a handcart, an old ferret hutch.

'I catch a few rabbits, the odd badger for a bit of fun. I don't use a ferret any more. . . . Nice drop of rain. It's been a dry year. You know what they say, "Up horn, down corn." You can't suit the crops and the cattle as well. I used to be a forage dealer. I haven't done it for years, all the cars did away with the horses. I can remember the first car to go down the High Street. You've seen the width of that street? It knocked a man off his bike. . . . Not all the changes have been for the best. The unions today, they can ask for anything they want and get it. It's all wrong. I've been through two world wars. Had the house requisitioned twice. Had soldiers billeted on us in the first war, the Bucks Yeomanry. You weren't asked if you wanted them, you had to. And in the second war, they put all the flour from the bakehouse in my loft. I don't know if they thought it would be safer there, the bakehouse was only the other side of the road. Seems we all knew how to work together then, I don't know. . . . The house used to belong to a tinker long time ago, there's still the old bellows up in the attic. My daughters say, "Why don't you have it all done up, clear it out?" I like to think of the people who were here before me. I like the history of places. All these back places used to be the old crafts, coopers and brewers and smiths and dealers.'

The village itself is divided into three parts. First, there is the old core of the village. Nearly all the cottages have been gutted and modernised, and their present inhabitants have no connection with the village. Then there are the council houses, which are the homes of those who formerly lived in the old agricultural labourers' cottages. The local accent is only heard from the people in the council estate. Finally, there are two private estates. The men work in the big towns or in London. Some of the women do 'village-y things', but for most it is another suburb, a by-product of a husband's career.

Many of the public footpaths are overgrown. Some have been incorporated into private gardens, others obliterated by building. Every time I asked about a footpath, the answer was always the same, the wording identical: 'Nobody uses them now.' This generalised vagueness originates with the encroachers upon public property, and it is dutifully echoed by people who have no real opinion on the subject. There is no longer resentment on the part of the villagers towards the newcomers: they are reduced now to a narrow portion of the bar in the two pubs, which have had their gardens concreted for the accommodation of cars, and their interiors turned into period lounges and charcoal grills. An old agricultural worker sits on a stool at the bar. A kind-looking lady who comes in asks him what tomorrow's weather will be. When she has gone he says, 'Why don't they listen to the bloody wireless?'

He started work when he was 11. The local schools always adjusted their terms to the harvest. 'Many a time I was fetched out of school if a horse needed shoeing. . . . When I started work I got ten shillings a week. Villages aren't villages now. If you get a function up at the village hall now, nobody comes. When I started work, I worked alongside my four brothers and my father, and my mother used to come up the fields where we were working with six dinners, all cooked separately. Harvest time you should have seen the rabbits. Farmer always gave you a harvest rabbit, you reckoned on that as your due. Only we helped ourselves, there was so many of them. Put one down each trouser leg, one inside your coat. Very often I've worked all day with a rabbit down each trouser leg, then got another one when it was time to go home. Now the harvest is over and done with in no time. We still get a good harvest supper, though.'

In the cottages, the visitors come and go, vigilant for signs of novelty: 'Have you seen her since she had that stroke? All one side of her face, it's terrible seeing what a fine woman she was.' In a glass case outside the post office, there are postcards advertising a Pedigree pram, some hi-fi equipment, a playpen, a teacher of the pianoforte. There is a card that says 'Wedding Dress for Sale. Never been worn. Also 24 invitation cards.' I say, 'Isn't that sad?' 'Well, don't be, it was her. She up and married somebody else at the register office two weeks before she was supposed to be married.'

The weather turns colder, fires are lit in the evenings. Memory and anecdote compete with *Policewoman* and *Kojak*. 'They still come for me to lay them out. I've laid out a few hundred in my time. One night, a chap down the village came knocking on my bedroom window with a lineprop, and I got up and he said, "Will you come, it's my mother." Well I didn't know her, but I thought, "Well, you've got to do it." And I went and washed her and laid her out. She was only a frail old lady, and as I lifted her up – it was the middle of the night remember – I got the shock of my life, her wig fell off. She was bald, poor old soul. . . . Anyway, next day the undertaker came to see me and said, "How much do I owe you?" I said, "Owe me?" He said, "Yes, the ladies in the village generally charge for it. Two guineas a time, I believe. They do it as a hobby, a sideline." Well I don't want money for an act of mercy.'

Grandma, over 90, oblivious of the TV adverts, talks in a thin wasting voice about rook pie and lamb-tail pie, wicker clothes-baskets of field mushrooms, bushes laden with blackberries and sloes and hazelnuts, elderberries, pig-killing time, trotters and chitterlings; and if her village is no more than an extended suburb, she will never know it.

4 March 1976

26
The Oss has his day

Angela Carter

You pass the Ambrosia creamed rice factory; then, after a while, the Mother's Pride bread factory on the Devon/Cornwall border. These two monuments to British traditional cuisine behind, you're into Britain's little Sicily, grim stone townships, grim sullen moors. . . . But we are bound beyond bleak Bodmin to the little town of Padstow, with its seafood restaurant, its steakhouse, its tropical bird garden. And it is May Eve.

Everywhere is hung with flags, and boughs of sycamore decorate all the doorways. Padstow is *en fête*. The Harbour Inn – stable of the Blue Ribbon Oss – is packed out, but a bit of dancing goes on. One agile man has stripped off his shirt, pissed out of his head, terpsichorally too extravagant to be a visitor.

The crowded bar sings the May Song, Padstow's own. It says: let us all unite, for summer is acome in today. But it will, in fact, come tonight, at 12 p.m. precisely. We shall sing in the summer in front of the Golden Lion, up the street.

The Lion has an elaborate sign on its front executed in Merrie England style. This announces that it is the stable of the Old Oss, or Red Ribbon Oss, one of the two hobby horses who will parade tomorrow's streets. The narrow access fills up as soon as the pubs close. Young kids sing and raucously dance the May dance and May Song while there's room to dance; before they pass out, anyway. Their dancing has been affected by discos. They only seem to know the one verse: 'Unite and unite', 'Rejoice and rejoice'. And the strange cry, 'Oss! Oss!' with its response, 'Wee Oss!'

In a lighted upper room of the pub, a man in purple underwear persists in sticking his bum out of the window. At first, in my innocence, I thought that this, too, was a folk tradition. But the growing hubbub of discontent in the crowd soon disabused me of that. After a while, people began to heckle him. But he didn't take any notice and eventually put a tape recorder on his window sill. It was playing the May Song. He must have recorded it earlier. A little flicker of alienation.

A cultured voice demanded total silence, so we could hear the bells. We hadn't heard the bells for years, it complained. And wasn't that the tradition? – that everyone waited quietly outside the Golden Lion until they heard the church bells ring, and then we got on with the night singing, as soon as it was actually May Day. Half the crowd muttered and grumbled, and the other half shushed them. Then somebody began to heckle the publican and his wife who'd appeared at a first-floor window. The bloke upstairs displayed his purple backside again, and turned his tape recorder up very loudly.

So we missed the chimes at midnight; but a stern woman, who commanded immediate attention, announced when they had taken place. I liked her immediately because she seemed genuinely hostile to visitors like me, trippers, though she assured us coolly that Padstow was glad to welcome its May guests, provided they didn't get in the way. Her welcome had the formal chill of an Aeroflot stewardess. Then she introduced the night song. It's slower, it's got special words. 'No hollerin', mind. Now I'll give you the key.'

Early to rise tomorrow. All but the most dedicated and the most curious are off to bed, though now the carollers will tour the town. There are special verses for rich men. ('You have a shilling in your pants/And I wish it were mine'), for married women, for young girls. Those who are visited like very much to be visited, have kept awake specially, come down to their doors to listen, provide the leaders with beer. And it must be a fine thing to be sung to in this antique fashion. It must refresh one's sense of home and continuance, even though lewd visitors are taking advantage of the promiscuous dark, the unexpectedness of everything, to neck in the churchyard.

Cool, dark air; a moonless night but fine stars; swishing trees, all very Hardy. The singers invoke the 'merry morning of May' again and again, and it is magic. Really. Even though a man in the crowd mutters to me that there's nothing to keep young people here; everyone stuck in their parlours in front of their tellies all winter; is serving Cornish cream teas to trippers a fit life for a man, I ask you?

We start at the Golden Lion; by 2 a.m. we have circumnavigated the town. When one of the visited plays back his aubade on a tape recorder, somebody sourly mutters that next year only one bloke armed with a tape recorder need make the tour. At the harbour, the hot-dog stand reluctantly puts up its shutters. In the ladies' public lavatory, already pungent and awash, a young girl grimly cleans her teeth. Goodnight.

Refreshed by a brief sleep, the town wakes about seven-thirtyish. Old men are out, decorating the base of the maypole with fresh flowers – furze, bluebells, cowslips so dewy they must have been picked this morning. The maypole is impressive enough to recall its totemic origins, tall as a telegraph pole and stuck all over with paper flowers and ribbons.

Children in maying gear, white shirts and white trousers, run about self-importantly already, wearing the colours of the respective hobby horses, red sashes and neckerchiefs, blue sashes and neckerchiefs. (You can buy them in the gents' outfitters, together with authentic Padstow sailor caps; and many have.) Cafes open, queues form. In the newsagent's a woman snarls: 'Drink and profit, that's all Padstow May Day is. An example of man's inhumanity to man.'

Another resident joins in. She hadn't been able to buy a loaf of bread, and she'd lived in Padstow all her life. Both agreed, while the newsagent sycophantically smirked and nodded, that May Day now was nothing to what it had been. Each lady, essential shopping completed, would presumably return home and sweat out the entire bright, beautiful May Day in a state of siege.

But we, we're waiting for the hobby horse. Drums herald it. Ten o'clock. Here comes the Blue Ribbon Oss, the first out. It starts from the Institute under a bower of green boughs. The road is so crowded, now, so many cameras going, that it can hardly dance properly, its partner, the Teazer, can hardly swing his club.

Nevertheless, it is appalling, magnificent.

Controversy rages amongst folklorists as to which is the most authentic survival – the Blue Ribbon Oss, started up again by a group of soldiers home from the First World War, or the Red Ribbon Oss, which has the support of the establishment of folklore preservationists. They both look alike anyway, but for the colours of the teams, the factional in-fighting, a few blue stripes on the Blue Oss and his beard of wool. Both are of vast antiquity.

The Padstow hobby horses, or Osses, are shining black monsters, grotesque, alarming, snapping, leaping, magic, beastly anachronisms. The Osses are, or were, a fertility symbol, a rain charm, a mark of death and resurrection, the summer-bringer, and now the glad harbinger of the tourist season to a region that would relapse altogether into more than Sicilian poverty without the extra revenue from the sale of cream teas, full-cream fudge, and Cornish-clotted-cream-sent-to-any-address-in-Britain-by-first-class-post.

Oss is built on an elm hoop, 5 feet 9 inches in diameter and 18 feet round. Over this foundation is stretched a gown of sailcloth, suspended from webbing braces on the shoulders of the dancer. On his head, the dancer wears a conical cap topped with a tuft of horsehair. Over his face is a mask of such striking design its origin is said to be African. In the nineteenth century, ships from Padstow went all over the world, the days when the maypole was a mast from the shipyard. If nobody did bring the mask back from West Africa, or Borneo, or Java, then God knows where it comes from. A ferocious red, black and white witch-doctor's mask, with red eyes.

The elm hoop boasts a vestigial horse's head and tail at either end. The entire apparatus weighs about 100 lb. The dancer makes several tours of the town, each tour lasting two and a half to three hours. It is tough work.

His partner, the Teazer, dances backwards before his spirited adversary. The marching band of melodeons, drums, accordions, plays the May Song. The teams march before and behind, arms linked, singing. Teazer, an elegant high-stepper, baits Oss with his patently phallic club; Oss makes ferocious darts and sallies at him, at the crowd. Once young married women pursued him, and young unmarried women fled him. If you were pulled under his skirts and danced with him, that was good luck. Which meant, you got pregnant. Great.

Sometimes Oss will die. He sinks down, a hush falls. Teazer

strikes Oss's frame with his club. We change to the second tune, a bizarre dirge about the whereabouts of King George. Who is 'out in his long boat. All on the salt sea-o!' Time has tampered with whatever it once meant, to make luminous nonsense of it:

> Up flies the kite
> Down falls the lark-o,
> Aunt Ursula Birdwood she had an old ewe
> And it died in her own park-o.

The festival walks a delicate tightrope between authentic bucolic rumbustuousness and squalid riot, and some bugger is always trying to film it, which the Blue Team, especially, can hardly bear, such are the tensions between local pride and local exclusivity and the desire not to be relegated into an exhibit in a living museum.

Mid-afternoon on May Day; a certain exhaustion, intimations of tomorrow's hangovers. Numerous coppers, hovering. More and more trippers. You can easily tell the trippers from the natives; the natives are wearing their best clothes. An embarrassing clown person in red nose, fright wig, check pants, silver boots, performs an inscrutable mime in front of the fish bar on the quay; hopeless! He's been upstaged by too much real street theatre. His private fantasy that he is enriching events (though nobody stops to watch him) adds a little estrangement to the scene; and now the teeny-drunks are reeling about. In an upper window of a house with a fine view of the sea, an old lady established herself early this morning and has jabbered at the crowds all day in a comminatory fashion. A pair of large dogs, succumbed to the festive spirit, fuck boisterously directly in the path of the Red Team; here they come again.

Shall we stay for the evening dance around the maypole? Somebody warns me there was a bit of fighting, last year. A crash of glass decides it; probably the newsagent's window. A head emerges from upstairs, gesticulating furiously, and two of the lurking coppers close in on a youth and lead him away. We pick our way over the puke and empty beer bottles to the car. Five miles outside Padstow it starts to pour with rain.

29 May 1975

27
The gambling class

Paul Harrison

On a cold and drizzly afternoon, the Mere bingo hall, Breckfield, stands out against the ruins of Liverpool redevelopment. The sky-blue paint crumbles off its stucco façade, crowned with crossed pairs of banjoes and fiddles in relief. At two o'clock a small pensioner, almost drowned in a long dark overcoat and flat grey cap, appears from inside, trots up and down, then parks himself in the glass booth under a bare light bulb and turns face forward the sign '10p admission'.

At 2.14 p.m. the first customer climbs up the mildewed steps: a woman in her forties, in a short navy skirt, mauve blazer, brown thigh boots and a blonde rinse. Another, in her late fifties, as down-at-heel as the first was smart, with a woolly bonnet pulled down over her forehead, a large and lumpy blue overcoat, and flat shoes. Then a girl about 20, with long black hair, suede coat with a fur collar, and white shoes. The habituees trickle in, around 20 of them; most of them in their fifties, a few dishier ones in their twenties; no one at all in between. A few quick pulls on the one-armed bandit, then they settle down in the dreamland decor, all mirrors and baubles and purple velvet, ready for the magic numbers to be read out.

Round the corner at the Mercury betting shop, movement continues throughout the afternoon, in and out through the frosted glass doors: a little old man about 60, unshaven and slightly tipsy; a young beau of 25 dressed in the latest continental gear, with styled hair; a bulky man of 50-odd with a heavy donkey jacket, muddy boots, and a khaki sandwich bag.

Liverpool is a cynosure of British working-class gambling. It has one of the highest densities of betting shops – six for every 10,000 population (Great Yarmouth tops the league with 7.24 shops per 10,000 people). It is the home of the two biggest pools promoters, Littlewoods and Vernons, who between them have 90 per cent of the turnover. It is also the place where Ernie mysteriously generates the random numbers for premium bonds.

Not a great deal is known generally about gambling and the working class. The global figures for spending on gambling indicate a prodigious national investment of time, money and nerves: a turnover of £2,700 million in the United Kingdom in 1973 – roughly on a par with the other vices, alcohol and tobacco, though in the case of gambling nearly 60 per cent of the spending goes back to the gambler in the form of winnings. The Churches Council on Gambling estimates that the real cost of gambling in 1973 was £441 million. But that does not include incidental costs like postage, postal order fees and travel. The Family Expenditure Survey for 1973 estimates that the average household spends 31p per week on betting – that is, payments less winnings. Betting on horses and dogs leads, with a turnover of £1,655 million, most of that spent off the course in Britain's 14,000 betting shops. Casinos (a middle-class mania) and fruit machines come next, with £300 million and £285 million spent in 1973. Pools and bingo are almost neck and neck – with £215 million and £210 million respectively. The Gaming Board has made its own survey of bingo. It estimates that 5½ to 6½ million people, 84 per cent of them women, play bingo regularly in the 1,813 licensed clubs – half a million every day.

All the surveys that have been made agree that around half the adult population takes part in some form of gambling – 60 per cent of the men and 40 per cent of the women. The latest survey, by Mintel, shows that the biggest gamblers are between 25 and 54 – 60 per cent of this age group gamble. Activity tails off then – only 50 per cent of 55–64-year-olds gamble (because they have finally learned that gambling doesn't pay?) and only 26 per cent of the over-65s (because they have no money?). Gambling increases as you go down the class scale, except among the very poorest. Over 40 per cent of the middle and upper-middle class (the ABs) gamble, against 56 per cent of the lower-middle class (the Cs) and

63 per cent of the semi-skilled working class (the Ds). But the unskilled workers (the Es) are least likely of all to gamble – only 29 per cent say they gamble.

Breckfield, the part of Liverpool I chose to look at, is one of those rare animals today, a close-knit working-class community that has escaped dispersal to the four winds by demolition – but only just. The heart of the area is shaped like a flatiron, with 10,000 or 15,000 people in a quarter of a square mile. Clearance has made a wasteland reaching right up to one of the long sides of the flatiron. Council estates are shooting up in a sea of mud, with corrugated iron fences that warn: 'Guard dogs loose.' Breckfield itself was, at one point, on someone's list for clearance. But now rehabilitation is the catchword instead of demolition, Breckfield is spared. The whole perimeter of the flatiron is lined with small shops, hundreds of them, dingy and battered, wire netting over the windows to protect them against soccer vandals going to the nearby Liverpool ground. (Spion Kop towers over Breckfield like a brontosaurus.) The 'Snug' cafe advertises its speciality – saus- age sandwiches. And Thomas Morris and Sons, pawnbrokers, offer 'Bargains in forfeited pledges', a windowful of gold wed- ding and engagement rings, memories in hock to keep the wolf or the bailiff from the door. The butcher displays meats to suit small budgets – cooked hearts, pork brawn, pigs' bellies and salt neck. More to our point, no one has far to walk for gambling. There are ten betting shops spaced out round the flatiron, and two bingo halls.

I spoke to a couple of dozen Breckfielders about what gambling they did. Three out of five gambled at least once a week – half of the women and two-thirds of the men. Only three gambled more than once a week. People's incomes varied from a £10 a week pensioner to a £4,000 a year supermarket manager with a working wife. In most cases, they spent less than £1 a week on gambling. Ten spent nothing at all, five up to 50p, five from 50p to £1, four more than £1. The biggest spender a 28-year-old single truck driver on £45 a week, staked £8.25 a week on betting and pools, though often getting a good deal of this back in winnings.

More interesting than the crude figures were people's attitudes and habits, in gambling or abstaining. I only met one committed opponent of any and all gambling – Thomas Finley, a waspish little pensioner with a hearing aid and staring eyes, who told me he thought gamblers were evil and foolish: 'I'm a Christian,' he said, 'and the tenth commandment says thou shalt not covet thy neighbour's goods. Gambling is coveting your ,neighbour's goods.' Most of the seven pensioners I talked to spent nothing or very little on gambling. William Hesketh, aged 70, finally absorbed the lesson that gambling didn't pay only ten years ago, after a lifetime of it. 'I gave up the pools in disgust when I won first divi, and it was only £3.50.' Even when he was betting regularly, there was a streak of rationalism in his bets. He would always back the first or second favourites in races – 'follow the money.' But the commonest reason the pensioners gave for not betting was poverty and thrift.

Edgar Leybourne, aged 71, a former chargehand in building maintenance told me: 'I've always had to work too hard to throw it away like that.' Even so, he and his wife Mary put 22½p a week on the pools. 'We just live in hope,' he said. 'It's a little interest at the end of the week,' said Mary. Although a participant, Edgar was cynical and suspicious of the promoters, almost as if he thought the whole thing was a fiddle: 'The bookies always win in the end. They're in it for the profit. I don't know anybody at all who's had a big win. That's the funny part of this pools business: it's all people out of town who win it, so you can't go and check up if it's true.'

Leybourne took the trouble to follow the clubs' form through the sports news, and fill in the draws on a skilled assessment of their probability. In fact, this approach was rare. Most people trusted to various forms of luck, rather than judgment. I caught Olive Sutton at her front door off to the afternoon shift at the tobacco factory, with a coat slung over her overalls, and a headscarf on. She fills in the same numbers every week on the pools. They were given to her by an astrologer who cast her horoscope. She earns a salary of £20 a week part-time, and uses 'her own money' for the 45p stake. 'I'd never use the housekeeping.' Like at least half the people I spoke to, when I asked her if she wanted a big win, she said she wouldn't know what to do with it. She just wanted 'a couple of thousand, to help the family out'; and she would make a big donation to a charity for spina bifida, because she herself had had a spina bifida baby that died. She was one of the few people who had any premium bonds – £50 worth. 'But we've never won a louse on one.'

The principal motive for doing the pools was, of course, the hope of winning: it wasn't just a way to pass or kill time, or meet people. This was also the case, I found, even with bingo, where the winnings are usually much smaller (though they can go up to £400 on the 'flyer', when several clubs are joining in the same game). But social contact is a more frequent motive here than with the other major forms of gambling. Elsie Snell told me she goes for the company, because 'if you're working you've got to have your bit of pleasure'. She is a widow of 58, and her four children have left home. She earns £14 a week (after tax) as a school cleaner, and spends £1 on bingo, which is about average for these people. 'I used to do spot-the-ball, too. But it's useless, you never win. You've got to be lucky to win and I'm not. Once I won £5 at bingo, and I was so excited I had a lump in my throat and I couldn't shout. Somebody else shouted before me and got the prize instead.'

Pools is an activity done in the quiet of your own living room, without the stimulation of other bettors in a gambling frenzy all about you. Combined with the fact that wins are so uncommon that the gambler gets no food for his obsession, this must be why it's rare to find a pools fanatic. Bingo and betting, for most of their participants, are a harmless diversion. But you get a fair number who have made them their principal hobby, and a very small number who have chosen them as their path to destruction. Elsie Snell has tales of the bingo maniacs. 'Some women buy six books a time and get through £10 a week. The one-arm bandits are worse than the bingo. I've seen a woman win £9, then put it all into the one-armed bandit. Some women take their babies to bingo, they have their baby on one arm and mark the book with the other. And there are one or two who leave their little kids at home, and can't pay the rent, and get up to their eyeballs in debt. There was one woman who was selling the clothes off her bed outside the hall, to get money to play. Her husband knocked hell out of her.'

Betting on horses is even more likely to become an obsession in Breckfield, and it can start at an early age. I met three addicts outside the Mercury betting shop. Anthony Nelson, a likeable lout in his late teens with long blond hair, started betting when he was 11, getting older boys to place the bets for him and watching the races on television. His eight brothers, his two sisters and both his parents all gamble. He is unemployed, and has only had one job since he left school – as a beer delivery boy. Betting fills up his day now: 'I get up at twelve o'clock and throw some money in my pocket and get down to the betting shop. I stay there till five, every day. That's all I live for, the horses. I try my luck on the first race, and if that goes down I try my luck on the second, and if that goes down I leave it. If I have a good win I say to me Ma, here's a couple of quid. If you're winning, you think, it's better than working, this. But when you lose, you say, I'd rather get a job. Basically I'd like another job. But I'd still want to do my betting.'

Ronald Harrison is married with three kids, and is also out of work, on £24.75 unemployment benefit. He gets £5 a week pocket money from his wife and stakes it all on the horses. When working as a general labourer, he has on many occasions gambled and lost his whole week's wages. 'Me and my wife have had murder over my gambling.' But though unemployment gives him far more time for betting, he now has to restrict himself to his £5 a week, of which he usually wins back about £3.

Kathleen Harper's husband died when she was 38, and she had eight children to bring up on her own: 'I've lost half my life,' she says. 'Now I'm 60, I might as well enjoy the last stretch.' She was one of the biggest gamblers I met: £5 a week on horses, 61½p on the pools, £1 on bingo and 15p a week on a charity draw. 'It was my son who started me off. He gave me three shillings and said put this on for me, and I'd never been in a betting shop in my life. He won £6. I thought, I must try this. It's a dead loss really like; but it just gets a grip on you. It's something to look at. But I've always got the food in. I've never left them short of a good dinner.' Kathleen bets for social contact, and even where she hopes to win, it is so she can give things to her family. 'One Easter I didn't have an egg for my grandchildren, then I won £5 and I got them eleven Easter eggs, one each. That's the idea what you do it for, to give it to your family. I often think about winning, but if I did, I'd put it all my kids.'

Few of those I spoke to said social contact was their main motive for gambling. But the betting shop, behind its blacked-out windows, is a meeting place with a ready-made excuse for conversation; the bingo hall, even more so. If you wait outside the Mecca on West Darby Road, where a lot of women from Breckfield go to play their bingo, you can see it's an occasion. They roll up in taxis, in twos, threes and even bigger groups. They tank up at the bar and sit down at their tables and get ready to start. The pools has none of this, though its social content is increased now that a lot of the coupons are taken in by collectors, who get 12½ per cent commission.

Informal betting on who will win the election or the Cup, is an essential part of life, at work and especially at the pub. The one-armed bandit in the Standard pub on Thirlmere Road takes £50 a week. The landlord, Danny Herlihy, is one of the biggest bettors. He has taken a bet of £100 that he couldn't down five pints of lager straight off: he did it in 15 seconds. He bet Davy James, a local solo guitarist, that he couldn't play 1,000 separate notes in a minute, and lost his £50. James crammed in 1,900 notes, electronically measured.

Gambling is a continuum – from total abstinence, to obsessive preoccupation. Those who really damage their own lives and their families through gambling are a very small proportion. Almost everyone I spoke to spent the same fixed amount on gambling each week, and were not so near the breadline that they were sacrificing anything important to do so.

Is gambling associated with a cynical attitude to society in general? I asked people if they thought most wealth in this country was earned by brains, hard work, luck or twisting. No one plumped for luck. Most people felt that their own money was earned by hard work, and other people's – big business, big trade unions, or welfare claimants – by twisting. But there seemed to be no relation between the degree of cynicism and the amount of gambling. Most of my respondents agreed that life was a gamble. In most cases they would quote the example that you could get knocked down in the street. One (a milkman) said it was a gamble whether you got a job you applied for or not. But when I asked if they took any other big risks, if they actually ran their *own* lives as a gamble, the answer was no.

On the other hand the fundamental uncertainty of their lives was apparent. They live more exposed to disaster than the middle classes, and less equipped to cope with it when it arrives. Even in my small sample, I came across two early widows, the woman who'd had a spina bifida child, and three unemployed men. Surprisingly, almost all those I spoke to spontaneously suggested that they were personally unlucky – they saw their habitual loss in gambling as a symptom of a general bad luck. 'I couldn't win an argument,' one woman told me stoically. Gambling is not really, for these people, an attempt to redress the balance of destiny, a small dream of escape, fame or fortune. Only one man (the biggest spender) said he would use his winnings to 'get out of this dump'.

Gambling is an integral part of social life and leisure. Winning the pools is a remote mirage deep in the back of a working man's mind. Winning on horses or bingo just doesn't bring in enough money to make any difference. And when people do win, the money is fed straight back, to buy small comforts or gifts, into their ordinary lives.

20 March 1975

28
A quiet day out at the match

Ian Walker

At half time a black Arsenal fan handed out Young National Front stickers. One lad on the train said he always imagined it was his Mum he was hitting when he was in a Saturday afternoon fight. A middle-class young woman who lived in Hampstead and worked for the civil service said she had been following the team home and away for seven years. The police horses wore plexiglass eyeshields and their riders had blue and white crash helmets. There were a few arrests. But as these excursions go, it was a quiet kind of day.

It had started out at King's Cross station at 8.30 in the morning. Arsenal and Chelsea both had football specials leaving at around the same time so everyone was on their toes, needlessly as it happened. A lot of beer was being drunk, but that was mostly because you're only allowed two cans on the train. Before we can board, Arsenal Travel Club officials, in red armbands, search our bags for booze and weapons.

As we pass Alexandra Palace on our left, two of the six policemen on the train are patrolling the carriages. They stop at a table occupied by two teenagers.

'How old are you son?'

'Fifteen, what about it?'

'I don't want to see you smoking.'

'Why? It's not against the law.'

'Yes it is. You have to be 16.'

The policeman grabs the cigarette out of the boy's mouth, throws it on the floor.

Robert had lit up again by the time I went over to talk to him and his friend Sean, who is 17. They never miss a game.

The previous Wednesday they'd made this same journey, up to Leeds. Sean takes home £30 a week as a trainee machine setter in north London. Robert is still at school, his Mum gives him some money, and 'Sean helps me out'. At £7.50 for the return fare to Leeds, plus £1.50 admission and then spending money, isn't it an expensive loyalty, following Arsenal away? 'A day out, isn't it?' says Robert, as we race through Welwyn Garden City station. 'We like going to different grounds and that; getting out of London.' But doesn't it mean you can't afford to go anywhere during the week? 'We never usually go out anyway during the week, just doss around.'

The amount of trouble you get into, Robert and Sean say, depends on the extent and the vigilance of the police protection: 'When we went to Liverpool, the cops said, "We don't like you Cockneys. We don't like you coming here. Find your own way to the ground." We had to walk past all these pubs with real unfriendly faces in them.' What happened? 'We got chased down the road, didn't we?'

In the next carriage up, John Taylor, apprentice electrician, is sitting on his own because 'me mate broke his leg last week'. A quiet sort of bloke, John doesn't care much for bother, but says that sometimes it's unavoidable. 'The home supporters are always out there waiting for you. The Leeds fans'll be waiting at the station, they were last year.' Last year, John says, Arsenal were winning 1-0 when Leeds had a goal disallowed, 'The stewards opened the gates and let all the Leeds fans in on the Arsenal. Had a big fight.'

The violence only annoys him, 'if there's a good match on: if the match is boring, I don't really care.' What about those headlines describing football fans as thugs and animals. 'They're true,' he says.

John has a skinhead haircut. About nine months ago I was attacked by a skinhead on a 253 bus in Camden Town. To that bloke a fight was just something which happened, and which was fun, when you were drunk. It was a bit like that for the lads from Bethnal Green whom I spoke to in an old-style BR compartment with a sliding door.

I slide it open, explain my business. 'Go on, I'll buy it,' says

Perry Tomlin. This is my invitation to join them. 'We're all mods,' says Perry, jumping up from his seat and running his thumbs under the thin lapels of his Tonik jacket, which is green, changing to bronze as it catches the light. As everyone introduces themselves, Perry prefixes the description with: 'You know, the well-known criminal.'

Perry says he's 15 next week. 'So he's 14,' says Stephen Jenkins who's a trainee chef and is sitting next to Mark Brewer, an apprentice butcher. The lad in the corner of the compartment, dyed blond hair, introduces himself as 'Jamie. This is my firm. Meet the firm.'

His leadership is noisily disputed while Perry tells me Jamie is on the dole. Stephen passes round a black-and-silver pack of Lambert and Butler. Apprentice engineer Terry Walker, wearing a red Fred Perry jumper, refuses a cigarette and opens a window, explaining he's got asthma. 'Against Man U last week we ran into Tottenham. I had to run into a restaurant cos I can't breathe.'

'And I'm the hero,' shouts Perry, leaping up again and beating his chest, Tarzan-style. 'I rescued him.'

'We don't look for trouble,' says Stephen. 'But if there's a ruck we steam in.' They proceed to enumerate, with a touch of pride, injuries received in the cause of Arsenal. 'I got done at Wolves, someone hit me with a bottle.' And 'I got done bad at Liverpool, broken nose.' And so on.

The train pulls in at Peterborough. A Leeds fan, in the baggy trousers that disappeared from London's boutiques over a year ago, is standing on the platform. Perry is immediately up at the window, out of which he is singing, 'Where *did*, where *did*, where *did* you get those clothes?'

'Leave it out. He's twice your size,' says Jamie languidly from the corner. A policeman strolls up, 'C'mon lads, take your seats. Don't stir the natives up.'

Clichés about dead-end jobs and Saturday afternoon glamour don't seem very apt when you're rolling up north on a train, everyone sitting around reading the *Sun*, playing cards, or gazing out of the window. But glamour, and power, is what it is all about. One day a week to see everyone running scared on the streets at the sight of you in this singing chanting wild bunch, 'Yeah, I follow Arsenal. Wanna make something of it, mate?'

Visiting supporters, if the balance of forces if favourable, aim to 'take' the end of the ground occupied by the mass of singing and chanting (young) home support. This is now the subject of conversation: 'At Brighton we had everything and we killed 'em. Everywhere you looked was Arsenal.' But grins turn to grimaces when they recall how, every year for years now, Tottenham have taken the North Bank at Highbury.

'Tottenham and Arsenal are worst rivals,' they explain. 'Whenever there's a local derby there's a fight.' They call Tottenham fans 'yids' because, according to Terry, 'years ago all their directors were Jewish.' And what do Tottenham call the Arsenal fans? 'Bubble and squeaks, meaning Greeks, but we ain't,' says Perry. 'We have a laugh, take the mickey. We don't mind a ruck, if there's a lot with us, know what I mean?'

When the balance of forces is unfavourable, it's less fun. Jamie says: 'At Everton last year we had to go up into the seats, there was only 50 of us. We had to leave ten minutes after half time. We was gonna get battered, we couldn't handle it.'

Arsenal's real hard cases don't travel by train. Mostly, they've been kicked out of the Travel Club for fighting, so they charter their own buses. 'The three leaders are Denton, Legsy and Jenkins. They've all got firms [gangs] behind them. They're hard little bastards. Two hundred against 20,000 and they'll still steam in. You can't get on the bus if you're gonna run.'

There has been a lot of talk of violence and Mark, the trainee butcher, tries to put things in perspective: 'People think we're mad. But we only go because we love football.'

'You might as well have a laugh before you're an old closet. Enjoy yourself while you're still young. Support your team,' says Perry, who at five foot nothing must live more on his wits than his fists.

'All I really work for is that,' says Terry, 'and to keep me Mum, buy clothes.' Perry agrees, saying, 'We don't really know what to do on a Saturday when there's no football. We just sit around the flats.' Apart from Terry, who now lives in Stoke Newington, these boys were all born and bred in Bethnal Green. Perry asks if I've heard of Bethnal Green and I nod. 'Hardest going. They're ruckers,' he says.

'Funny thing, Violence. . . .' says Stephen, and I interrupt him to ask what I'd asked John Taylor, how he feels about tabloid headlines describing fans as no better than animals. 'You feel proud,' he replies. 'You think it's really good.' The others nod.

But these boys are sharp, they've got some idea of PR, too. It's time to put me straight, time to tell me they are not obsessed with violence, and that they do understand why they grew up as they did. Stephen here becomes the spokesman:

'We are a load of thugs, but you're brought up in Bethnal Green. You're just walking down the street, some geezer hits you and it's a fight. You learn when you're young how to look after yourself. . . . Also, when you're a little kid and come home saying you've been beaten up, all our Mums say, "Well, hit 'em back. Stand up for yourself."'

Jamie picks up the story: 'You got your old lady nagging you all fucking week and you can't do nothing about it. It just builds up and builds up, until it's Saturday and you get out there. . . . Bam.' He is standing up, eyes closed, throwing punches into thin air. 'Bam. If I'm clocking someone, I see my old lady there.' Everyone falls silent for two seconds, respectful of that confession, and not knowing quite how to follow it. Until Jamie sits down again, laughs, so everyone can laugh.

These lads used to be skinheads before the present mod revival, which Terry says is 'just another trend', though one he'll follow. I mention Sham '69, the now defunct skinheads' band, whose farewell concert was broken up by the fascist British Movement. I then find out they've all been on National Front marches, 'Well mainly on Anti-Nazi League things, running round the outside, chanting that.'

('It's just another craze,' says Terry, wearily.)

They've also all been to Rock Against Racism carnivals. 'Oh, yeah, I went to Vicky Park,' says Perry. 'Everyone went for the music anyway.' I say I don't like racists and they look embarrassed, not belligerent. 'We know some coloured geezers,' says Stephen. 'They're all right. All except Pakis.'

'What's wrong with Pakis? Don't cause any trouble, do they?' demands Jamie.

This gets nowhere, and I'm wondering if their families are National Front? Stephen says his aunt wasn't 'till she got robbed by blacks. But my Mum isn't NF, there couldn't be a bigger socialist going.'

'My Mum said she was going to vote National Front, but she voted Liberal,' says Terry smiling at the absurdity of it all.

The train stops at Doncaster station, where there are large
numbers of Leeds fans. Perry, safe in the knowledge no one is
getting on or off, is again yelling sartorial insults out of the
window.

Jane, the posh-sounding young woman who lives in Hampstead and works for the civil service, is sitting right at the back of
the train with her two girl friends: Julie Blay who's a sorter at the
post office and Lynn Davis, a student of photography. Lynn's
Dad used to play for Arsenal Reserves in the 1950s. She is wearing
the tight blue jeans and black suede spiked heels she'll be in
tonight when she meets her boyfriend down the pub. 'Men don't
like girls who know more about football than themselves,' she
says. 'It insults their vanity.'

These three, aged between 18 and 21, have all been travelling
away with Arsenal for six or seven years. 'We don't get as much
hassle as the guys,' says Julie. 'It's verbal abuse, but we just
ignore it.' She goes on to say that at the last away game she picked
up three sets of darts. *'All thrown from the seats,'* she emphasises.
'They say all the trouble starts from the terraces. But that's just
not true.'

The trouble is, in Julie's view, exaggerated by the press and
often provoked by the police. 'They enjoy a good fight as much as
anyone else. Also, you've spoilt their Saturday afternoon.
They're bloody well going to spoil yours.'

Feminists, I'm saying, regard football as a macho ritual, which
. . . 'Most feminists are just frustrated old bags,' interrupts Lynn.
The others laugh in agreement. The train is pulling into Leeds
station.

A corridor of policemen make it plain where we have to walk.
At the end of the corridor is a steel gate behind which we wait
while we are searched again for weapons. Arsenal FC enamel
badges are regarded as potential weapons. One middle-aged
Scotsman, who has the entire Arsenal team tattooed on his chest,
doesn't think much of this. 'It's a fucking disgrace when you have
to take your badges off.' Told to get our 21 pences ready, we're
finally driven off in double-deckers, three policemen to each
bus.

Outside the ground a posse of riot police, on horseback,
wearing blue and white crash helmets, are by the sign which has
'Entrance for Visiting Supporters' painted in white. But it's only

12.30, kick-off is not till 3, so we all queue up for bright-red frankfurters and plastic cups of almost milkless tea. This comes to 50p.

Over the road from the entrance, six National Front posters are stuck on an empty redbrick end-terrace. Fifty yards down the street, a billboard says 'Wisdom. The Choice Is Yours' under a photograph of false teeth in a glass. Most of the Leeds fans haven't arrived yet, but one struts past. On his white T-shirt is written in blue capitals: YORKSHIRE REPUBLICAN ARMY.

The gates open at 1 p.m. We pay £1.50 and there's one hour of sitting around smoking, playing cards, another of swapping chanted abuse with Leeds supporters, from whom we are separated on all sides by blue steel bars.

'Arsenal, where are you?' sing Leeds. There's still only the 200 or so of us who came by train. But Denton and his firm's arrival is theatrically timed, five minutes before kick-off. Denton himself leads the charge of 100 crop-haired teenagers on to the terraces and there's pandemonium as they try to scale the barriers. Police move in, fists swing. The disturbance only lasts two minutes, but long enough for Stephen Jenkins to now point dolefully at a swollen red eye which will in time be black. A couple of Arsenal fans are escorted from the ground.

'Are we all settled in now?' asks one cop, through his teeth.

'Aye, I'm reet fine, lad. How are you?' replies the Arsenal fan. It is a poor attempt at the Yorkshire accent.

'I'm fine. Let's keep it that way,' says the policeman, leaning over to grab the fan's arm. The rest of the exchange is drowned out in a roar signifying the game's start.

An electronic scoreboard instructs us to 'Give Jimmy Hill a wave. We're on *Match of the Day*.' Leeds sing 'Jimmy Hill's a wanker.' Arsenal disagree. And the dialogue continues throughout the game.

Taunts are as much about the relative merits and demerits of Yorkshire and London as they are about the two teams' past glories and humiliations. Leeds chant, 'York-shire.' Arsenal sing, 'Maybe it's because I'm a Londoner.' Both sets of supporters mimic the other's accent. Arsenal assert that moral superiority which they feel comes from travelling to away games, being 'real supporters'. 'Do you ever go away?' they demand. Ignoring this, Leeds instead bring up the shameful defeat of the last few seasons. 'Tottenham, North Bank, Easy, easy.' Which gets the lame retort, 'Ea-aye-addio, we won the cup.' Repeat.

Leeds score a goal just before half time and their fans sing 'one nil' to the tune of *Amazing Grace*.

At half time, in the crush for lukewarm pies and hot Oxo, Denton is distributing Young National Front stickers. Denton is black. Members of his firm dutifully stick these messages about white youth and repatriation to their jackets. One black youth has two 'Repatriation, Not Immigration' stickers, one 'Fight Communism' and one 'White Youth Before Immigrants' sticker, all affixed to the front of his anorak. The same black youth was, some two hours later, arrested at Leeds station.

Denton, some say, is a member of this organisation, which seeks to eliminate humans of his colour from the motherland. I don't believe it. I couldn't get near enough to speak to him, but he is either playing some kind of sick joke on himself, or else the joke is on his disciples ('These dummies'll take NF stickers off a black?'). The remaining possibility is that he's taken the goal of winning white acceptance to its ultimate, logical, and absurd, conclusion.

Football crowds goad black players in two main ways. One is to chant 'National Front', the other is to ape the grunt of apes. Both taunts came from the Leeds fans terraces after half time, when the Leeds fans saw that Denton was some kind of leader.

Arsenal's response was first to chant 'National Front' back at Leeds, with Denton and the other half dozen blacks joining in, then to group round their leader, pointing and singing, 'We got the hardest nigger in the land.' Denton meanwhile is doing a passable imitation of the dance the men in the *Black and White Minstrel Show* used to do – you know, the way they opened their mouths, stretched back their heads and shivered splayed-out palms?

I ask the Bethnal Green contingent about Denton's real political preferences, but they just shrugged and laughed. For them, I suppose, black members of the NF are no more, no less, bizarre than friends from the same block of flats fighting each other on Saturdays if they happen to follow different teams.

Leeds United v. Arsenal ended in a 1-1 draw. A lot of us missed the Arsenal goal because it was just after half time and we were still in the pie queue.

The only time the chanting had got really venomous was when Arsenal were awarded a penalty. 'You're gonna get your fucking heads kicked in,' we were told, at high volume, a few thousand index fingers pecking in our direction. Just as well the penalty was missed. A home defeat brings violent revenge. As it was, Leeds fans couldn't be bothered hanging around outside until the lock-up period was over: visiting supporters are confined to the ground till most of the home crowd have dispersed.

When our gates finally did open, police herded us back on to the buses, back into the same walled-off section of the station we'd been kept in on the way up, until the train was ready to leave platform 12.

Once on the moving train I thought we were safe. This, apparently, was not the case. A steward came round telling us to draw the curtains (it was now a beautiful late summer's late afternoon), just in case any bricks were aimed at the windows.

Conversation turned to the possibility of clashing with Chelsea at King's Cross. We were due back at 8.45 p.m., but our train was late. Chelsea's was due back at 9.15 and there was no telling whether they were on time. 'They've come all the way down from Newcastle, they'll be half pissed and they lost too. They'll be just in the mood for some aggravation,' said a tattooed veteran of these excursions.

This man, probably in his mid-thirties, then went on to recount adventures he and his mate had in Amsterdam, when Arsenal played Ajax. Everyone showed polite interest.

Most of the train were either asleep, trying to sleep, or playing cards. Stubble being burned on the fields outside Peterborough looked dramatic in the dusk; beautiful if you like that kind of thing. The man with the tattooed arms was now telling another anecdote: a mate of his had acquired a square yard of the Highbury turf after an offer in the local paper. This was a few years back, when the old pitch was taken up to build an under-ground heating system as protection against snow and ice. This man's mate had given the square yard pride of place in his garden, in the middle of the flowerbed and away from the rest of the lawn. Even the man with the tattoos thought this was going a bit far, especially as the square, he told us, was now faded and bare.

Chelsea were nowhere in sight at King's Cross. Just as well for the lads from Bethnal Green: they had a party to go to. The three girls rushed off to their dates. The man with the tattooed arms reckoned he could go and get an Indian takeaway and still be home in time for *Match of the Day*. One more Saturday night.

13 September 1979

29
The Triple-X boys

Paul Willis

Bill-the-Boot, Sammy, Slim Jim and Bob, the Triple-X motorbike boys, never wore helmets and goggles. These destroyed the excitement of wind rushing into the face, and the loud exhaust beat thumping the ears. The point of fast driving was the experience, not the fact, of speed. They despised sports cars, though these can go as fast as motorbikes. On a bike, high-speed riding is an extremely physical experience. The whole body is blown backwards. (At the Triple-X club, the boys would often tell one another: 'I was nearly blown off.') And when even a slight bend is taken at high speed, the machine and the driver need to go over at quite an angle in order to compensate for the centrifugal force. The experienced driver becomes part of the bike and intuitively feels the correct balancing at high speeds. If there is anything wrong, he will say it is the motorbike's fault.

The dangers and the excitement of bodily wind pressure exist, of course, for the conventional motorcyclist, too. But he is partly removed from the rawness of the experience; he is contained and sealed by his gear. He makes decisions, and controls the motorcycle, at one remove from the direct experiences which made the control necessary. His clothing is as streamlined and smooth as possible, to prevent unnecessary drag.

For Slim Jim or Bill-the-Boot the experience is very different. The equivalent of gale-force wind is tearing into the living flesh. Eyes are forced into a slit and water profusely; the mouth is dragged back into a snarl; and it is extremely difficult to keep the mouth closed. They make no attempt to minimise the drag effect of the wind. Jackets are partly open and are not buttoned down around the throat; belts are not worn; there's nothing to keep the jacket close to the skin; trousers are not tucked away in boots and socks; and there is nothing at all to prevent the wind from tunnelling up their sleeves.

There was one boy in the group at this Birmingham club – Percy – who rode conventionally. But the rest, for example, preferred large cattle-horn handlebars. This meant sitting upright, hands and arms level with the shoulders. This increases drag, and ironically also limits the top speed of the bike. But it improves handling ability, and dramatically increases the sensation of speed.

The conventional motorcyclist, who likes speed, lowers the handlebars and puts the footrests further back. His body can lie then virtually flat along the bike and present the minimum surface for wind resistance. Tiny windscreens on the handlebars may protect what little frontal surface area of the rider is visible. The whole outfit negates the effects and characteristics of the motorbike. It is the technological answer to the problems technology has created. Uniformity, anonymity, featurelessness, encircle the rough, rearing, dangerous qualities of the motorcycle.

The Triple-X motorbike boys accepted the bike. Their lack of a helmet allowed their long hair to blow freely back in the wind. This, with their studded and ornamented jackets, and their aggressive style of riding, gave the boys a fearsome look, which amplified the wildness, noise, surprise and intimidation of the motorbike.

The bikes themselves were modified to accentuate this. It was common practice to remove the baffles from the silencer box on the exhaust, in order to allow the exhaust gases from the cylinder to carry their explosion directly into the atmosphere. The effect was sometimes startling. The metal piston, exploding down the metal cylinder and abruptly and inevitably reversing up again, brought its power and impersonal ferocity right out into the vulnerable zone of human sensibilities.

An alleyway led up the side of a church to the coffee bar of the Triple-X. Members often parked their bikes along this narrow passageway. They stood by them, talking, starting and revving their bikes, discussing technical matters or any matters at all. It could be extremely intimidating to walk up this narrow aisle. The noise was often overwhelming. The loud thumping of the engines seemed to promise sudden movement and action – but none came.

Death on the motorbike held a particular awe and even attraction for the motorbike boys. Here is a selection of their comments on this subject.:

BILL-THE-BOOT: I think it's the best way. I'll have a bike until I'm about 35, you know. I think it's the best way to die . . .

BOB: The thing is . . .

BILL-THE-BOOT: Hey, it's me . . . I'd like to go quickly mind you, out like a light, 'bang' . . . fast like about 100 miles an hour . . . hit a car you know . . . smash straight into something.

SAMMY: I'd hate to grow old, I see some old people and I think, fuck, if I was like you I'd go under the first bus.

AUTHOR: Well, why don't you finish yourself off with drugs and die that way?

SAMMY: Oh, bollocks to that, I'd sooner kill myself on the bike any day. Just blash down the road, giving it almighty stick, and fucking that's it. I don't want to know I was going to die, you know what I mean, but if I was going to die I wouldn't mind on a bike – fucking great!

SAMMY: I'd like to die racing down the road, down the bastard, give it almighty stick, give a Jag a go, and then you know, a fucking big lorry comes, 'crunch', that's the end of you . . . nice eh?

This is not a simple 'death wish'. To die through stupidity or obvious incompetence is not the point. Death should only come after physical limits have been pushed to the full, after the body has made massive attempts to control the machine. Death would thus be out of the rider's hands; he could do nothing more to save himself. This explains the fatalism in the way they talked about death on the motorbike. It was not a specific choice to be made with total free will.

At a simple physical level, the group was rough and tough. Many social exchanges were conducted in the form of mock fights, with pushing, mock punches, sharp karate-type blows to the back of the neck. Slim Jim had been a Teddy Boy in earlier years. He used to say that he could never understand why so many people seemed to take objection to him, and why he was so often forced into fighting. It was true of them all that they came to this club, the Triple-X, partly because other clubs, and often public cafes, would not have them. Their style could be described simply as the notion of 'handling oneself' – of moving confidently, in a very physical and very masculine world.

A dwarf used the club regularly. He was much too small to ride a motorbike and he did not wear motorbike gear. Clearly, he was also much too small to be effective in a fight. However, in a crucial sense he could handle himself, and he was undeniably popular in the club, especially with Slim Jim and Bill-the-Boot.

A common form of exchange with the dwarf was again the mock fight. Slim Jim and Bill-the-Boot would go through an elaborate fight routine and suddenly pretend to be overpowered or mortally injured. The dwarf went along with these fictions. He would stick his fists up, adopt the flashy footwork of a professional boxer, and hit his adversary with what was probably all of his strength. The dramatic downfall of his opponent was greeted with puff-chested pride, strutting, and baiting, aggressive shouts, worthy of Muhammed Ali. Thus, although the dwarf lacked physical strength and mastery, he made up for this with the symbolic masculinity and rough 'matiness' of his style.

This masculine style owed nothing to the conventional notion of the healthy masculine life. Where individuals became involved in sport – ordinary organised sport, for example – it was to spoof the whole thing. Rules and conventions were ignored. Old sweaters and jeans were worn, instead of neat sports clothing. This was not due to material or social deprivation, but to a conscious unwillingness to be trapped by convention. These bike boys would not engage in any safe channelling-off of aggressive feelings that might have endangered the normal course of life. For the Triple-X boys, that would have been dishonest. Masculinity and aggression were mixed in with normal life.

Their attitude to music at the club matched their lifestyle. The quality the boys universally disliked in music was slowness and dreariness. The quality they prized was fastness and clarity of beat. They preferred singles to LPs: singles were more responsive to the listener. If you disliked a particular record, at least it only lasted for two and a half minutes. And to play an LP was also to be committed to someone else's ordering of the music. LPs are more popular with an audience which is prepared to sit and listen for a considerable period, and with a certain extension of trust, so that unknown material can be appreciated and evaluated. Approximately since the Beatles' *Sergeant Pepper*, 'progressive' groups particularly have tried to produce LPs imaginatively conceived as units which are meant to be taken as a whole at one sitting. The Triple-X boys are not like this. They are usually moving about, engaged in other activities. They respond to music only when it is not 'boring'. Their preference for singles is so overwhelming that the absence of a single version of a song is invariably held as being *prima facie* evidence of its inferiority:

BOB: The Stones are, well okay, it's not as good as Chuck Berry's then. Have you heard Chuck Berry's?

SAMMY: Yeah, but it's only an LP, it ain't on a single.

There seems to be an integral connection between rock music and riding fast:

BOB: It helps like, the sound of the engine . . . try and get a beat in my head, and get the beat in my blood, and get on my bike and go.

SAMMY: If I hear a record, a real good record, I just fucking wack it open, you know. I just want to wack it open.

BOB: You can hear the beat in your head don't you . . . you go with the beat don't you . . . I usually find myself doing this all of a sudden [moving head up and down], with my feet tapping on the gear or something stupid like that. . . . Once you get the beat in your head, you really go, you start going.

SAMMY: Yes, the beat of the motorbike, the beat in your head, you want to beat the traffic. . . . The more the engine roars, the more I have to give it, and I think you bastards.

BILL-THE-BOOT: Once I've heard a record, I can't get it off my mind, walking or on the bus, humming it, or singing it you know. I think that's in your head . . . you know . . . if you were on a motorbike, it'd drive you mad that would, it's all in my head, you're bombing down the road.

It isn't just that the music or the bike reflect or parallel the boys' own feelings. The music and the bike have become *part* of their feelings. Those feelings could not exist without the music and the bike. The powerful rhythm of the music, along with the fierce throb of the bike, *became* their power and masculinity, their confidence and their aggression.

The music gave the coffee bar in the Triple-X club its final stamp of authenticity, as a real motorbike cafe. The music purged it of alien elements. Visitors found the full, bustling, loud room unnerving and were glad to get out. The boys' behaviour was at its most spontaneous, open and natural in the coffee bar. The loud, strident music symbolised and generated all the important values – movement, noise, confidence. The very air was fuller and more friendly to breathe. Other 'adventures' always ended up here. It was a sort of home.

29 March 1973

30
Soccer's tribal wars

Paul Harrison

Cardiff City versus Manchester United: the match in Cardiff last Saturday was billed in advance as the biggest bloodbath of the season. United fans were notorious; reputedly the toughest mob in the country. Cardiff rowdies had run amok a week earlier in Bristol, smashing windows and knocking down old women. Most dailies had run stories about expectations of violence – the *Daily Mail*'s headline was 'The street of fear'.

The day began with a bad omen: an ageing fan collapsed and died in the queue for stand tickets. Early arrivals among the Manchester supporters charged up St Mary's Street, howling, 'We're the best-behaved supporters in the world', while shoppers scuttled out of the way like geese.

Apart from a few such minor incidents, police preparations seemed to have paid off. There was no trouble on the supporters' special from Manchester. Arriving fans were pushed down a separate exit, lined up with their hands against the wall, and frisked. Outside, a solid wall of police and dogs was funnelling the fans away from the centre, over the river Taff, and straight down Ninian Park Road, a mile or so long, with a thin blue line stretched along it, one policeman every 25 yards. A few windows were barricaded, and one family – Mam in curlers and Gran with no teeth – were outside their house to defend it with their Alsatian. But there was no trouble yet.

At the ground, precautions were even more thorough. Fans from the opposing sides were filtered into two separate entrances. The terraces, Grange End behind the goal for Cardiff, and Bob-bank for United, were separated by an 8-foot metal fence, with police keeping a clear no-man's-land 30 feet on either side. And on the way out, the two crowds were to be channelled along two separated routes. Police planning looked foolproof.

But the chanting started more than an hour before kick-off. At about 2.15, someone from the Cardiff side threw the first stone, then the bricks started flying: if they couldn't get at each other on land, then they could always fight a missile war, and there was plenty of ammo flying around: the workmen who put the fence in had not swept up the chunks of broken concrete around the supports. Swathes opened up in the crowds on either side as they saw the brickbats coming. I saw three people hit in the face, one above the eye, one in the ear, one on the nose, blood streaming down them. Great cheers went up when a hit was scored, or when the police dragged someone out on the opposite side. Equally, when these things happened to their own side, you could see lads with their faces screwed up in grimaces of anger and indignation.

Incidents of especial cowardice whipped up the fury further. Cardiff fans had sneaked round into the Bob-bank toilet and were waylaying innocent United fans as they relieved themselves. From the same toilet a massive saw-toothed disc of concrete curved up into the air before ploughing down into the Grange End Cardiff mob.

Things quietened down when the match started, though only imperceptibly. About a third of the Manchester supporters and a quarter of Cardiff went on chanting and singing, hardly noticing what was happening on the pitch. If you might get hit in the side of the head with half a brick, you couldn't afford to take your eyes off the air. The furore lasted for an hour and a half: by half-time, it was far more muted.

After the game, on their separate route to the station, a few United rowdies, cheated of their scrap with Cardiff, put in around 30 windows and beat up the few householders who were brave or foolhardy enough to try and stop them. Police who had lined the route before the match were nowhere to be seen. At the railway station, police shut the entrance gates after the main mass of United supporters ('reds') had gone through. A couple of hundred reds found themselves locked out in Central Square, as

Cardiff City fans massed and began taunting them, and there were a few violent skirmishes.

The police net, at the end of the day, was seen to be full of great ragged holes, though they arrested nearly 60 people. Dozens of boys had worse wounds from stones than they would have had from boots, and in their frenetic concentration on keeping the fans apart, the police had left unprotected the residents along the ground-to-station route.

It was an astonishing spectacle, and for an unfamiliar observer it was as ritual, as incomprehensibly alien, as stone-age war in New Guinea. After conversations snatched with dozens of fans while dodging the missiles, I find none of the conventional explanations adequate, except as factors in a much more complex equation. The state of the game – though it may have been at the origin of football hooliganism in the late 1960s – doesn't seem to play a part any more. Of course, violence on the pitch condones violence among fans, and the gradual departure of the working-class family man for the TV in his own lounge has left the terraces with no sobering influences.

There is an element of truth in the boredom/deprivation explanation. Most of the committed rowdies I met at the match on Saturday came from just a few areas. In Cardiff, from Canton and Grangetown, rows of terraced houses with few open spaces, and from Llanrumney, a massive council estate with an appalling record of vandalism. Yet I found few from the most deprived parts of Cardiff – from the mostly coloured Butetown, or from crumbling Splott, planning-blighted, choked with fumes from the steelworks. Most of the Manchester fans I spoke to came from Salford rather than Moss Side.

For the youngsters I spoke to, the match is a bright spot in a week of routine work or school – and petty quibbles from parents, since most of them, aged between 12 and 20, still live at home. There were painters and decorators, ice cream salesmen, van-boys, bank messengers, apprentice carpenters, labourers, slaughtermen, and a fair number of schoolboys. Wages ranged from £15 to £40 a week. Supporting is an expensive hobby especially for the thousands of United fans from outside Manchester who have to travel even for the home matches. Most of those I asked spent £5 or more a week on football – fares, scarves, badges, meals, drink – £100 or £200 in a season. Not a pastime for the newly or nearly wed. But they all thought it well worth it: 'It's a day out', 'There's nothing else to spend our money on round our way', 'You go to places you've never seen before.'

All this might help explain who joins in the rowdy gangs, but it doesn't explain the weird activities the gangs get up to. There's the mass chanting: a medley of bragadoccio; insults to virility, bravery and legitimacy; and open threats.

From United: 'If you want us, come and get us'; 'Manchester aggro'; the rather quaint 'We are United fans/And if you're a City boy/Surrender or you die./We all follow United'; 'part-time supporters' (meaning they don't go to away matches).

From Cardiff: 'Ole ole ole oo, who the fucking hell are you'; 'Come and have a go at Cardiff aggro'; 'You're going to get your fucking heads kicked in'; 'Supertaffs'; 'Wankers'; and 'Bloody English, all illegitimate, all illegitimate, all illegitimate, (repeat) Bastards every one!' And the worst taunts of all: 'Aberfan' from the United side, and 'Munich '58' from Cardiff.

Then there are the gestures: rhythmic clapping and raising of arms, holding up scarves horizontally, waving them round the head (all as simultaneous as a Chinese display of gymnastics), getting your friends to lift you up while you make V-signs, slowly and sensually, with both hands.

Most striking of all are the uniforms and adornments. Cardiff fans had not developed this art: most were dressed in modern Italian-cut clothes or denim jackets. United have cultivated it to the exotic perfection of Mount Hagen aborigines. They wear scarves round their heads and waists, and knotted round their wrists, like a hybrid of pirates, apaches and headhunters. They wrap Union Jacks round themselves like cloaks, daubed in white paint with fearsome slogans like 'Doc's red army'. The 'Cockney reds' (United fans from London) had the wildest garb: one with a baggy overall patched with tartan, no shirt or vest, baggy brown pants and a red and white bob cap. Another with crew cut, brass earrings, bead necklace, blue cardigan, vast khaki trousers held up with thin braces, and inscribed with the team's names, Union Jack worn like a saree, and shiny white boots. 'We only dress like this for away matches,' he said.

All these things combined go to reinforce the impression of a new tribalism, which as well as these externals has its own mythology, rules, stereotypes and values. The prime value is loyalty to the team and to your fellow-supporters. This means you must retaliate to any insult against the team and you must unquestioningly go to the aid of a fellow fan in trouble, regardless of the rights and wrongs of the situation. One cry like, 'They're beating one of us up in the toilets,' and 100 people would charge towards the scene.

Though you must always retaliate to insult or attack, in theory you never start it yourself: 'We'll be nice and quiet; but if they come over here, we'll fucking murder them'; 'We never start a fight but we always finish them'; 'I don't cause no trouble, I just find it.' In fact, unprovoked attacks are frequent – but they are always rationalised as revenge for some previous insult. The 'hostage' principle also applies – you may wreak vengeance at random on any member of the opposing side for a provocation from any other member of that side. (Even police at the match, under tremendous strain, at times worked this way on Saturday.)

Other myths in the self-image of the tribes: the tribe, like Falstaff, are always fighting against superior numbers, they never use weapons other than those to hand like bottles and stones. The other side is invariably seen as not human: 'They're like cannibals/animals'; 'They're the worst crowd in Britain.' The other side are cowardly, carry weapons, and only attack at least two to one.

Finally, there is what one might call the Bedouin syndrome. The enemy of your enemy is your friend. So Bristol supporters had come along to cheer United, and Manchester City fans to support Cardiff. But your friend of one moment can become your enemy of the next – so while Barry and Cardiff fans unite against the English, they'll be at each others' throats when they play each other.

These are the elements of the culture. They are not new this season. The soccer fans' tribal culture inevitably leads to escalation. There are those whose principal sport is starting the ball rolling.

In Cardiff I happened to bump into one such. His story is almost incredible; but because of the group he was with and the incidents I had seen them involved in, I tend to believe it. He was a great barrel of a man, with red hair and a beard, called Frank (he wouldn't tell me his second name, 'out of respect for his parents'). He was 26 and a lorry driver from Canton in Cardiff.

'I go to a match for one reason only: the aggro. It's an obsession, I can't give it up. I get so much pleasure when I'm having aggro that I nearly wet my pants – it's true. I go all over the country looking for it. I couldn't sleep all last night, I got so worked up looking forward to this match. My mother hid my shoes this morning.

'Every night during the week we go round town looking for trouble. Before a match we go round looking respectable [he had a shirt and smart trousers on]; then if we see someone who looks like the enemy, we ask him the time. If he answers in a foreign accent, we do him over, and if he's got any money on him we roll him as well.'

At Saturday's match Frank and his hangers-on paid to go in the Cardiff end, then found they could not get at the United fans. So they went out of the ground and paid again to go in to Bob-bank. They scrapped their way through to the toilets. 'Then we saw one of our lads – he wears irons on his legs – out on the deck getting his head kicked in. There were only eight of us against 20 of them, but we were beating them till the police came. This scarf I got here [a United scarf], the bloke I got it off was bleeding from everywhere in his face when I'd finished. So once again Frank proved that he's still number one. You've got to keep on proving yourself that way.' Frank was obviously a highly respected leader among his followers, and they would do exploits of bravado just to win recognition from him. A single provocation from someone like Frank, given the tenets of the culture, is bound to spark a riot.

Only a few fans were really vicious in this way; but the fans reach the pitch full of frustrated aggression, which has been built up by successive minor clashes with police. One of them complained to me:

'We were provoked by the police all the way from Manchester. They pushed us around in the station at Manchester, they got at us all the way down in the train saying, "Sit down, get your feet down, stop smoking." You get to Cardiff and they've got the dogs ready for you. All the way to the ground they keep pushing you back on the pavement, then when you get in the ground they manhandle you and arrest your mates for nothing. The other side get you hopping mad and you can't get at them because of the fence. You come out seeing red. You hit out at anything that moves.'

The working-class people of Ninian Park Road had the misfortune of being in the way as targets for the redirected aggression. It was frightening to see how the incidents had brought out the potential for violence in them, too. One huge man, who had been kicked on the face and still showed the scars, had brought out a large hammer and was standing defiantly by the broken window. His wife was arguing with a policeman, because the police had not protected them. 'Let the police go, they're no fucking use,' the man shouted. 'There were 20 louts onto me, three times I got a kicking, and the police let them. That's your bastard coppers for you.' This got the young policeman's back up. 'Put that hammer away or you'll get locked up.' 'If you won't protect us we've got to look after ourselves.' 'I'm not arguing, put it away.' Next door, the husband had borrowed an Alsatian for the day and was deliberately letting it strain at the leash. 'I'm going to get a twelve-bore shotgun for next time, and the first guy who tries anything I'll fire it right up his arse.'

It was a day of mass unreason: everyone was reacting to stereotypes, clinging to group images, flailing out at the nearest one of 'them' who happened to be around. Boot boys like Frank sparked off the violence for kicks, and the tribal culture did the rest. Press, police, public and supporters were all involved in the equation. And it cannot be solved simply by controlling one of the factors.

5 September 1974

31
Down the Rhondda terrace

Lincoln Allison

It is a crisp winter morning. The mist has cleared, unveiling a blue sky and brilliant sunshine. Across the road could be almost anywhere at this latitude, from Canada to Siberia and back again the other way, because there are just fir trees and snow and the last of the mist drifting away from them. But the near side is unquestionably Welsh, even if you did not know that this place was called Mynydd Beili-glas.

The long steep ridge of Craig y Lyn stretches away for a couple of miles, pristine and pure white except where it is so steep and rugged that the grey rock speckles the face. Below that is the black-green forest, with snow in the firebreaks. And then brown grassland, dotted with mining villages towards the horizon and, beyond that, Merthyr.

But the real giveaway is the sheep, which, while I am looking at the view, has wandered up to within a couple of yards of me and is staring quizzically at me. This confirms one of my prejudices about Wales. In England, people think sheep are silly and harmless; in Wales, it is the other way round.

I go south, into the Rhondda. It is like walking into a huge monochrome abstract painting. There are great stretches of conifer in various stages of growth, giving way to the valley, two miles across, the sides almost sheer like a great trough. There are sheep pottering busily about: although it is an A road, there is no traffic. In fact, there is a complete silence. Three sheep come to look at me, looking over the rim into the valley. I am looking down at the first sign of industry, a drift mine, like a black amphitheatre, where a tractor is moving far below. One sheep crosses the road, the other two think about it and then follow. They have clever faces, these sheep.

The road, which has been running along a ridge, finally hits the valley bottom at Treherbert. By now the valley has filled out with a great swathe of man-made shapes, dominated by the immensely long lines of grey terraced houses. It strikes me that this is a form of life which is manifestly 'industrial', but certainly not urban. Nobody in Treherbert lives more than a couple of hundred yards from the mountainside. I start to walk down the valley, on the main road.

Mediocre writers often get themselves, or their characters, from one place to another by implying that it is the place which changes rather than they who move: 'France became Italy' or 'Leicestershire became Nottinghamshire'. It is a usage I find irritating, but it seems unavoidable here. Treherbert *does* become Treorchy, somehow incorporating Pen-yr-englyn and Ynswen on the way. Between the two, the terrace of houses only relents for perhaps 300 yards, and then only on my right. The centres of places, if they can be called that, are only distinguished by having more shops.

Extrapolating from the map, I begin to think of the Rhondda as one long terrace, 20 miles from end to end. Then this thought turns into a fantasy, of the whole of Wales being a single terrace, hundreds of miles long, with no two adjacent window frames painted the same colour. The whole landscape is similar to the valleys of north Lancashire and west Yorkshire, but this seems to be the extreme version.

There are few pubs, but quite a lot of clubs. Most of them are called 'working men's' clubs but the biggest and most prosperous in appearance – after Treorchy has become Pentre, with Ton ranging up the hill to my right – is the Ton and Pentre *Conservative* Club. This seems to belie the radical image of the Rhondda, the huge Labour and substantial communist traditions. But then I remember what several Welshmen have told me about the Conservative clubs of the valleys: 'See, you don' 'ave to *vote* Tory, do you? But they always 'ave the best snooker tables.'

I have passed through Ystrad Rhondda and Llwyn-y-pia and reached Tonypandy. The valley has become wider and flatter now. There is less snow on the surrounding hills, but they are as rugged and steep as before. It is after mid-day. I relax my pace and saunter round Tonypandy.

Now I already know something about Tonypandy, about how a series of riots in a prosperous, raw, new mining community in the early years of this century became mysteriously transformed by rumour and the passage of time into a symbol of class struggle, remembered long after any genuine class conflicts were forgotten. But there is no evidence to be seen of either the myth or the historical truth.

Tonypandy seems like a quiet and well-to-do country town. Beyond the tall grey solidity of the Edwardian shops in its main street there are the wooded hills, glowing a pale brown in the sun. It is the sort of place where you expect to see English tourists buying anoraks and walking boots. There are few graffiti, except at the railway station, and very little dereliction or unoccupied buildings.

There is an empty shop and what used to be a bookie's and a derelict chapel with the roof coming off, which has a SOLD notice on it. There are a handful of youths standing talking in the street, but no more than you see anywhere these days, and many women going about their business exchanging quick, cheerful comments with one another. I buy some new bootlaces from a man who calls me *bach*, which I thought real Welshmen didn't do.

I make my way to the White Hart, a solid, town-centre sort of pub. There is a single big bar inside, but there are only half a dozen people in it, even at lunch time. I order a pint of Welsh bitter.

Next to me, as I sit, is a notice where three names have been put down to travel as supporters with the White Hart RFC. Opposite that is a notice which says DON'T HIT THE LANDLORD, HE'S ONLY A DWARF, though he seems very little shorter than most Welshmen. One man by the bar is saying, 'Excellent prop forward, 'e was,' and demonstrating a rucking technique. I think to myself that I could have written all this without actually coming here.

After a while, more of a crowd develops round the bar, a collection of dark-haired, stocky men in anoraks and rugby club sweaters. The news is on, very loudly, on the big colour television. Nobody pays any attention to it, not even when Joe Gormley is interviewed about the future of the coal industry. Nor do they pay any attention when the Welsh news comes on, first in

Welsh, then in English, with what seems to be an interminable list of Welsh factory closures. There is more attention, though, and some raucous laughter, when *Crown Court* is on, with a witness describing the fight he had with his Irish wife.

A chunky, dark-haired man with tinted glasses joins the group. In reply to 'How's tricks?' he says, 'We've never 'ad it so bad, man,' and repeats 'Never 'ad it so bad' with a huge beaming smile as if he had just said the opposite. I have a strange sensation of reality being at two levels.

Leaving Tonypandy, I climb the side of the valley into Pen-y-graig where a number of rows of terraces stand at different angles on the hillside. Two boys are kicking a rugby ball on one of the streets. There is something marvellously random about a rugby ball on a steep cobbled street. If it is allowed to land, anything can happen.

I am out of the Rhondda valley now in the narrowest sense and into a subsidiary chain of dwellings. This takes me to places with the surprisingly English names of Williamstown and Edmonds-town. These seem to be rougher and poorer places. Much of the way, the terrace faces across the road to the sheer cliff of Mynydd Dinas which towers 700 feet directly above the houses.

The bottom of the hill is an area which the people in the terraces use for all sorts of purposes. There are pigeon lofts and old cars in various states of decay, chickens scrabbling about and a couple of rather down-market ponies. Such cars as are parked are very old and corroded. The people look poor, too, both the adults, standing and talking, and the children sitting on the steps of the houses. All in all, it is a bit of a shanty town and reminds me of parts of Lancashire that I know.

Up beyond Trebanog I decide to cut across the hills to Ponty-pridd so I leave the road and go into Rhiwgarn. This is a new estate higher than almost any other settlement in the Rhondda on the edge of open country and what is, today, the snow line. It seems bleaker by far than anywhere else I have seen. Not only is it high and exposed, but the brown, pebble-dashed houses and flats lack that sense of solidity and cosiness which the old terraces have.

I make my way through a hole in the fence, out onto open country and toward the top of Mynydd-y-Glyn. Soon I am completely alone, beyond the marks of any other footsteps and ascending a great, bare plateau of snow. There is no sound except for my boots crunching into it. Turning round I can see below a great sweep of the valley, perhaps eight or nine miles long, the endless chain of terraced houses being sometimes thick, sometimes thin, but never completely broken. I stumble on a hidden rock and my feet whip away from under me on the hard snow. I land quite heavily, but there is no harm done. It occurs to me that if I had broken my leg, I might have lain and died of exposure within sight of thousands of houses.

These hills are like the Pennines, only more so; the intimacy of the inhabited valley and the wildness of the hills are both more extreme than anything in lowland England. As I sit there for a moment I notice that the other side of the valley, probably because it faces south, has less snow. It looks as though someone had decided to paint the hills white and just finished off the dregs of his old tin of paint on the top and gone off to buy another one.

In order to descend into Pontypridd, I have to go through a mature forest. By local standards it is small, about three square miles, but the trees are packed so close that it is only possible to make progress through the firebreaks and felled areas. I zig-zag, making slow progress, down into the valley. I do not like such planted forests; they lack any sense of life and character. And to me, they are made slightly sad places by the relics of the open countryside which they contain: often a bit of dry stone wall, usually collapsed; once the remains of a farmhouse.

I approach Pontypridd through another kind of shanty town, with horses and pigeon lofts and little vegetable patches on the edge of the woods. I pass a rugby pitch with sheep grazing on it and then into a part of town which appears to be called Merlin: at least there is a Merlin fireplace factory and a Merlin School of Motoring and a Merlin pub which has an enormous plaster statue of the wizard, about 8 feet high. On my way into town, I pass Pontypridd rugby club with its new stand and its tall posts, striped black and white. The town itself seems somehow more urban than the rest of the valley, a miniature of one of the great industrial cities, dark and intimate and rather shabby.

I sit on a sheltered seat in the park to jot down a few notes. A man of about my own age suddenly joins me. He is small and wiry and wears a lumber jacket and those shoes, no longer fashionable, with big toecaps and heels. He thinks I am lost because I am looking at the map, but I explain that I am looking at where I have been. But he sits down next to me, anyway, drunk in a mellow sort of way and smelling of stale beer. He becomes fascinated by my ordnance survey map. 'Good map, this, eh?' he says. 'What?' 'Bloody good map.' He points to many places on it, pronouncing the unprounceable names in a fluent, sing-song voice and seems intrigued that they are, on the map, where they really are. He is from a farm which he calls 'Gethlyooch . . . up the back o' Ponty'.

For a time we sit and talk about life and farms and forests and jobs and money and beer and houses until it is getting dark. Then he wants me to go with him to see something. But as we walk it occurs to me that we are going very much in the wrong direction for me. In any case, where is he taking me? And why? I have suspicious thoughts, but my judgment is that he is lonely and bored. I tell him I want to go back and catch the train. He looks at me in a pained way and we part.

Actually, I want to continue my notes and I do so on a bench by the bowling green in the last light until, to my surprise and embarrassment, he comes up to me again. We resume our conversation as before, but it is interrupted by the park keeper who is closing the gates. He shouts at my companion, 'Get out, boyo,' he says, 'You're not allowed in 'ere. You 'ad me once, but the bloody dog'll 'ave you next time.' 'What did you do?' I ask as we get back to the street, walking briskly. 'I 'it 'im once, see,' he says. 'Well, not so much 'it 'im really. Pushed 'im a bit. Cheerio for now.' And he turns away as I go to leave the Rhondda.

A middle-aged woman is saying to her companions, 'Course they'll 'ave to give us a bloody 'oliday, now. 'E's the Prince of *Wales*, innee?'

9 April 1981

32
Aberdeen in winter

Lincoln Allison

Balmedie Beach, Gordon District, Grampian Region, Scotland, on the shortest day of the year. I am standing on a sandhill, part of a range that stretches indefinitely north and south. It is not yet dawn. In the west a full moon shines over the sparse, low-lying countryside, dotted with white farmhouses. In the east the sun is reddening wisps of cloud, above a sea which is neutralised to a flat calm by a west wind.

Beneath my feet the sand is frozen, and has a crisp, powdery texture. Directly above me a helicopter, two headlights shining in front of it, makes its way north-east to the rigs. Then another and another within two minutes, following exactly the same path. They are coming from Aberdeen, which is dimly visible to the south as the top halves of a set of tower blocks.

There is something exciting, almost illicit, about being here. I rarely see the dawn; I have never been to Scotland except in summer. I had a clear sense of going somewhere different as the 125 train, a kind of huge sports car on rails, accelerated out of Berwick and past the sign which marks the border. Already it seemed a bigger, wilder, tougher country.

On the left were little frozen valleys which had never felt the impact of the winter sun, now setting huge and red. The hills were covered in snow, and the coast above Berwick is much more rugged than the Northumberland coast. Such building as can be seen is distinctively Scottish in style.

I am here to visit Aberdeen. I already have a composite image of the place: granite, shrewdness, civic pride, fish, prosperity, cold, grey, oil, Americans. By now the sun is up, re-emerging in the way it disappeared 17 hours ago – as a great red ball.

I have collected my thoughts and start to walk south along the clean, flat, golden beach. It is an exhilarating walk as the sun turns from red to yellow and creates dazzling reflections across the sea. There are many boats, in various stages of decay, beached along this stretch. They include the *Coastal Emperor* (Aberdeen), which is over 100 feet long, rusting away in a dignified, upright position at the top of the beach: an 'adventure playground' designed by fate. I assume that nobody dies when a ship beaches on a coast like this, and that the cost of re-floating is prohibitive.

First sight of Aberdeen – from a sand ridge between a golf course and the River Don – isn't pretty, because half a dozen tower blocks dominate the middle distance. A foghorn booms away from the lighthouse on the north pier, though it is a clear day, I make my way upstream past some drab council houses, painted white but stained with damp and moss.

Ordinary domestic architecture in Scotland – which means primarily the council house – is markedly drabber and drearier than its equivalent in England. It is partly that so few people in Scotland own their own homes, and that there is a long tradition of low-rent, low-cost accommodation. But they do less to decorate houses than the English do. Yet dignified buildings in Scotland – hotels and town halls and the like – are often far more elaborate and decorated than in England.

Ignore the road bridge, which takes the A92 traffic north toward Peterhead, and follow a path up the river. The Don is very wide and still here, with steep, wooded banks and an island in the middle. It reminds me a little of the river banks in Durham. But the river suddenly narrows and I cross it by the high, narrow, stone Brig O' Balgownie which has been there since 1320. South of the bridge is what seems like an ancient Highland village, with cobbled streets and old cottages. The illusion is preserved from the sight of those tower blocks by the height of the river and the trees. A new mini-van, labelled Women's Royal Voluntary Service, drives away up the steep street.

I follow it up Don Street and then go through a gap in the wall to get into Seaton Park. There now happens one of those great bonuses in the life of a middle-distance walker, which make up for such things as ice-cold rivers. As I negotiate my way carefully down the steep and greasy steps, which lead into the park through the leafless trees and the cawing rooks, I realise that the competence and fitness and the smart scarlet tracksuits of the men playing football in the park below can only mean one thing. Right in front of me, obstructing my line of progress, is the entire squad of Aberdeen FC, the Dons, champions of Scotland.

Almost immediately I become involved in an intense argument. There are about a dozen people, true fans, watching the practice game, in which one side wears neat green bibs over its track suits. I ask an old man to identify some of the players for me, and he does so enthusiastically; then continues to talk about football, offering the opinion that Aberdeen would be 'murdered' if they had to play in the English First Division.

This enrages the man next to us. He is in his late twenties, a short, stocky, handsome man with black hair and moustache, and wearing a scarlet, padded waterproof. He is standing with his small son, and he turns to us and mouths the word 'Crap' with angry emphasis, though in the style of a man who is driven by intellectual conviction rather than a spirit of aggression.

An argument begins. It focuses on the recent European Cup games between Liverpool and Aberdeen. The structure of the argument is as old as sport itself. Did Liverpool win so easily because they are fundamentally better and for immutable reasons (the old man's view)? Or was it mere contingency, a consequence of injuries, fouls, refereeing decisions and Liverpool's luck in getting ahead (the young man's view)? It is, of course, irresoluble, like most good arguments, and it takes some time to fail to resolve it.

Their different levels of faith are repeated in their views of the players. The young man tells me, 'There's guid young players here, really guid; players that are goin' ter be the greet names o' Scottish fitba'.' We watch Gordon Strachan, the wee man, and already a famous player, tackling back in his own penalty area as if he were playing against England. But then another player, slim and dark-haired, is pointed out, and the young man tells me that he has 'more skill than anyone ah've ivver seen; more skill than Charlie Cooke, even'. But the old man says, 'Ach, he's makin' nae progress, man. He can play on a Mondie mornin', he cannae play on a Sat'die.'

I learn a lot about Scottish football in this conversation, and one thing that is agreed is the lack of an adequate reserve league in which Aberdeen's youngsters can learn their trade. As we look at the tall and elegant figure of Marc de Clerck, the reserve goal-keeper, the young man says, 'He's in the Guinness Buk o' Records, ye ken.' I ask why, and am told, 'In the hist'ry o' fitba, he's the only Belgian goalie tie score a goal for a Scottish side in England.' Apparently, it happened during a League Cup match at Berwick when de Clerck netted with an enormous punt.

Overlooking Seaton Park on its south side is St Machar's cathedral, with its dumpy twin spires. There is nobody around, and I am alone inside. Its eerie twilight and Presbyterian plainness contrast with the fine day outside and the hustle of the football only a quarter of a mile away. This is the beginning of Old Aberdeen (known as the Auld Toon if you own a teashop), and I go south down its main artery, which starts as Chanonry, be-comes High Street, and then College Bounds.

There are low courtyards of cottages, large, stern, manse-like houses and intermediate friendly little terraces. Then there are the more elaborate buildings of the university, with their gothic arches and cloisters. Walking into the quadrangle of King's College, I am reminded immediately of Oxford. The porter is called a sacrist and the stone is grey instead of golden-brown. And the impression is intensified by the two people I see in the quadrangle. One is a plump, middle-aged academic, the other a slim young Chinese. As they pass, the don says, in an English accent, 'How are you? . . . Not too cold for you, I hope.' The traditional call of the dutiful teacher to the foreign student. The Chinese boy beams and nods and then walks on.

Further south, down Spittal, the gaps between the houses to the east reveal views of Pittodrie football ground, the gasworks and the sea. What with the architecture and the calls of seagulls and the view, I am constantly assuming that I am in a seaside resort rather than a fairly large city. At the bottom of Mounthooly there is a huge new roundabout overshadowed by blocks of flats with 14 storeys, so the old town is entirely behind me.

I follow King Street to the town centre. It is broad and busy, flanked by uniform, tall, plain grey buildings. There is a strange brightness because the sun is shining on the dampness of the road, now that the frost has melted. Apparently the plainness has nothing to do with culture nor religion, but is simply because the granite is so hard and difficult to work. In Castle Street, though, there is a contrasting elaboration in the Scottish baronial grandeur of the town hall and the Salvation Army citadel.

I walk east, and Aberdeen suddenly becomes a resort. The amusements and cafes are surrounded by the flat grass of the Queen's Links. As in other resorts, dogs are being walked briskly along the promenade, and some people are just sitting in their cars looking at the calm sea. A fat man smoking a cigarette in a turquoise Rolls-Royce looks very bored. Then, at the tip of the north side of the Dee, I reach the amazing Footdee (pronounced Fidee). It is a little Hebridean fishing village of low cottages and narrow cobbled streets, and in it old ladies potter round tiny gardens. But it is right next to the docks, and the ends of some of its streets are overshadowed by oil storage tanks.

The docks themselves seem busy and important. The *Ben Viking* (Kristiansand) is leaving, its stern half a tangle of mysterious pipes. Lorries come and go, and strange machinery is being welded on the quay. It seems rough, tough and prosperous; but there is also a lot of dereliction, big areas of scruffy, unused ground and blackened stone buildings which are falling down.

I am hungry now and I find a small caff, in what seems a poorer area on the south side of the Dee. Everything is half-cooked and re-heated and I choose Scotch pie, beans and chips, 75p. It is hot and the portions are big. Across the road, on an unused shop, I can see posters which show Mrs Thatcher as a laughing vampire with the slogan: NO WONDER SHE'S SMILING. SHE'S GOT SCOTLAND'S OIL.

Across the road, in the Victoria bar, I impulsively order a pint of light. It is the worst beer I have ever tasted, thin, fizzy and metallic. Then I realise that all the tables have decanters on them, and that it is normal here to drink chasers. I order a malt whisky which makes the light taste better. Because of a legislative miscalculation, Scottish pubs can open all day now, and there are people here who have no intention of leaving. The largest group of men are swearing and talking about racing in an incomprehensibly thick accent, and the woman next to me is saying to one of her male companions, 'Ye've nae soul, Charlie, ye've nae soul.'

In the short afternoon, I go up Torry Hill. At first, I am confused by this area. The people and the cars look thoroughly working-class, but they live in great, grey detached manses. Then I realise that each front door has two numbers on it, and there are different numbers on each of the side doors. Yet another peculiarity of Scottish housing.

On top of the hill there is a panoramic view southwards – of industry with hills as a backcloth, from the new sewage plant they are building on Nigg Bay, across the modern industrial estates of Tullos and Altens. Down at the bottom of the hill, I finally find the smell of fish (for which Aberdeen used to be famous) in the little fish warehouses and packing plants of Ferryhill. Two Yorkshire lorry drivers ask me the way.

I go back to the city centre, to the lights and big shops of Union Street. It is dark now and I am tired, in no mood to jostle with the big crowds of shoppers. The evening paper says that an Aberdeen skipper has been detained for using illegal nets in the Faroes. A middle-aged man reprimands a passing youth for swearing. In a quieter part of the street, the A1 Employment Agency has vacancies for tool pushers, mud sprayers and the like. But you need experience.

What of the Yanks? Apart from the odd accent and a stetson near the station (which might well belong to a Glaswegian), I have seen no evidence of the American presence in Aberdeen. On the whole, they play little part in the life of the city, having their own school, newspaper and shop. So I make my way past dignified Georgian granite houses to the American Food Store in Midstocket Road. It is a small supermarket where you can buy taco shells and Hershey bars and Little League baseball bats. For old times' sake, I buy some tortillas. But having done so, I calculate that I have paid approximately *twenty times* what I used to pay for them in California.

Finally, long after the sun has gone down, I visit one last corner of Aberdeen, the Winter Gardens in Duthie Park. It is a botanical garden, a complex of greenhouses not unlike those in Kew and Edinburgh. But it is dark now and the tropical foliage is lit by hundreds of tiny nightlight candles. Some line the paths, some are carried by children, and some float on the ponds. A brass band is playing near the entrance, and the place has the atmosphere of some fantastical, tropical grotto. It is a strange and, perhaps, intentional contrast to the hard, grey, ancient, modern, proud city which owns it.

5 February 1981

33
The valley without the chapels

Jeremy Seabrook

The early Victorian centre of Aberdare is like that of a country town, with its inns and war memorial, and the primitive trestles set out for the Saturday market. But what gives the town its distinctive Welsh appearance is the archaic grace of the chapels which tower over all other buildings.

Many of them face each other in competitive denominational defiance, with a plaster inset in the pediment, announcing the date of their foundation, of their enlargement, and finally of their rebuilding – mostly before the early 1900s, the time of the last major religious revival in the communities on the South Wales coalfield. Nearly all in the same style, the chapels are temples of slate and stone, built to accommodate five or six hundred people. Some of them are now sadly ruinous, others still lovingly tended by the elderly and dwindling congregation.

If coal and the chapels dominated the valleys, the depletion of the coalfield over the last half century has its counterpart in the exhaustion of the chapel culture. But the waning of their influence, with the intertwined epic of suffering and resistance, has led, not to the sense of exultant liberation that might have been expected, but rather to a sad feeling of discontinuity and loss.

Calfaria, mother church of the Welsh Baptists in Aberdare, stands back from the road behind iron gates. A dusty white globe, with CALFARIA in black letters, surmounts one gatepost. Dark yew trees creak in the wind, and have scattered their scarlet berries among the elegant slate tombstones and the funerary monuments, testifying to the virtues of colliery officials, virtues of which the workpeople saw little.

Inside, the church is beautifully preserved. Waiting for its sparse congregation on Sunday morning, it has a serene and expectant dignity. The floor tiles – beige, blue and maroon – have been polished, and the pews gleam a bright chestnut colour. The metal pillars supporting the balcony are painted pink; the balustrade, decorative wrought iron, is black and gold. Each pew – and there are 70 of them on the ground floor – has an enamelled white numberplate.

The glass in the plain windows is faintly tinted, which transforms the cold November light to a dull rose colour. On a carpeted dais, there is a row of padded and polished Victorian chairs, where the deacons sit. There is a cherub carved on the wooden panel of the lectern; the carvings around the clock are of leaves and garlands of flowers. A bowl of white chrysanthemums stands on a side table. Calfaria now has less than 70 members; 'the saving remnant', as the minister says.

Not all the chapels are as well maintained as Calfaria. Others have fallen into ruin, have been smothered by ivy. Their leaded windows are buckled, or have been filled in with breeze blocks. The plaster has been gradually eroded so that the names are indistinct – Bethania, Carmel, Soar, Sion, Bethel.

Of course, many people will tell you, what drove us from the chapels was the narrowness and the complacency, the hypocrisy of the coal owners and of those who tried to ingratiate themselves by appearing conspicuous in the chapels favoured by the bosses. 'The chapels were corrupted. People went out of habit or social conformity'; 'It was all prohibitions. Dancing and drinking, all the pleasures of the poor were forbidden'; 'If a girl got pregnant, she would be cast out.'

One old lady, who hadn't abandoned the chapel told me, 'Sunday was a day apart. We went to church, came home, and changed out of our best clothes; then we changed back into them for Sunday school, came home and changed again; then back into them for evening service. On Sunday you were not allowed to sew on a button or pick up a brush to sweep the floor.'

But the dislocation goes deeper than a simple reaction against such oppressive disciplines. Belief is not invalidated by being abused by the coal owners or an exploitative system, any more than absence of belief justifies the uncomprehending discontinuity between generations that has occurred in more recent years.

'There are two different tribes living in the valleys now,' said a member of Sion, daughter church of Calfaria, 'the young and the old.' And they do seem to exist uneasily together, gliding past each other in the streets of the old pit villages, with very little contact between them.

On Saturday night, the town centre – still called *y pentref* (the village) by some of the older people – is taken over, occupied almost, by the young: exuberant groups going from pub to pub, looking for something to do, eating out of silver foil dishes and plastic containers as they go, climbing the scaffolding around a chapel, throwing Coke cans into the road.

Late on Saturday night, half a dozen boys, sing to the tune of *What do you Get when you Fall in Love*:

> What do you get when you drink twelve pints?
> A ten pound fine and a year's probation,
> And a roughing up at the police station,

and aim the remains of their chips at the grey statue of Griffith Rhys Jones, on the plinth of which it says, 'The South Wales Choral Union, composed of 500 voices, won the chief choral prize valued at one thousand pounds in open competition at the Crystal Palace London in July 1872 and 1873.' A restless energy flows through the streets on Saturday nights; and the old people stay away. 'I am a destructive cunt,' somebody sprays onto the blind end of a row of houses.

But then, on Sunday morning, a more sparse and very different population fills the streets. Old ladies with felt hats carry ancient, gilt-edged Bibles, with walking sticks to help them negotiate the steep streets, grave and decorous. A faint whiff of camphor and strong mints accompanies them on their way to the under-heated chapels which they have attended every Sunday for 70 or 80 years.

If the young have, for the most part, been released from the joyless disciplines of chapel and pit, they have also been disinherited from the other side of that life: a sense of secure identity, anchored in a tradition of music and singing, of mutual improvement societies, penny readings, drama and oratorios; a world in which it was possible to be an intellectual and a working man.

'They were like lawyers, some of the men who worked in the pits then.' 'In the Miners' Institute library, you would find Josephus' *History of the Jews* next to a book on mining engineering and the plays of Shakespeare.'

The question which has been asked again and again, in all working-class areas, poses itself with greater clarity in South Wales. Why was the relief from that old poverty and dispossession – which we longed and fought for above everything else – paid for in such a cruel way, with such sacrifice to us in human, cultural and spiritual terms?

Of the old, the young say, 'I don't listen. I'm not interested. They go on and on. They exaggerate: how they had to sit on orange boxes and steal food before they could eat. They're jealous of us.' And the old say, 'They don't know what we've suffered and they *don't* care. You can't tell them anything.'

You can't tell them anything. That sentence, which I must have heard a dozen times, expresses the extent of the cultural fault-line between the generations, the breakdown in transmission. You can't tell them, because their experience has mostly been formed, not by coal and chapels, but by the promises of what money can buy.

Two young miners sit on the window sill of a pub in the centre of town. One of them says, 'I always swore I'd never go down the pit. But when it comes to it, you see all them who haven't got a job, and you're glad of it. Chapels? They don't mean anything to me. They could be made into something useful.' 'Disco,' his mate grins.

'You need to spend £15 for a decent night out, twelve pints, cigarettes, taxi fares. I don't want to get married till I'm about 25.' The other one says, 'I've been courting for a year and a month. Looks like I'll have to get married. I suppose I'll have to shoot her if I want to get out of it.' He smiles deprecatingly. It's only a joke but, underneath, there is already a sense of the world closing in, of the limiting and narrowing of the years. 'There's only one real way out, and that's to win the pools.'

A boy and girl have come back home from London for the weekend. They go from pub to pub, looking for old school friends. They are a handsome couple. She has bleached white hair and black Ali-Baba trousers. He has dark hair, a stud in his ear and in his nose, black velvet jacket and pointed shoes.

'We don't want to just get married and have kids. If you stay here, the pressure is on right from when you leave school. I worked as a nurse and typist here. I'm managing a boutique in London.' The boy says, 'I did an engineering apprenticeship, but when I finished I wanted to get out of Aberdare. I'm just working in a warehouse now. I don't care about work.'

They say they left the valley, not because of work, but for the sake of the entertainment London provides; a new reason to add to the multiple causes that have driven so many people from the valleys. She says, 'I come back once every six weeks. My Mam misses me.' 'Do you miss her?' She wrinkles her nose and says, 'I miss her cooking.'

Three girls sit on a bench outside the public lavatory. A bleak raw evening; a smell of urine and disinfectant. They are 15; all attractively dressed and made up. They have come from Penrhiwceiber, a few miles down the valley, and are waiting for Lynette's boy friend. Hayley says she hasn't got a boy friend at the moment.

She shows her wrists, which are covered with sticking plaster. 'She's always doing that. She cuts her wrists whenever she loses her boy friends. She gets too involved. You shouldn't.' 'I can't help it.' 'Anybody can help it.' 'Not me. Love is the most important thing to me. Anyway, I don't cut them very deep.'

I was reminded of an old miner I had met earlier in the week. He told me that, when his wife died, nine years earlier, the chapel had been his backbone. 'I don't know what I would have done but for the chapel. It had given us so much comfort and pleasure in life. Where else would I take my grief?'

In the cafe on Saturday afternoon, an anxious young woman, laden with carrier bags, sits on the opposite side of the buff Formica table. I smile at her, and she starts to talk eagerly. She is waiting for the bus to go home:

'I wish I didn't have to. I've been shopping for my father. He had a stroke. He can't do anything for himself. My Mam and Dad are separated. I don't blame her for leaving him. He always liked his drink and his women. He was always off gallivanting. I don't know if that's what caused it, his stroke. He's in a wheelchair now. I'm the only one he's got, and I don't look after him because I love him, I do it because there's nobody else. My brother calls by in the car; he never stays five minutes. He's not old, my Dad, he's only 53. But he isn't grateful. He's always criticising everything I do. I gave up my job a year ago. I wish I hadn't. I couldn't get one now even if I wanted to. I was working in a shop.' She says suddenly, 'You don't mind me talking to you? I can see you want to get away from me. Everybody does.'

The stories that the old tell are very different. Visiting them in the plain and frugal dignity of their houses, the memories that the young don't want to hear come pouring out: memories of the 'Welsh knot' in the late nineteenth century, when children were forbidden to speak Welsh in school. The Welsh knot was hung round the neck of any child heard speaking Welsh, and they passed it on in turn to anyone they heard using the mother tongue. The child who was wearing it at the end of the day was beaten.

Then there are the even more ancient stories of distant migrations from the north and west into the valleys to find work in the coalfield; stories of walking over the mountains to church; the old barns in which the chapels were founded – memories lovingly transmitted.

I spent an evening with an old miner and his wife, who is superintendent of Sion Sunday school; a warm and including hospitality, a sharing of memories of a time when she had a relative in every street in Cwmaman – one of the nine villages around Aberdare. Mr Williams is 100 per cent disabled with pneumoconiosis, and ceased work 18 years ago. Normally he sits huddled in the hearth from November to April, because one of the symptoms is that it is impossible to keep warm.

They talk of their shared childhood in Cwmaman, with alternate laughter and sudden bursts of melancholy at the intensity of their recollections, as they try to recall the nicknames of the people they knew. 'There was Sarah Bendrws, Doorstep Sarah, who spent all day minding other people's business; Dai Legs-and-Braces; Tom Bacon-and-Cabbage; Will Thomas Cup-of-Tea. I was known as Tom Williams Bright-Eyes, because I had a greyhound called Bright Eyes.

'Where I worked at first, the seam was only 26 inches high. You were worn out by the time you got there. The trousers I wore would stand up by themselves with the salt from my body. But the men used to sing hymns underground. You would discuss what the minister said at chapel, even though all the while your lungs were filling up with the dust, and nobody cared. The owners here used to be the Llewellyns, you know, the ancestors of Roddy Llewellyn. But they weren't bad employers.'

Mrs Williams brings out a plate of Welsh cakes she had made. She is the one who usually gives meals and accommodation to visiting preachers. 'I don't make Welsh cakes for the preachers now. One of them once said, "Oh, there's always Welsh cakes wherever we go." Since then, I've stopped making them. We call them *teisan pregethwr*, preachers' cakes. Of course, we say *tishan*, that's the hearthstone Welsh we always spoke at home. When our daughter was learning Welsh at school, we had to learn to say it properly. You lived in two worlds when we were young, the world of *Cymraeg yr aelwyd* – hearthstone Welsh – and the English world of school.'

The idea of different worlds was echoed by a young teacher I spoke to, a man who is devoted to the culture of the valleys, but who recently stopped going to church:

'My grandfather was church secretary for 50 years. Commitment to the church informed his whole life. And my mother was brought up in the same spirit, and this strength was passed on to me and my brothers.

'All my mother's brothers and sisters left Aberdare. The girls went away to service. My mother stayed to look after her mother and grandmother. This means that my cousins and I live in different worlds. My brother and I are the only two in our generation to speak Welsh.

'Because the expression of Welsh Nonconformity was Welsh, it has been doubly impoverished. It has been attacked by the furthest effects of secularism as well as by the lack of knowledge of Welsh. I found it left me with a personal crisis, having been brought up in the fifties and sixties with values that were already socially obsolete. Not personally obsolete: I have sympathy with the moral code, the view of life, the language, the religious and spiritual tradition; but that is alien to my contemporaries. I feel more at home with those older than myself.

The Welsh desertion of Nonconformity has affected politics, too; not at the level of voting perhaps, of electoral support for Labour, but the deeper feeling. As the religious belief has decayed, so has the moral force of the secularised belief that grew out of it. Almost all those in the congregation I spoke with had

been committed to socialism. Some of them had gone over to
Plaid Cymru, some had become disillusioned with politics. Most
felt that the values they had cherished had been deformed or
corrupted. One man put it like this, 'The Labour Party has lost its
strength because it has come too far from its roots – it changed,
accommodated itself too easily to capitalism – while Nonconformity has been dislocated by holding on too fast while the
world around it changed.'

The outcome has been similar in both traditions, but it has
worked in opposite ways. 'The Labour left is talking a language
people have lost, just as the old Nonconformity is. Their call to
arms does not connect.' The teacher said, 'The emergence of Plaid
draws on a strong but vague sense of resentment and loss.'

The sense of loss is defined more precisely among the members
of the congregation of Calfaria and Sion. 'We used to have a
Sunday school of 200 children. Now I have to give my grandsons
tenpence each a week to get them to come to Sunday school.'

'The Union of Baptists used to have a scripture examination
every March. I conducted three classes in our vestry. Each child
would have to go in front of an examiner, and be asked questions
on the catechism he had had to prepare. It was as much of a to-do
as sitting for the school examinations.'

'When we had our *cwrdd y mawr*, the big anniversary services,
I've seen the chapel packed, the aisles overflowing, you couldn't
get them all in. Then, when we put on *The Dream of Gerontius*,
Samson, what an event it was. Everybody got excited for months
beforehand.'

'Of course, the difference between the denominations was
more marked then. Some would refuse to co-operate with the
others. People thought they had the whole truth. Although I'm
a convinced Baptist, I wouldn't say a non-Baptist was not a
Christian. But infant baptism was taboo with Baptists at one
time.'

'The community was a family of families. People were not
afraid to take responsibility for one another. Now what you hear
is, "I don't want to get involved." What else is there in life, if not
to get involved one with another?'

'We had a culture that was local but not parochial.'

But in spite of the thinning of the congregation, and the
insistence that it is the blows of two world wars and the depress-

ion that have caused the defection, there remains a patient but anxious conviction that the renewal will come, must come. The gospel remains visible and unchanging, they say. No one has been turned away. People will come back.

On Sunday morning, I go with the senior deacon and his two sisters to Sion in Cwmaman. Although they now live in Aberdare, they still return to the church of their childhood, the spirit of which remains more vital than most others. Cwmaman is one of the most unaltered of the pit villages, except that there are no longer any pits. It runs along a small side valley, about three miles from the centre of Aberdare. The streets are of sombre dressed stone, with bright red-brick rustication around the doors and windows. But some of the earliest cottages were built with rough uneven stones taken straight from the riverbeds.

Since the disaster at Aberfan in the neighbouring valley, the industrial landscape has changed. All the tips and the rusting machinery and decaying pitheads have been dismantled; a physical counterpart of the erasure of memory of the young. The split remains of ruined and gutted mountains have been levelled, and children's playgrounds installed, with bright red and blue plastic roundabouts and swings (a sad and guilty gesture, perhaps, for the lives of children lost at Aberfan). There is a slightly eerie feeling that the reason for the existence of these places has gone; but the settlements remain. And everyone insists that the old neighbourhood support and feeling are still there today, even if less intensely lived.

There were about 25 people at morning service in Sion; most of them over 60. There were a few younger men. A man who works for the National Coal Board was with his son, who is studying Welsh at A level. 'My son can speak better Welsh than I can. My parents were both native Welsh speakers, but when they started courting, they began to talk English. Welsh was the hearthstone language. It was felt to be too intimate for courting, which was more formal then. But then they carried on with English after they were married.'

The church has no regular minister now. A visiting preacher comes each week. Today's preacher is a man in his late forties, training for the ministry. Although Sion is less grand than Calfaria, there are the same polished pews, there is the same evidence of loving commitment. The deacons sit on the dais below the lectern. They turn and face the congregation for the hymns. The preacher reads from the Bible.

It is the story of the Prodigal Son: a resonance that echoes over the rows of empty pews, a metaphor that addresses itself to those who have defected from their roots and their belief. To hear the parable in the unfamiliar music of a foreign language is intensely moving. You have a powerful sense of faith, detached from its particular object, an almost abstract expression of a profound and lasting human need. Because it is no longer a militant or majority belief, it is all the more poignant.

In this cavernous place, with the pewter November light filtered through the dusty windows, the sound swells plaintively, and seems to express the homeless hunger and objectless longings of all those people outside the church. When the congregation sing – the hymn is *Cwm Rhondda* – they fill the church with passionate intensity. You feel that surely these people are justified in their serene certainty that those who have gone away will come back; even though the way of their returning will almost certainly not be in the forms that are familiar. When they talk of the darkest hour and the ebb tide, the worship of Mammon and Baal and false gods, at this moment it is impossible to believe they are deluded.

Out on the main square, the pubs are opening. An old woman goes to the paper-seller and begs to be given a newspaper. The young boy says, 'I can't give you one for nothing.' I buy her a copy of the *People*. She turns to me: an old blue raincoat smeared and worn, a dingy pink knitted hat, brown boots. She says, 'It's my birthday today. I'm 80. Do you know, I started to play the piano when I was three. I've played in all the chapels in Cwmbach and Aberaman. But that's a long time ago. I've lost everyone belonging to me.'

She goes off across the war memorial, turning over the wreaths of poppies, collecting scraps of wastepaper which she thrusts into her bag.

24 December 1981

Contributors

Lincoln Allison, born 1946 in County Durham but brought up in the Lancashire Pennine town of Colne. Read PPE at Oxford, teaches politics at the University of Warwick, and has published a book on environmental planning. In 1979 he began to write a series of 'walks' for *New Society*. His book, *Condition of England* (1981), includes some of the English walks.

Paul Barker, born 1935 at the Brontë end of the West Riding. Read French at Oxford. Taught at the École Normale Supérieure in Paris, then joined *The Times*. Editor of *New Society* since 1968. Books he has edited include *A Sociological Portrait* (1972) and *Arts in Society* (1977).

Angela Carter, born 1940 in Eastbourne and brought up in south London. Was a local newspaper reporter before going on to read English at the University of Bristol. Novels include *Shadow Dance* (1966), *The Magic Toyshop* (1967), *Several Perceptions* (1968), *Heroes and Villains* (1969), *The Passion of New Eve* (1977). Has also published two collections of short stories, two children's books, and the study, *The Sadeian Woman* (1979).

Helen Chappell, born 1955 in Stanmore but brought up partly in Singapore. Read social and political sciences at Cambridge. Winner of Catherine Pakenham Award for young women journalists. *New Society* staff writer since 1981.

273

Norman Dennis, born 1929 in Sunderland. Took degree at London School of Economics and is now Reader in Social Studies, University of Newcastle-upon-Tyne. Wrote *Coal is Our Life* with Cliff Slaughter and Fernando Henriques (1956). Other books are *People and Planning* (1970) and *Public Participation and Planners' Blight* (1972).

Eileen Fairweather, born 1954 in London. Read English at the University of Sussex. Has worked for *Spare Rib*, and as both performer and playwright in fringe theatre. Her article is based on material which Penguin will be publishing in a book on women in Northern Ireland, of which she is joint author along with Melanie McFadyean and Roisin McDonough.

Tom Forester, born 1949 in London. Read sociology at the University of Sussex, followed by a politics degree from Oxford. Labour and industry correspondent of *New Society*, 1976–80; now freelance writer. Wrote *The Labour Party and the Working Class* (1976), and edited *The Microelectronics Revolution* (1980).

Paul Harrison, born 1945 in Oldham. Read modern languages at Cambridge, then took a political sociology degree at London School of Economics. On the staff of *New Society*, 1972–5; now freelance writer. Books: *Inside the Third World* (1979) and *The Third World Tomorrow* (1980). He is now working on a book on the inner city.

Peter Marsh, born 1946 in Leeds. Qualified in child care, and was a superviser at a remand home and housemaster at an approved school before reading psychology at Oxford. Was co-director of Contemporary Violence Research Centre, Oxford University, 1977–9; now teaches psychology at Oxford Polytechnic. Books include *Aggro: the Illusion of Violence* (1978); and with Desmond Morris, P. Collett and M. O'Shaughnessy, *Gestures: their Origin and Distribution* (1979).

Howard Parker, born 1948 in Preston, and brought up in Liverpool. Took social science and criminology degrees at the University of Liverpool, where he now teaches social work. His books are *View from the Boys* (1974), *Social Work and the Courts* (1979) and *Receiving Juvenile Justice* (1981).

Ken Pryce, born in 1941 in Kingston, Jamaica, and brought up there before going to the University of York to read social sciences. He did graduate work at the University of Bristol before going to the University of the West Indies, Trinidad, to teach criminology. His book, *Endless Pressure*, was published by Penguin in 1979, and his article in the present collection draws on different parts of it.

Jeremy Seabrook, born 1939 in Northampton. Read modern languages at Cambridge. Has been an adult education tutor and social worker; now a freelance writer. With Michael O'Neill, has written plays for the Royal Court, television and radio. Books include *The Unprivileged* (1967), *City Close-Up* (1970), *Loneliness* (1973), *The Everlasting Feast* (1974), *A Lasting Relationship* (1976), *What Went Wrong* (1978), *Mother, Son* (1980), and *Unemployment* (1982).

David Selbourne, born 1937 in London but brought up in Lancashire. Read law at Oxford. After working in industry and teaching in Birmingham, went to Ruskin College, Oxford, as tutor in social and political theory; Aneurin Bevan Memorial Fellow, 1975. His publications include *An Eye to India* (1977), *An Eye to China* (1978), *Through the Indian Looking-Glass* (1981), *The Making of A Midsummer Night's Dream* (1982), and various plays.

Ian Walker, born 1952 in Birmingham. Read English, and social and political sciences, at Cambridge. Taught in east London, spent two years on the dole, worked for the *Leveller*. Staff writer at *New Society*, 1979–81; now with the *Observer*.

Stuart Weir, born 1938 in Surrey. Read history at Oxford. Worked on the *Oxford Mail* and *The Times* before going to work for Child Poverty Action Group and Shelter. Assistant editor of *New Society* since 1977. An editor of, and contributor to, *Manifesto: a Radical Strategy for Britain's Future* (1981).

David White, born 1943 in Surrey. Read English at Oxford. *New Society* staff writer, 1970–81. Now freelance journalist.

Michael Williams, born 1948 in north London. Read English at University of Liverpool. With *Liverpool Daily Post, Birmingham Evening Mail* and *The Times* before joining *New Society* in 1979.

Paul Willis, born 1945 in Wednesbury. Read English at Cambridge. Research fellow at the Centre for Contemporary Cultural Studies, University of Birmingham. Books: *Learning to Labour* (1977) and *Profane Culture* (1978).

Peter Woods, born 1934 in Great Yarmouth. Has degrees in history from the University of London; in the sociology and psychology of education from the University of Bradford; and an Open University PhD. Taught in West Riding schools before becoming senior lecturer in education at the Open University. Author of *The Divided School* (1979) and editor of several other books.

Sheila Yeger, born 1941 in High Wycombe. Read English at Oxford. Formerly a community worker; now a playwright and television writer. Television includes *Angels* (BBC) and *Starting Out* (ATV). Plays produced at Bristol Old Vic, Edinburgh Festival, Soho Poly, The Orange Tree. Has also published a novel, *For Maddie with Love* (1980).